Praise for *Advancing* **Differentiation**

"If you find it difficult to navigate the often-perilous landscape of differentiation, Dr. Cash is the guide and guru you need. His gift to you is this survival kit. Use it well!"

—**David Michael Slater,** teacher and author of over twenty books for children, teens, and adults

"My graduate students call this the 'blue book,' an apt title for a volume that defines value in education. They routinely report that they keep their copy on their desks long after their course is over. The second edition is even stronger than the first, with its increased focus on concept and capacity building. Many view differentiation in standards-based classrooms as an impossible dream, but Richard Cash joyfully and capably provides valid and viable strategies for teachers who know in their hearts that there is more to education than one-size-fits-all thinking."

—**Frances R. Spielhagen, Ph.D.,** professor of education and director of the Center for Adolescent Research and Development (CARD) at Mount Saint Mary College

"*Advancing Differentiation* is a game changer! This book helps me navigate through the challenges of differentiation by providing rigorous and practical methods that help my students uncover the deeper layers of learning."

—**John Born,** 7th-grade social studies teacher

"*Advancing Differentiation* is a fantastic resource for teachers and teacher leaders to develop their understanding of differentiation. This book provides a number of powerful tools for teachers to develop their questioning skills, embed critical thinking into their classrooms, and create a learning environment that will motivate and engage a diverse range of learners."

—**Jake Duke,** STEM curriculum developer, Bellevue School District

"Cash adeptly blends advanced content, complex thinking, and conceptual understanding with the technologies of twenty-first century learning. This second edition lays out the essential components of a differentiated classroom including emphases on teaching big ideas through critical and creative thinking and problem solving. Cash blends theoretically sound ideas regarding curriculum and instruction with clear guidance for applying differentiation in authentic learning spaces. This is a great book for teachers and curriculum designers."

—**Todd Kettler, Ph.D.,** assistant professor, College of Education, University of North Texas

"One of the most inspiring and practical books I've read in years . . . I was blown away by how useful all the chapters will be to our profession."

—**Rick Wormeli,** writer and teacher trainer, author of *Fair Isn't Always Equal* and *Differentiation: From Planning to Practice*

"Amazingly comprehensive . . . [this] book is an excellent resource for administrators and classroom teachers alike. Dr. Cash provides countless practical applications [and] makes a case for differentiation for the purposes of raising student achievement and Response to Intervention (RTI), in addition to the increasingly diverse populations our districts encounter in the century."

—**Anne Roloff, Ph.D.,** past president of Illinois ASCD and assistant superintendent for Curriculum and Instruction, Niles Township High School District, Skokie, Illinois

"How I wish I had this book when I was a principal. I had many new, young teachers, and this outstanding approach to teaching would have made my life as a mentor much easier. The clear writing, commonsense approaches, and suggestions and charts will give any teacher—new or seasoned—confidence and motivation. A fine, practical addition to our field."

—**Judith Roseberry,** consultant, past president of California Association for the Gifted

"Cash not only provides the big picture of the landscape of differentiation, he clearly demonstrates his expertise in both the art and the science of teaching. He consistently advances his message that all students can learn at high levels and deserve rigor and challenge. This is an essential book for teachers as they encourage new ideas and creative productivity in their students in the current educational landscape."

—**Felicia A. Dixon, Ph.D.,** professor emerita of psychology, Department of Educational Psychology, Ball State University

"Cash's approach to differentiation is refreshing, authentic, and practical. He takes a complex philosophy and brings it alive through his writing . . . This publication should be in the hands of all teachers."

—**Jaime A. Castellano, Ed.D.,** assistant center director at the Luciano Martinez Child Development Center, West Palm Beach, Florida, and professor at Florida Atlantic University, Boca Raton.

"Richard writes with a clarity that appeals to both the novice and the seasoned educator. I've yet to read a more comprehensive teacher guide. *Advancing Differentiation* just moved to the top of my recommended list!"

—**Jeff Danielian, M.Ed.,** teacher resource specialist, editor-in-chief of *Teaching for High Potential*, National Association for Gifted Children

"Dr. Cash takes differentiated instruction to a new level of urgency and pedagogical quality . . . This book is a breath of fresh air."

—**Scott J. Peters, Ph.D.,** assistant professor, Department of Educational Foundations, University of Wisconsin–Whitewater

Advancing Differentiation

Thinking and Learning for the 21st Century

Revised & Updated Edition

RICHARD M. CASH, Ed.D.
Foreword by Diane Heacox, Ed.D.

Copyright © 2017, 2011 by Richard M. Cash, Ed.D.

All rights reserved under International and Pan-American Copyright Conventions. Unless otherwise noted, no part of this book may be reproduced, stored in a retrieval system, or transmitted in any form or by any means, electronic, mechanical, photocopying, recording or otherwise, without express written permission of the publisher, except for brief quotations or critical reviews. For more information, go to freespirit.com/permissions.

Free Spirit, Free Spirit Publishing, and associated logos are trademarks and/or registered trademarks of Free Spirit Publishing Inc. A complete listing of our logos and trademarks is available at freespirit.com.

Library of Congress Cataloging-in-Publication Data
Names: Cash, Richard M.
Title: Advancing differentiation : thinking and learning for the 21st century / Richard M. Cash ; foreword by Diane Heacox, Ed.D.
Description: Revised & updated edition. | Minneapolis, MN : Free Spirit Publishing, 2017. | Includes bibliographical references and index.
Identifiers: LCCN 2016045725 (print) | LCCN 2016056566 (ebook) | ISBN 9781631981418 (paperback) | ISBN 1631981412 (paperback) | ISBN 9781631981425 (Web PDF) | ISBN 9781631981432 (ePub)
Subjects: LCSH: Individualized instruction. | Thought and thinking—Study and teaching. | Education—Curricula. | BISAC: EDUCATION / Inclusive Education. | EDUCATION / Classroom Management. | EDUCATION / Teaching Methods & Materials / General.
Classification: LCC LB1031 .C38 2017 (print) | LCC LB1031 (ebook) | DDC 371.39/4—dc23
LC record available at https://lccn.loc.gov/2016045725

Free Spirit Publishing does not have control over or assume responsibility for author or third-party websites and their content. At the time of this book's publication, all facts and figures cited within are the most current available. All telephone numbers, addresses, and website URLs are accurate and active; all publications, organizations, websites, and other resources exist as described in this book; and all have been verified as of November 2018. If you find an error or believe that a resource listed here is not as described, please contact Free Spirit Publishing.

Edited by Meg Bratsch
Cover and interior design by Emily Dyer

10 9 8 7 6 5
Printed in the United States of America

Free Spirit Publishing Inc.
6325 Sandburg Road, Suite 100
Minneapolis, MN 55427-3674
(612) 338-2068
help4kids@freespirit.com
freespirit.com

Free Spirit offers competitive pricing.
Contact edsales@freespirit.com for pricing information on multiple quantity purchases.

Dedication

To my parents, Elizabeth and Cecil Cash, who taught me how to think, encouraged my creativity, and told me I could do anything I set my mind to.

This book was born out of ideas I've gathered and generated throughout my years as a teacher. None of this would have been possible if it weren't for the exceptional mentoring and guidance I received from my friend and colleague, Mrs. Barbara Ford. Mrs. Ford, thank you for helping me become who I am today.

Acknowledgments

Thank you to Craig Feltmann for always believing in me, supporting me, and cheering me on in this process, and for making it a big deal. I don't think I could have done it without you. Special thanks to Dr. Diane Heacox, whose work has been a catalyst for change in classrooms around the world. Diane, you are a great collaborator, someone who makes me think at that next level, and fun to be around.

To the best editor I've ever had, Meg Bratsch: your finesse with my thoughts made me look good. You were a joy to work with.

I also want to thank my brothers Robert and John Cash, my sister Susan Swinick, and my dear friend Jennifer Stevens for never letting me get too big for my britches.

I greatly appreciate all the support and encouragement I received from my colleagues in the Bloomington Minnesota Public Schools, especially Dr. Tim Anderson and Sue Ostlund. You work hard to keep me humble.

Thank you to all the teachers who created examples for the materials in this book, especially my friends in the Washoe County Public Schools GATE department—I'm amazed by your creativity!

Finally, I extend my sincerest appreciation to my goddesses: Barbara Dullaghan and Julie Donaldson. Your passions for excellence, insights into learning, and love for the students keeps me grounded in why we do what we do!

Contents

Reproducible Pages viii
Figures ix
Foreword by Diane Heacox, Ed.D. xi
Introduction 1
   The Next Level of Differentiation 1
   The Importance of Thinking Skills in
      Today's World 2
   About This Book and Digital Content 3
   How to Use This Book 6

Part One
Taking Differentiation to the Next Level

Chapter 1: Defining How Differentiation Looks in Today's Classroom 10
   A Primer for Differentiation:
      The Whats, Hows, and Whys 10
   Dispelling the Myths of
      Differentiated Instruction 15
   Visible Differentiation: Supporting Teachers
      Through Observation Practices 18
   Technology Use in the
      Differentiated Classroom 19

Chapter 2: Defining the Essentials of a Differentiated Curriculum 28
   Skills for a New Century 28
   A Hierarchy of Knowledge: Factual,
      Procedural, Conceptual 29
   Four Steps to Defining the Essentials
      of Curriculum 30
   Mapping a Concept-Based Plan
      of Curriculum 42

Chapter 3: Advancing Differentiation to New Levels Through a Rigorous Curriculum 55
   What Is a Rigorous Curriculum? 55
   Hallmarks of a Rigorous Curriculum:
      Effective, Engaging, Exciting,
      Enriching (E^4) 56
   Infusing Rigor Into Your Curriculum 59

Chapter 4: Motivating and Engaging Learners 66
   What Is Motivation? 67
   Understanding How the Brain Learns 68
   Strategies to Motivate and Engage Students . . . 74
   Using Assessment to Motivate and Engage . . . 77

Chapter 5: Developing Student Self-Regulation 100
   Self-Regulation Theory 100
   Building Self-Regulation Through
      Goal Setting 102
   Building Self-Regulation Through
      Mindset 102
   The Student-Centered Classroom 103
   Using Centers and Stations to Develop
      Self-Regulation 107
   Five Understandings for Developing
      Self-Regulation for Learning 109

Chapter 6: The Teaching and Learning Continuum: Building Success Through Autonomy 113
   What Is the TLC? 113
   Why Build Autonomy? 114
   Framework Supporting the Teaching and
      Learning Continuum (TLC) 115
   The Four Levels of the TLC Model 116
   Assessment That Builds Autonomy 120

Part Two
Putting Thinking Skills to Use in the Classroom

Chapter 7: The Thinking Classroom.... 126
- 10 Skills for the Future Workforce 127
- What Is Thinking?....................... 127
- Divergent Thinking vs. Convergent Thinking 128
- Characteristics of a Thinking Student....... 129
- Characteristics of a Thinking Classroom 129
- Characteristics of a Thinking Curriculum ... 129
- Methods for Developing Intellectually Disciplined Thinkers................... 130
- General Strategies to Improve Student Thinking 135

Chapter 8: A Framework for Thinking: Digging Deeper into Bloom's Taxonomy 146
- A Brief Introduction to Bloom's Taxonomy... 146
- Performing Automatically to Performing Consciously 147
- Building on Bloom's 147
- Putting It All Together: The Digging Deeper Matrix (DDM)....................... 157

Chapter 9: Critical Thinking: Developing Reasoned Thought 159
- What Is Critical Thinking? 159
- General Critical Thinking Strategies 160
- Critical Thinking Strategies in Reading 161
- Critical Thinking Strategies in Writing 165
- Critical Thinking Strategies in Mathematics......................... 166
- Critical Thinking Strategies in Science...... 166
- Seven Critical Questioning Strategies to Use Daily 167
- Critical Thinking Tools 169

Chapter 10: Creative Thinking: Stepping Outside the Box........... 182
- What Is Creative Thinking? 183
- Characteristics of Creative Individuals 183
- Strategies to Develop Creative Thinking 184
- Creative Thinking Activities 187
- Creative "Sponge" Activities 191
- Additional Creative Activity Ideas 191
- Building a Creative Classroom............. 192

Chapter 11: Problem Finding, Problem Solving, and Decision Making........ 196
- Characteristics of Effective Problem Finders, Problem Solvers, and Decision Makers 196
- Finding Problems 197
- Solving Problems 197
- Decision Making........................ 203

A Final Note 211
Conclusion......................... 213
References and Resources 214
Index............................. 219
About the Author.................. 227

Reproducible Pages

> You may download these forms at **freespirit.com/AD-forms**.
> Use password **2engage**.

Chapter 1
10 Elements of a Differentiated Classroom 21
10 Elements of a Differentiated Classroom Survey 22–23
Classroom Indicators of Differentiated Instruction 24–27

Chapter 2
Concept Development Worksheet 49
Breaking Down the Essentials................. 50
Concept-Based Curriculum Map (Four-Term)..... 51
Concept-Based Unit Plan 52–54

Chapter 3
Principles of Curriculum and Instruction for Advancing Learning........................ 61
Classroom Practices for Advancing Learning 62
Walkthrough Checklist of Differentiation for Advancing Learning........................ 63
Guide to Tiering Assignments and Activities................................ 64–65

Chapter 4
25 Strategies for Developing a Boy-Friendly Classroom 81–82
Strategies for Creating a Brain-Compatible Learning Environment...................... 83
Brain Breaks................................. 84
I Chart...................................... 85
What Interests Me: Topic Preview 86
KIQ Chart 87
Rank Your Interests 88
Guidelines for Creating a Passion Project 89–90
Motivation Strategies Based on Student Interests 91
Sternberg Model of Abilities: Learning Preferences Activity 92–93
Motivation Strategies Based on Student Learning Preferences....................... 94
Four Square Concept Map...................... 95
3-2-1 Exit Slip/Entrance Ticket................ 96
Roundtable Review........................ 97–98
Motivation Strategies Based on Assessment 99

Chapter 5
Student Checklist for a Student-Centered Classroom 111
Teacher Checklist for a Student-Centered Classroom 112

Chapter 6
Teaching and Learning Continuum (TLC)...122–123

Chapter 7
Checklist of Characteristics of a Thinking Student......................... 137
Checklist of Characteristics of a Thinking Classroom 138
Checklist of Characteristics of a Thinking Curriculum 139
Teaching Thinking Skills: Lesson Format Template..................... 140–141
Guided Thinking Template.................... 142
Student Perception Questionnaire 143
Work Plan................................... 144
Student Reflection Log 145

Chapter 8
Digging Deeper Matrix (DDM) 158

Chapter 9
Spider Diagram 173
Compare and Contrast Graphic Organizer 174
Cross-Impact Matrix (CIM) 175
Infer: Justify Your Thinking.................. 176
Positive, Negative, Interesting (PNI).......... 177
Consider All the Issues (CAI) 178
Priority Ladder.............................. 179
Synthesis 3 + 1 180
Structured Thinking Organizer (STO) 181

Chapter 10
Norms of the Creative Classroom............. 194
Encouraging Creativity...................... 195

Chapter 11
Five Whys to Therefore 206
If-Then Mind Map for Decision Making 207
What Would Happen If . . . ? 208
What? So What? Now What? 209
12 Steps to Group Decision Making........... 210

Figures

Figure 1.1 The Pros and Cons of Technology Use 20
Figure 2.1 21st Century Workforce Skills 28
Figure 2.2 21st Century Curriculum Model 30
Figure 2.3 200 Abstract Concepts 32
Figure 2.4 Concept Development Lesson Sample 34–35
Figure 2.5 Relationships–Rigor–Relevance: The 3 Rs of Sense-Making for Deeper Understanding 36
Figure 2.6 Concept Development Worksheet: Example 36
Figure 2.7 The Pyramid of Knowledge 37
Figure 2.8 Breaking Down the Essentials: Example Math Standard 38
Figure 2.9 Breaking Down the Essentials: Math Example (Lower Grades) 40
Figure 2.10 Breaking Down the Essentials: English Language Arts Example (Upper Grades) 41
Figure 2.11 Interconnected Concept Model: Example 42
Figure 2.12: Concept-Based Curriculum Map (Four-Term Example) 43
Figure 2.13: Concept-Based Curriculum Map (Three-Term Example) 44
Figure 2.14: Concept-Based Unit Plan: Example 46–48
Figure 4.1 The Cycle of Motivation 68
Figure 4.2 The Brain's Domains 68
Figure 4.3 The Hindbrain 69
Figure 4.4 The Midbrain 69
Figure 4.5 The Reptilian Brain 70
Figure 4.6 The Cerebral Cortex 70
Figure 4.7 The Four Lobes of the Cortex 71
Figure 4.8: Students' Needs, Wants, and Requirements 73
Figure 4.9 Pathway to a Motivating and Engaging Classroom 74
Figure 4.10 Rank Your Interests: Example—The Nervous System 75
Figure. 4.11 Using Assessment as Feedback to Students 78
Figure 4.12 Four Square Concept Map: Example 78
Figure 4.13 Read-Write-Pair-Share and Think-Pair-Share 79
Figure 4.14 1- to 3-Minute Coaching/Consultation 79
Figure 4.15 Tiered Review/Practice 80
Figure 5.1 Self-Regulation for Learning Model 100
Figure 5.2 Four Stages of Self-Regulation 101
Figure 5.3 Cycle of Progression of Achievement 102
Figure 5.4 10:2/20:2 Rule 106
Figure 5:5 Five Understandings for Developing Self-Regulation for Learning 110
Figure 6.1 Gradual Release of Responsibility Model 115
Figure 6.2 TLC Level 1: Didactic Instruction 117
Figure 6.3 TLC Level 2: Facilitated Instruction 118
Figure 6.4 TLC Level 3: Coached Instruction 118
Figure 6.5 TLC Level 4: Consultative Instruction 119
Figure 6.6 Assessment That Builds Autonomy 121
Figure 7.1 Divergent Thinking 128
Figure 7.2 Convergent Thinking 128
Figure 7.3 Teaching Thinking Skills: Lesson Format Example 131

Figures (continued)

Figure 7.4 Guided Thinking: Math Example. 133
Figure 7.5 Guided Thinking: History Example. 133
Figure 7.6 Asking Good Questions Cycle 136
Figure 8.1 Bloom's Taxonomy 1956. 147
Figure 8.2 Implementing Bloom's Revised Taxonomy. 148
Figure 8.3 Bloom's Revised Taxonomy with Additional Assessment Layer 149
Figure 8.4 Digging Deeper into Bloom's: Science Example (Lower Grades). 150
Figure 8.5 Digging Deeper into Bloom's: History Example (Upper Grades). 151
Figure 8.6: Digging Deeper into Bloom's: Math Example (Intermediate Grades). 152–153
Figure 8.7 The Three Stages of the *Understand* Level. 154
Figure 9.1 Spider Diagram: Example—Biological Systems 161
Figure 9.2 Advanced Compare and Contrast Graphic Organizer: Examples. 162
Figure 9.3 CIM: Examples. 163
Figure 9.4 Sequencing and Prioritizing Graphics 164–165
Figure 9.5 PNI: Examples (Lower Grades). 170
Figure 9.6 PNI: Example (Upper Grades) 170
Figure 9.7 Priority Ladder: Example. 172
Figure 11.1 A Linear-Cyclical Problem-Solving Process. 198
Figure 11.2 Five Whys to Therefore: Example 198
Figure 11.3 If-Then Mind Map for Decision Making: Example 199
Figure 11.4 What Would Happen If . . . ? Example. 199
Figure 11.5 What? So What? Now What? Example 200
Figure 12.1 Connecting Differentiation and 21st Century Thinking and Learning. 212

Foreword by Diane Heacox, Ed.D.

As teachers, we are frequently presented with new educational paradigms, school and government initiatives, and an ever-expanding list of "do's." This is what keeps us engaged and learning, but it can also feel a bit overwhelming.

Today's students differ greatly from each other and their learning needs vary even more dramatically than ever. Such classroom disparities require educators to think differently about teaching and learning. Richard Cash's *Advancing Differentiation: Thinking and Learning for the 21st Century* is a comprehensive resource that enables teachers to deepen their understandings of differentiation as well as prepare our students for their tomorrows.

Teaching for an increasingly more diverse world means infusing more complexity and rigor in learning, focusing on conceptual knowledge beyond subject-specific knowledge, employing strategies to engage and motivate learners, building student self-regulation skills and learning autonomy, and developing students' thinking proficiencies. This is no small charge. However, the insights, ideas, and easy-to-implement strategies in this book enable you to critically examine your current classroom practices. Planning templates are offered to easily guide you in developing new teaching habits and routines.

The first six chapters provide ideas for optimizing curriculum and instructional practices to increase student achievement. Richard defines the essential elements of curriculum for the twenty-first century, as well as ways to motivate and actively engage students in the learning process. Focusing on best practices, he also includes an overview of how the brain learns and the impact of culture and gender on learning.

This revision contains many new concepts and ideas to explore and put into action in your classroom. Particularly helpful is Richard's step-by-step process for developing concept-based learning. He contends that for our students' futures, we need to place less emphasis on factual knowledge and a greater focus on procedural and conceptual knowledge. He provides a curriculum map template and unit planning tools to guide teachers thoughtfully through this shift in their curriculum.

Additionally, new templates and figures deliver fresh insights into designing tiered assignments and embedding technology, experimentation, inquiry, and problem solving in authentic learning tasks. Our understandings of the effects of poverty on learners, as well as the importance of self-regulation skills, are deepened in this edition.

Advances in technology have altered the very nature of pedagogy. The tools of technology and the tremendous access to information have changed the act of teaching. Richard considers both the positives and negatives of classroom technology and challenges us to consider that the efficiency of technology in supporting learning is enhanced through the thinking and learning habits of our students. This revision also examines how the "flipped classroom" may enhance differentiation in your classroom.

The Teaching and Learning Continuum (TLC) in Chapter 6 may be of particular interest to teachers. We want our students to take more responsibility for and control of their learning. However, students do not necessarily develop skills of autonomy independently as they mature. The TLC model suggests that in order to move all students toward greater autonomy, we must change the role of the teacher and the learner. Specific strategies for guiding students to greater levels of autonomy are clearly outlined in this chapter and throughout the book.

The final four chapters focus on the skills essential for our students' success in the future. Richard introduces us to the foundations of thinking proficiency: critical reasoning, creative idea generation, problem finding and solving, and decision making. He coaches us in our efforts to formally introduce thinking skills to students, bring the skills to the students' consciousnesses, and embed the skills in our curriculum and lessons. He provides generous examples of lessons bridging many grade levels and curriculum topics. Graphic organizers provided for thinking skills will save you preparation time. Richard's concept of "digging deeper into Bloom's" will change the way you use the Bloom's Taxonomy model in your classroom.

Advancing Differentiation is your go-to resource as you extend your practices in differentiation and increase your focus on twenty-first century skills, dispositions, and attitudes essential for a progressively more complex world. All educators—from novices to master teachers—will find next steps in their professional development within the pages of this comprehensive book. Strategies, templates, tools, and examples will make your work in preparing your students for their futures both doable and practical. Enjoy this engaging and enlightening book as Richard Cash guides and coaches you in developing new habits in teaching and learning.

Diane Heacox, Ed.D.
Author of *Differentiating Instruction in the Regular Classroom* and *Making Differentiation a Habit*, coauthor of *Differentiation for Gifted Learners*, and Professor Emerita of Education at St. Catherine University in St. Paul, Minnesota

Introduction

> We are now at a point where we must educate our children in what no one knew yesterday, and prepare our schools for what no one knows yet.
>
> —Margaret Mead, cultural anthropologist

Mrs. Donaldson is a sixth-grade teacher in a suburban school district. Her 30 students come from four continents, speak seven different languages, represent every major ethnic group, range in economic status from disadvantaged to wealthy, differ intellectually from developmentally delayed to gifted, and are a genuine cross-section of social and emotional needs. One thing her students have in common is they are all learning. She has made an effort to know each student as an individual, understands their learning preferences, is familiar with their interests and cultural backgrounds, and continually assesses them to find out what they know and don't know, what they are and aren't able to do, and what they understand and don't understand. While she has constant demands on her time as a teacher, she's made it a priority to differentiate her instructional strategies as well as her learning environment. It's paying off in her students' success and in her classroom's efficiency. Mrs. Donaldson's not an expert on differentiation—and she doesn't need to be—but she's on the journey toward proficiency.

I have observed and worked with hundreds of teachers like Mrs. Donaldson; they inspired me to write this book. In our challenging time of new standards, evolving high-stakes testing, efforts to eliminate the achievement gap, and constant political pressure to improve student performance, I am continually amazed by these teachers' passions for ensuring every child is not only prepared to meet standards and pass tests, but is truly prepared for future success.

The Next Level of Differentiation

Today's classroom is far different from the one many teachers, parents, and business professionals encountered during their own 13-plus school years. Advances in technology like one-to-one tablet or laptop initiatives, continued developments in learning and brain theories, and expansion of knowledge are just a few of the forces requiring educators to change the way they teach children. In addition, student needs today vary more dramatically than ever. Students come to our classrooms with preparation ranging from early exposure to vast amounts of information to limited access to reading materials. Student learning differences are developing and being identified earlier and are more wide-ranging. These differences include sensory processing disorders; emotional and behavioral issues; differences in memory, abstraction, or sequencing ability; dyslexia; ADHD; autism; degrees of English language proficiency; and various levels and types of giftedness, among many others. Such disparities require us to think differently about how we design our curriculum and deliver instruction.

When we truly know our students, we are better able to meet their needs and direct our curriculum and instruction toward ensuring their success. However, the curriculum many of us use in our classrooms, in the form of textbooks and other classroom learning materials, is often not enough to meet the myriad needs of learners and prepare them for their futures. While retaining fidelity to a standards-based curriculum is essential, it also is our job as teachers to adapt and enhance this curriculum when needed to ensure our students' success. This often means infusing more rigor and conceptual knowledge into the curriculum, employing specific strategies to engage and motivate students, building students' self-regulation skills and learning autonomy, and, perhaps most importantly, making certain our students are not just learning but also are *thinking*.

The Importance of Thinking Skills in Today's World

As Margaret Mead so aptly stated, "Children must be taught how to think not what to think."[1] Beyond the need for a rigorous curriculum and differentiated instruction is the core need for thinking skills. In today's differentiated classroom, students and teachers must work together toward a common goal of thinking proficiency. In addition to subject-specific knowledge, thinking skills are crucial to students' future success in their work, personal, and community lives. Thinking skills, most generally, include the ability to take in and make sense of new information and connect, apply, and transform that information into unique and novel ideas. Proficiency in thinking involves the capacity to analyze information and find problems, evaluate evidence through critical reasoning, and then creatively synthesize ideas to generate new knowledge.

Our students must be equipped to think differently, cogently, and flexibly to thrive in today's world. A 1991 school improvement research report cited, "In the twentieth century, the ability to engage in careful, reflective thought has been viewed in various ways: as a fundamental characteristic of an educated person, as a requirement for responsible citizenship in a democratic society, and, more recently, as an employability skill for an increasingly wide range of jobs."[2] Now in the twenty-first century, with the fast and furious advances in technology, vast increases in the amount of information at our fingertips, diversification of the workforce, and the "flattening" of the world through global trade and communication—it is more crucial than ever that our students be taught these skills of effective thinking. Being able to think, both critically and creatively, is the characteristic that will determine whether our students succeed as members of today's workforce and society, and tomorrow's.

The Partnership for 21st Century Learning, a national advocacy organization in the United States, has defined five essential competencies that help employees and citizens be successful in this century. They include *adaptability*, *self-direction*, *cross-cultural skills*, *productivity*, and *leadership*. In addition, the organization has identified the five major interdisciplinary themes these thinking skills will likely be centered on: *global awareness* and *financial*, *civic*, *health*, and *environmental* literacy.[3] Similarly, the Global Digital Citizen Foundation, "a nonprofit organization dedicated to cultivating responsible, ethical, global citizens for a digital world," suggests that students need to be proficient in "transparency-level skills" of:

- problem solving
- creativity
- analytic thinking
- collaboration
- communication
- ethics, action, and accountability[4]

Thus, effective thinking skills are imperative for our students to develop into individuals who are able to locate and prioritize information, employ ever-advancing technologies, retain and continually build on essential knowledge and skill sets, and contribute innovative solutions to increasingly complex societal and environmental problems. Proficient thinking will also enable students to relate to people of diverse backgrounds, maintain functional relationships, manage their individual goals and identity, make wise financial and personal health choices, and participate as informed citizens in a democracy.

An engaging, rigorous curriculum that infuses high-level thinking skills, delivered through authentic differentiated instructional practices within a student-centered classroom

---

1. Mead, M. *Coming of Age in Samoa: A Psychological Study of Primitive Youth for Western Civilisation*. New York: William Morrow, 1928.
2. Cotton, K. "Close-Up #1: Teaching Thinking Skills." *School Improvement Research Series Report*. Northwest Regional Educational Laboratory (NWREL), 1991.
3. The Partnership for 21st Century Learning (p21.org/our-work/p21-framework).
4. The Global Digital Citizen Foundation (globaldigitalcitizen.org).

environment—this is what will ultimately guarantee our students' current and future successes.

About This Book and Digital Content
What's New in This Revised Edition

Since the original release of *Advancing Differentiation*, I've had the great pleasure of working with numerous schools and districts around the world to improve education for all students. With the help of educators from those schools, I've gained new ideas and made refinements to this text. The purpose of this revision is to share with you the most up-to-date practices in differentiating curriculum and instruction.

Although updates were made throughout the book, the most significant changes occur in the early chapters. Those chapters give you a clearer understanding of what can be differentiated and how to best achieve the results you are seeking. Also, Chapter 1 discusses the crucial question, *Why differentiate at all?* Teachers, educational coaches, lead teachers, and administrators will find useful self-assessment surveys, observation forms, and new ideas for increasing proficiency in classroom differentiation.

Chapter 2 provides ways to address the changing needs of the future workforce. As our world moves at lightning speed, so too must our approaches to students' learning processes. An articulated curriculum design defines the differences between strategies and skills and refines the levels of conceptual knowledge. Schools and districts I work with have provided exceptional examples of ways they have aligned their curriculum by using the concept-based map and unit plan.

Other new elements and ideas include:
- designing authentic learning and tiering assignments and activities (Chapter 3)
- working with students living in poverty (Chapter 4)
- using learning centers and stations to develop self-regulation (Chapter 5)
- developing activities that promote autonomous learning (Chapter 6)
- teaching students the steps to asking good questions (Chapter 7)
- additional examples of the Digging Deeper Matrix (DDM) (Chapter 8)
- more critical thinking templates (Chapter 9)
- encouraging creativity in math (Chapter 10)

About *Advancing Differentiation*

As suggested in the title, *Advancing Differentiation: Thinking and Learning for the 21st Century* is intended to move you from where you are now in the procedures of differentiation to the next level of infusing the thinking and learning skills essential for student success and college and career readiness. The book is divided into two parts, both focused on evolving your practice of differentiation. Part One helps you better articulate the content (what you expect students to learn) and how you organize the environment (brain-compatible learning) so your students are more successful in acquiring and achieving standards and goals. You will be introduced to methods for defining the essential components of your curriculum and ways to motivate, engage, and build your students' responsibility in the learning process. Part Two is focused on the process (how students think through the learning) and products (how students can eloquently show what they have learned). The book's second half guides you through infusing and implementing 21st Century Skills. It defines the various levels of thinking and provides a wealth of practical strategies that can be applied to any classroom.

Together, the two parts of this book combine the concept of differentiation with the skills our students need for success in the twenty-first century. When considering the actions of differentiating content, teachers must be aware of the concepts, procedures, and facts they want their students to understand, be able to do, and know. Conceptual levels of learning are supported through the execution of procedures and implementation of facts. It is these understandings of concepts that move our students to greater degrees of success in today's world. Being able to aptly apply skills and procedures in multiple contexts and in automatic ways gives students the mental time and energy to problem solve, reason critically, and think creatively. This all is supported with a strong knowledge base in and among disciplines.

The essential goal of this book is to help teachers create a classroom environment that identifies and embeds twenty-first century skills within the curriculum, reinforces these skills through instructional practices, and requires the generation of creative and original products. Additional goals are included in the following list.

The Goals of This Book

- To clarify how differentiation can be taken to the next level in today's classroom
- To provide methods for defining the key components of your curriculum: what students should understand, be able to do, and know
- To offer ideas for creating effective unit-based and essential questions
- To examine what constitutes a quality, rigorous, concept-based curriculum
- To lay out a framework to help you create effective, engaging, exciting, and enriching learning opportunities that guide all students to deeper levels of thinking
- To present research and evidence-based information on student motivation and engagement
- To offer an overview of how the brain learns, including the impacts of gender, ethnicity, and cultural background on learning
- To supply useful strategies and helpful assessment formats that can increase student achievement
- To provide valuable tools for developing student self-regulation and responsibility in learning
- To offer a unique design for increasing student autonomy in the learning process
- To outline numerous strategies for infusing the skills of critical and creative thinking, problem finding, problem solving, and decision making
- To define essential tools for building a classroom centered on student learning and thinking proficiency

Part One (Chapters 1–6) leads you through the process of taking your current differentiation practices to the next level. In order to masterfully differentiate instruction, you must have articulate knowledge about how your curriculum is designed. Knowing what goes into the construction of curriculum will help you define what is essential, learn how to increase rigor, motivate and engage your students, and thus develop lifelong learners.

Chapter 1 explains how, with the ever-changing demographics and needs of students, differentiation takes on a new immediacy in today's classrooms. *Differentiated instruction* is a crucial strategy within leading instructional paradigms such as Multi-Tiered System of Supports (MTSS) and Response to Intervention (RTI). Many myths surround differentiation: what it is and is not, what it can and cannot do. This chapter dispels these myths in both the classroom and school culture of student success. It also presents Figure 1.1 The Pros and Cons of Technology Use and discusses the impact of technology use on classroom instruction. Included in this chapter is the 10 Elements of a Differentiated Classroom Survey. This handy tool can be used as a personal self-awareness gauge or as a building-wide focusing tool for professional development.

Chapter 2 outlines the *essentials of the curriculum* you deliver in the process of differentiating. The focus of this chapter is to relate the three levels of knowledge construction: what your students should understand, be able to do, and know. These levels also relate to the three types of knowing: conceptual knowledge, procedural knowledge, and factual knowledge. Factual knowledge includes the terminology, specific details, and basic elements that students must be acquainted with to work within the discipline. Skills, procedures, techniques, and thinking strategies are all examples of procedural knowledge. The highest level of learning is conceptual knowledge, which provides students with a framework for understanding the relationships between disciplines—from classifications, to principles and generalizations, to theories and models. Conceptual knowledge is also defined in levels of abstraction from universal to content-based to self-regulatory.

Chapter 3 defines and asserts the need for a *rigorous curriculum* that is effective, engaging, exciting, and enriching (an "E^4" curriculum). The chapter highlights the need for all students to engage in conceptually based complex learning tasks that allow them to explore content through various learning modes. Students are stretched in their learning when they complete authentic tasks. Additionally, students gain ownership of the learning when they engage in substantive conversations about content that is relevant to their lives. Ideas for increasing authentic learning and tiering assignments and activities are included in this chapter.

Chapter 4 guides you in creating a learning environment in which students develop the intrinsic desire to learn. *Intrinsic motivation* is achieved when learning tasks stimulate students, develop their interests, and foster appropriate skill development. Engaging students in interesting, fun, and personally meaningful tasks makes them want to learn. This chapter offers suggestions for developing a classroom that is based on student choice and is intrinsically motivating. It explores learning preferences and how you can use them to improve achievement. It provides instructional ideas related to gender and cultural differences and working with students in poverty, as well as various brain-compatible learning strategies and examples. Robert Sternberg's model of "Successful Intelligence" also is explained and related curricular formats are offered. Finally, this chapter outlines a *three-phase assessment process* that both motivates students and helps you determine their readiness levels. Assessment *before* learning identifies which skills and processes students possess at the beginning of each lesson. Assessment *for* learning is the systemic, ongoing, dynamic process of collecting and analyzing data to improve student learning. Assessment *of* learning identifies how close the student came to achieving the learning goal. This section offers tips and suggestions for assessment application and grading practices.

Chapter 5 provides strategies for encouraging *self-regulation* and building a student-centered classroom. When students have an awareness of their own learning process, it helps them monitor their progress, make changes and adaptations when necessary, understand the usefulness of various learning strategies, and recognize the direct relationship between effort and learning. Five key elements are defined for mobilizing resources to improve student self-regulation. The chapter also shows you how to use the theory of mindset to assist learners in developing metacognitive awareness to achieve their goals. Finally, reflection on the learning process is critical to understanding successes and gaps in learning. Several ideas are offered for developing efficient reflective practices. You will also gain a greater understanding of how to use centers and stations in your classroom to develop students' self-regulation.

Chapter 6 discusses the benefits and goals of student *learning autonomy* and introduces the Teaching and Learning Continuum (TLC) model. Teaching students to be self-directed learners is fostered through a gradual transformation in student and teacher roles. Without a progressive instructional design, students may struggle in conducting quality independent learning. Building on a synthesis of research on teaching and learning, the TLC offers a framework for the changing roles and responsibilities of both teacher and student. As the learner gains skills toward self-guidance, the teacher becomes more consultative. Also suggested are classroom strategies, practices, and activities for developing each level of student independence and autonomy.

Part Two (Chapters 7–11) guides you in implementing effective high-level thinking skills in your differentiated classroom. This section articulates and defines the concept of thinking and offers ways to integrate thinking skills into any curricular area, topic, or grade level. It also provides a template to use as an overlay to enhance and extend material offered in textbooks.

Chapter 7 asserts that the foundations of *thinking proficiency* are critical reasoning, creative idea generation, problem finding and solving, and decision making. This chapter explains the need for both divergent and convergent thinking, and defines the characteristics of a thinking student, a thinking classroom, and a thinking curriculum. It also provides methods for developing intellectually disciplined thinkers.

Chapter 8 constructs a *framework for thinking* by using Benjamin Bloom's Taxonomy of Learning and Robert Marzano's Advanced Taxonomy of Learning to explore various questioning techniques and lesson designs. This chapter provides you with strategies to move learners from basic to complex levels of thinking, and from automatic reproduction to conscious self-awareness in the learning process. Examples of the Digging Deeper Matrix (DDM) will show you how to advance learning for all students.

Chapter 9 discusses *critical thinking*, which entails making decisions based on the evidence at hand. Without sufficient training in critical thinking and reasoning, students often use emotion, opinion, or instinct to make decisions. This chapter presents strategies and curricular ideas for how students can form questions to build relevant claims and inform the decision-making process. Helpful graphic organizers and examples are also included.

Chapter 10 emphasizes the importance of *creative idea generation* in the classroom. As our world changes more rapidly each year, our students must be provided with the skills to develop their own creativity and creative thinking abilities. The ability to think "outside the box" is framed through fluency, flexibility, originality, and elaboration (FFOE). This chapter defines these four elements and articulates curricular connections. Strategies for supporting a creative learning environment are also introduced. Of special note are the ideas for encouraging creativity in mathematics.

Chapter 11 illustrates the process of approaching learning through the lens of *problem finding and solving* in order to engage learners more completely. For students to solve problems, they need a tool kit filled with many diverse tools. This chapter provides problem-finding techniques, problem-solving strategies, as well as decision-making skills.

Finally, the **Final Note** and **Conclusion** review the key points of the text and also revisit the issue, presented in Chapter 1, of technology in the classroom and discuss how it can be successfully incorporated as an important component in thinking and learning for the twenty-first century. Included is a graphic depicting the connection, made throughout the book, between differentiation and twenty-first century thinking and learning.

The digital content (see page viii for how to download) includes all of the reproducible forms from the book as PDFs. Many of the forms can be customized on-screen before printing them out. In addition, a slideshow presentation is included for use in professional development.

If you wish to use the book in a professional learning community or book study group, a PLC/Book Study Guide with chapter-by-chapter discussion questions and teaching suggestions is available. You may download the free guide at freespirit.com/PLC.

How to Use This Book

Advancing Differentiation brings together essential elements of curriculum design and the latest research on thinking and learning. This book is a culmination of my journey as a student of learning. I've connected the theoretical ideas into practical, proven strategies that can increase students' achievement and ultimately lead to their future success.

My intent with this guide is to support classroom teachers, teacher coaches, school administrators, and curriculum developers in enriching and enhancing the learning experiences of all students. I also believe this book serves as an excellent resource for teacher education college courses. The ideas, strategies, and techniques fit within any content area, grade level, or ability level. While sample figures and templates may illustrate higher grade levels, they can easily be adjusted for lower grade levels, and vice versa.

By using the 10 Elements of a Differentiated Classroom Survey in Chapter 1, you may decide to pursue various directions. You may choose to go through the book chapter by chapter, building a rigorous curriculum and a thinking classroom from the sequential flow of the text. Or, you may choose to review the text in its entirety, examine your current practices, and then select individual chapters that can help you refine what you are already doing to ensure all of your students are thinking and learning. For example, you may find that your existing textbook materials do not offer enough information about concept development or provide for rigorously engaging activities. You will then want to focus your attention on Chapter 3: Advancing Differentiation to New Levels Through a Rigorous Curriculum.

If you are a specialist outside the role of a classroom teacher—such as a teacher coach, curriculum coordinator, gifted and talented specialist, or school administrator—this book can be a valuable resource. How do you help teachers understand how curriculum is designed? In what ways can you help teachers and students create their own essential questions? How do you get students to think effectively in this age of standardized testing? How do you infuse thinking skills without having to remove something else from the curriculum? You will find the answers to these questions and more within these pages.

You may be asking yourself, "Where do I begin? How do I get started? What do I need to know?" I suggest starting small. Get a taste for success. Take one idea or topic from this book and make it work for you and your students. I've arranged each chapter to provide a general overview of the theory that grounds the practices, and then give plenty of examples of how to apply the ideas to your classroom. Not every idea presented here will work for you, but many can be adjusted and modified to fit your students and curricular needs. I hope that you will find this text to be an essential resource in your classroom, school, and district to engage your students in the art of thinking, increase their achievement, and ensure lifelong success.

Enjoy!

Richard M. Cash, Ed.D.

PART ONE

Taking Differentiation to the Next Level

The following six chapters serve as a valuable resource in building your portfolio of differentiated curriculum and instruction practices. The art of differentiation is about being proactive in meeting *each* of your students' learning needs. Having a greater storehouse of ideas, strategies, and techniques can better prepare you for the diversity of these needs in the twenty-first century.

Defining How Differentiation Looks in Today's Classroom

Differentiated instruction is a way of taking into account the needs and wants of others without relinquishing our own needs and wants, or dominating and controlling the other person. In that way, differentiated instruction is more than just a method of teaching; it is a way of being human.

—Carol Ann Tomlinson, author and educator

As a teacher these days, you have likely been introduced to a plethora of "new" initiatives that can improve how your students learn. Integrated math, whole language, standards-based assessment, newly designed standards—the list goes on. For years, teachers of gifted and talented students (such as myself) have been required to use the strategies of differentiated instruction, because not all gifted students are gifted in the same way. Outstanding pioneers of gifted education such as John Feldhusen, Joseph Renzulli, Joyce VanTassel-Baska, and Sandra Kaplan instructed teachers of gifted kids how to identify their students' strengths and limitations, build units based on higher order thinking skills (or HOTS), and create lessons that were loaded with critical reasoning and creative thinking. This education of gifted and talented students was known by the acronym GT. I see now, however, after many years working with a broader group of students, that what we have learned in gifted and talented education can be applied to *all* students at varying degrees of sophistication. I now call GT: great teaching! This book is full of GT ideas, strategies, and techniques for every learner.

A Primer for Differentiation: The Whats, Hows, and Whys

Differentiation is not simply the act of creating a variety of options for students or making some activities more or less structured. The theory behind differentiation is to focus on individual learners and be aware of where they begin their learning and where they need to go. We need to know the steps along this pathway and provide students with appropriate guidance toward achievable goals. To do this, we identify what our students need to know, be able to do, and understand to be successful in this new century. This chapter examines *what* can be differentiated, *how* it can be differentiated, and most critically, *why* it needs to be differentiated.

What Can Be Differentiated?

Differentiate Environment: The Where and When of Learning

In past centuries, to learn meant going to school where the textual information and teacher knowledge existed. That no longer holds true today. Information of all kinds is available from multiple resources, most specifically the Internet. Our students may now be doing more learning outside the classroom than inside it. The environment of learning has changed dramatically with the advancement of technology and new understandings of how learning happens.

Differentiating the learning environment involves many more dimensions than simply the classroom arrangement. Though classroom arrangement is powerful, we need to think beyond the room's four walls. Consider using a "flipped classroom" as a way to differentiate the environment. A flipped classroom rearranges classroom instruction and homework. In a typical classroom, the teacher delivers content through direct instruction or other pedagogical methods, and then students take work home to practice the new content. In a flipped classroom, content is delivered through short videos (or other mediums) viewed by students at home, and the teacher works directly with students to practice the new content during class time. While there is no single model for a flipped classroom, the underlying concept is to reverse what students do in and out of the classroom in order to increase students' engagement, decrease incorrect practice, and involve the teacher more directly in students' learning.

DIFFERENTIATION IDEAS FOR FLIPPED CLASSROOMS

Flipping the classroom is more than just having kids view videos at home. Think of it as time-shifting direct instruction to outside the classroom, while providing more face-to-face time with students inside the classroom. Consider what can be gathered outside the classroom (such as facts and background knowledge) and how it might be delivered.

Use a flipped classroom for:
- previewing a topic
- pre-teaching vocabulary
- reteaching lessons
- posing questions
- gaining prerequisite knowledge
- teaching various levels of courses within one room (such as world languages or mathematics)
- students with different learning needs or requiring extended time
- leveled activities based on readiness
- enriching and enhancing topics of study based on interest
- self-paced learning
- independent or self-directed learning
- learning stations or centers
- reviewing for quizzes or exams

Ways to flip:
- host an online Moodle or Blackboard conversation (using internal servers)
- create movies by lesson, topic, or unit using video editing software
- have students create videos of topics as final assessments that can then be saved each year for other students to view for pre- or reteaching, review, or self-paced learning
- use selected websites, such as Khan Academy
- assign Internet searches on topics of interest
- make a video of your lectures and provide them to students on DVDs, flash drives, or in a shared cloud storage folder for home viewing
- provide students with screen captures of your direct instruction
- create digital presentations with voiceover instruction
- assign audiobooks

Flipping requires:
- careful planning and additional work on your part (at least at first)
- knowledge of new technologies and presentation formats
- time to create recordings of instruction
- student access to technology outside of school
- preparing students to take responsibility for consuming material at home
- motivating students to gather information at home
- revising class time to involve highly interactive and hands-on learning
- forward thinking in situations when technology fails or students are not prepared

Benefits of flipping the classroom:
- promotes student-centered learning
- greater student engagement through technology

- students learn to take responsibility for and control over their learning
- visual learners enjoy learning through seeing
- students can consume material at their own pace
- students can reconnect with the content if they need review or reteaching
- as students apply new learning, the teacher is present to offer real-time feedback
- better student-teacher interactions
- can improve student achievement
- can improve students' attitudes toward learning
- makes home connection more valuable because parents can see what is being taught

Differentiate Content: What You Want Students to Learn

The content, or curriculum, is what you want your students to learn. More than just what you teach, what you want students to *learn* is the focus of differentiation for the twenty-first century. Content is defined as what students need to know factually, be able to do procedurally, and understand conceptually. Many ideas for increasing the depth and complexity of your content will be shared in later chapters.

Differentiate Process: How Students Own the Learning

Some students enjoy working in groups, while others like to learn alone. Some students need more scaffolds or practice to develop skills, while others need less time and practice. The learning process involves the lessons and activities students engage in to acquire skills and develop conceptual understandings. Throughout this book, multiple options are presented for differentiating lessons and activities.

One of the most effective ways to differentiate the learning process is through the use of flexible grouping. The practice of grouping has a long and sometimes stormy presence in education. When used poorly, such as using long-term stable or tracked groups based on students' abilities, grouping has been shown to have a negative effect on students. However, small-group instruction when used wisely—such as grouping students by readiness to learn a new set of strategies, by interest for deeper learning, or by learning preference to increase motivation—can have a positive academic and affective outcome for students.[1] *Keep in mind:* Grouping alone does not improve achievement. It is the differentiation of curriculum and instruction within the groups that improves achievement.

BENEFITS OF GROUP WORK

Grouping helps build these 21st Century Skills:
- cooperation
- collaboration
- communication
- risk-taking
- flexibility
- motivation
- engagement

10 TIPS FOR PRODUCTIVE GROUP WORK

Ensure that:
1. Students know the reasons for and benefits of group work.
2. All group members are clear about the rules, procedures, and norms.
3. Group type matches task outcome.
4. Group size fits the function of the task (a suggested size is three to five students).
5. Group members receive feedback about their performance.
6. Group membership is flexible when the group is functioning below expectations (you have the right and duty to shift membership to ensure productivity).
7. All members feel part of the group and have duties to fulfill.
8. Group membership is balanced to bring out the best in each member.
9. Group leadership is selected democratically by individuals.
10. Students practice efficient movement in and out of the group.

---

1. Ward, B. A. "Instructional Grouping in the Classroom." Washington, DC: Office of Educational Research and Improvement (OERI), U.S. Department of Education, November 1987; Hattie, J. *Visible Learning*. New York: Routledge, 2009.

WAYS TO FORM GROUPS
- pretests/assessments/tests
- sign-ups
- survey/inventory
- peer-selection
- social webs
- self-selection/self-identify
- teacher selection

SAMPLE GROUP TYPES

Interest-Based
Students are arranged according to their interests. This can be changed by unit or by periods of time. The benefit of this type of grouping is that students focus attention on developing their talents and interests and connect new learning to prior knowledge. Interest-based grouping can also be an opportunity to introduce more complex, enriched topics into the content.

Readiness-Based
Following an achievement assessment, students with similar skill levels are grouped together to achieve a higher level of skill development. Materials must be tailored to the students' skill level with the goal of moving students to the next level. The benefit of this type of grouping is that it can offer advanced learners the option to work more independently and it can provide more teacher involvement for students with greater instructional need.

Learning Preference–Based
Students are grouped by likeness in learning preferences to complete a task. When completing a product, it may be beneficial to pair students with different preferences and each partner assumes a critical role (appropriate to his or her preference) in the completion of the product. For example, students who prefer creative modes of learning develop the product idea, students who prefer practical modes of learning ensure the product's usefulness and appeal, and students with analytical learning preferences keep the project on time and within budget.

Jigsaw
Each student or group of students receives a different part of the content and is responsible for learning the material. Then, students from different content groups are grouped together to share their information and teach the other members about the material.

Literature Circles
Small groups of students receive different texts with the same/similar theme or topic. Students spend part of the time within like groups to discuss questions and the other part of the time in unlike groups (similar to jigsaw groups) to discuss the similarities and differences among the various texts. The benefits of this grouping type are that it exposes students to various pieces of literature, demonstrates how authors use literary elements to convey meaning, and illustrates the different ways readers interpret literature.

Row/Column Grouping (by rank order)
Based on achievement assessment, students are ordered by rank using the following format. Students can then be grouped by column (achievement-based groups) or by row (heterogeneous groups). The benefit of column grouping is that there is a span of ability with a greater chance of students learning through role modeling. Keep in mind, however, that the greater the ability difference, the less likely students will role model.

Achievement-based group ↓	Heterogeneous group →		
	1	11	21
	2	12	22
	3	13	23
	4	14	24
	5	15	25
	6	16	26
	7	17	27
	8	18	28
	9	19	29
	10	20	30

Friendship/Colleague-Based
Grouping students based on their social connections can be an effective tool for developing comradery and inclusion. The critical element of friendship/colleague grouping is productivity. If the group becomes dysfunctional, you have the right and duty to change group membership.

Clock/Map Partners
Using a clock face or map, students select partners for particular times or locations. For example, a

student might choose: Sarah = 3 o'clock, Tom = 6 o'clock, Marilyn = 9 o'clock, and Derek = 12 o'clock; or Sarah = USA, Tom = Indonesia, Marilyn = France, and Derek = Ghana. When the teacher says, "Pair with your 3 o'clock (or USA) partners," students know with whom to pair. The benefit of this type of grouping is that partnerships are prearranged, which can make transitioning from a large group to small groups more efficient. (*Note:* The clock times are not meant to correlate with actual times of the day when grouping occurs, they are merely a group-naming device.)

Cooperative Groups

In cooperative groups, each member performs a specific role, such as leader, timekeeper, or note-taker. The benefit of this type of grouping is that it teaches students how to work together and to understand that each member adds value to and helps complete the task.

Study Buddies

Study buddies are prearranged partners who can assist one another in learning, completion of homework, or completion of a task during or after class time. Study buddies can meet virtually or in person. The benefit of this grouping method is that each student is assured a partner in learning. Study buddies can be chosen by the students or arranged by the teacher based on similar or complementary personalities, needs, or other characteristics.

Barometer Groups

A barometer group is a randomly selected small group of students that the teacher calls upon to gather data (formative assessment) to find out how well instruction is working, evaluate the classroom environment, or offer advice for adjustments to content, process, product, and environment.

Random Groups

Random grouping can be used when all learners are confident in the material or the learning. Students are randomly placed into groups to complete a task. The benefit of this type of grouping is that it exposes students to diverse ways of thinking and learning and can build a greater sense of community in the classroom.

Differentiate Product: The Way Students Demonstrate Their Learning

All students should be assessed on the same standards and tested in the same way on local, state, and national tests (most likely in a paper-and-pencil or online format), however, these forms of assessments may not always represent what the student has learned. Students can represent the product of their learning in many ways: what they know, are able to do, and understand. Some students enjoy making presentations while others may want to write about their learning. This is why product differentiation is a useful tool in the learning process. Chapter 4 provides several ideas for how to use assessment to motivate and engage students, and a model for assessment that can build learning autonomy is shared in Chapter 6.

How Can Learning Be Differentiated?

Differentiate by Readiness: Prepare for the Now

Readiness is not the same as ability. In some cases, you may take natural ability into account when designing lessons or activities, but mostly you are teaching to a student's skill development, which has to do with his or her preparation for the learning (or readiness). Some students come to school prepared with a great deal of skill development and background knowledge, while others have had limited experiences and will need more options and supports throughout the learning. Using readiness as a form of differentiation ensures that all students encounter challenge through respectful tasks and build toward achieving or exceeding standards.

Differentiate by Interest: Engage Through Choices

Every child has an interest in something; finding out what students are interested in can attach them to the learning. Additionally, getting students interested in the learning can have a significant effect on their desire to achieve academic goals. Interest is considered to be the highest form of engagement in learning—if you can tap into a child's interest, she or he will pay attention to the learning longer. Additionally, consider ways to pique students' interest in the lessons and topics. More ideas on discovering and piquing student interest can be found in Chapter 4.

Differentiate by Learning Preference: Respect Different Ways to Learn

Each of us learns in different ways. Some people enjoy reading about new topics, while others would rather have someone tell them about it. Some students enjoy learning in a group while others prefer to learn independently. And some students prefer creative learning activities, while others perform better on practical tasks. Considering how a student likes to learn and perform can be an effective way to engage and motivate students. Chapter 4 includes ideas for building lessons and activities based on the various ways kids prefer to learn.

Why Differentiate at All?

As stated previously, our classrooms are far more diverse and full of more distractions than any other time in history. We also have significant neurological evidence that supports the varied ways people prefer to learn. If we approach learning from only one direction, we most likely are not going to address the learning needs of the majority of our students. Planning for the differences in your classroom by offering options, choices, varied structures, and different ways of doing and showing work can significantly increase student motivation and achievement.

However, you won't be differentiating everything all the time. At times during instruction you will provide information to the whole class in one way, such as during a presentation or demonstration. Or, sometimes all students might need to work on the same task to prepare themselves for standards assessments or state testing. These tasks won't be differentiated. If, after an assessment, you find some students need more help or scaffolding, then differentiation becomes a factor.

When deciding what and how to differentiate, you need to have a clear *why*, or reason, for the actions of differentiation. Those reasons will come from your assessment data. Whether using pre-assessments, formative assessments, or summative exams, this data should inform you about variations in instruction or differing tasks. Always be specific about why you are differentiating to make your labors of creating differentiated learning successful. Throughout the remaining parts of this book you will find valuable assessment ideas to assist you in defining the "why" of defensible differentiation.

Dispelling the Myths of Differentiated Instruction

Often due to a lack of the basic information just provided, many teachers fear differentiated instruction. The numerous myths that surround the idea can sometimes stifle a teacher's willingness to begin the process of differentiating. Following is a collection of some of those myths and how they might be addressed to encourage teachers to move forward.

Myth #1: Differentiation is another word for individualization.

▶ **Reality:** Differentiation is *not* synonymous with individualization. All teachers individualize to some extent. When a teacher meets one-on-one with a student, individually answers questions, or modifies instruction based on an individual need, this is both individualization as well as differentiation. Individualization gained a bad reputation during the 1970s when teachers were expected to write individual lessons for students. This is not differentiation. Differentiation aims to meet individual needs through a quality curriculum and effective and efficient instructional practices that target groups of students based on learning readiness, individual interests, and preferred ways of learning—not through creating 30 or more separate lesson plans for every unit.

Myth #2: In a differentiated classroom you will see all the kids doing something different.

▶ **Reality:** All students should be provided relevant, meaningful, and challenging learning opportunities. Every lesson and activity should consider the individual students within the class, but not every child will be doing something different. There will be times when small groups of students or individuals will be engaged in different projects or independent or self-directed studies, and other times when all or most students are engaged in the same activity. Teachers in a differentiated classroom take on the role of managing the learning process. Just like in any work setting, not every worker is doing the same thing, but a good manager is clear about what each worker is doing and where each worker is in the process. So too in a differentiated classroom, the teacher, like a good manager, oversees and coordinates the learning process of each student, some in groups and some individually.

Myth #3: Differentiation will change everything and solve all of our teaching problems.

▶ **Reality:** Differentiation will not solve all your problems; it is not the magic potion that will instantly raise student achievement. Being a teacher who is mindful of his or her students' academic, social, and emotional needs is what will help address learning gaps, increase motivation to learn, and ultimately lead to a rise in student achievement. Differentiating curriculum and instruction means providing intervention strategies and techniques so that every student is successful. Differentiation doesn't happen in isolation or without a team effort. Just like in the Multi-Tiered System of Supports (MTSS) or Response to Intervention (RTI) model, differentiated instruction requires teachers to use data to make decisions about learning, employ effective practices, and reflect on the outcomes of its implementation. This is what differentiation can do to ensure all students meet or exceed expectations.

Myth #4: In a differentiated classroom the teacher does not teach.

▶ **Reality:** In a differentiated classroom the teacher is the key to student achievement. However, the role of teacher changes from the "sage on the stage" to the "guide on the side." There will be times when teachers may need to directly instruct, as well as times when students direct their own learning. Chapter 6 presents a teaching and learning continuum that supports students in gaining more autonomy in their learning. Though differentiation is nothing new, teachers must now be proactive about planning instruction to optimize student learning. They have thorough knowledge about what they want their students to learn; research effective practices to deliver instruction; implement quality strategies before, during, and after instruction; continually monitor student learning; and reflect on how well students have mastered material before moving on to the next topic.

Myth #5: You can't differentiate when you are trying to prepare for high-stakes testing.

▶ **Reality:** "Evidence clearly suggests that for most students, mastery and understanding come through, not after, meaningful interaction with ideas."[2] The first important objective of differentiation is for students to understand the content deeply. When students understand the content, they are *more* prepared for standardized tests rather than less, and their knowledge is not isolated to discrete bits of information applied in unreal situations. Students learn more deeply when allowed to connect information to previous experiences and knowledge, apply learned material in authentic situations, and exercise skills in problem solving, creative thinking, and critical reasoning. The second important objective of a differentiated classroom is to prepare students for all kinds of content delivery, including those that are undifferentiated (such as standardized tests). All assessments, including standardized tests, are tools that direct the plans for instruction as well as offer feedback to the learner. Teachers who differentiate use quality assessment strategies throughout the learning process including those that model standardized tests.

Myth #6: Differentiation is mainly for gifted students.

▶ **Reality:** Differentiation is for all students. A differentiated classroom is centered on students' readiness, interests, and learning preferences—not on ability alone. Some students will require more complex and in-depth material, while other students will require more scaffolding and foundation construction to support their learning experiences. When differentiating based on your students' abilities or achievement, it is critical to keep in mind that your gifted and advanced students do not get "more" work, they get "more challenging" work. Tasks must be respectful not only of students' abilities but also of their time. In differentiated classrooms, teachers apply principles of gifted education to all students.

Myth #7: Differentiation is just a way to group or track students.

▶ **Reality:** Tracking is the practice of permanently assigning students to a particular level of instruction with very little differentiation included. In a differentiated classroom, teachers routinely employ the strategy of flexible grouping practices, which include grouping students by interest,

---

2. Tomlinson, C. A., and J. McTighe. *Integrating Differentiated Instruction & Understanding by Design: Connecting Content and Kids.* Alexandria, VA: ASCD, 2006: 8.

ability, learning preference, academic strength/limitations, or gender. Teachers plan instruction so students move in and out of groups to interact with a variety of peers throughout the learning process. Sometimes students will work with like-ability students and sometimes with students who have different skills and/or abilities. In other cases, some students learn best while working with others and some learn best by working alone. This strategy takes into account students' interpersonal and intrapersonal strengths. The type of grouping depends on what outcome you expect from the activity.

Myth #8: Grading isn't fair in a differentiated classroom.
▶ **Reality:** Not all kids learn at the same rate. Therefore, grading in a differentiated classroom takes on an entirely different meaning. When teachers know *what* they want students to know, be able to do, and understand and *how* they want students to represent that knowledge, and they have developed quality grading criteria, then grading becomes about identifying students' acquisition of knowledge and mastery.

Grading in a differentiated classroom must be equitable and represented through a "photo album" of student growth. Three types of assessment are used in a differentiated classroom to ensure students are learning the material. Preassessments are used to find out what students know or don't know, are able or not able to do, and understand or don't understand before instruction begins. Formative assessments are used as checkpoints for how well the students are accumulating the information taught and provide the teacher with feedback about teaching strategies and pace. Summative assessments are used to mark students' achievement of goals set forth in a unit of study. You will employ all three of these assessment strategies to create a "grade" of how well the student gathered information and mastered content. Remember, it is *not* about the grade, but rather about what the student learned.

Myth #9: With everything teachers have to do, they can't be expected to differentiate, too.
▶ **Reality:** Differentiation of curriculum and instruction should not be separate from all other school initiatives. Differentiation is Multi-Tiered System of Supports (MTSS)/Response to Intervention (RTI); structured instruction, Sheltered Instruction Observation Protocol (SIOP); Positive Behavioral Interventions and Supports (PBIS); Advancement Via Individual Determination (AVID); guided reading; integrated math; college and career readiness; and the list goes on. All the initiatives that schools employ to provide safe and quality learning environments and to improve student achievement are methods of differentiation. Simply put, whatever it takes to ensure that every child is ready for the next step is differentiation. Differentiation is embedded within the educational systems; it is not a separate initiative.

Myth #10: Differentiation takes too much time that I don't have.
▶ **Reality:** Differentiation *will* require a considerable time investment initially, but in the long run it will actually save you time as a teacher and increase the overall efficiency of your classroom. Begin by creating your own mindset of doing whatever it takes to get students to be proficient in what you know to be essential about your content. Start small, work on one strategy at a time, develop expertise, and build a knowledge base. Every hour you invest now in planning and implementing differentiation will save you an hour in the future and will enable your students to succeed and progress more quickly.

Differentiating curriculum and instruction is *not* easy. It takes many hours for teachers to define what is essential for students to know, be able to do, and understand; figure out how best to provide engaging experiences for students to acquire this information; present information through multiple activities that assist students in applying the learning; create effective assessment strategies that can appraise where students are at in the learning process; and finally, offer authentic modes of production where students can demonstrate their knowledge. Differentiation is a teaching process that takes time and patience . . . but it is entirely doable.

The 10 Elements of a Differentiated Classroom on page 21 is for you to refer to as you read this book. Each of these elements will be explored in more detail throughout. Also included is the 10 Elements of a Differentiated Classroom Survey on pages 22–23. Use this survey to assess where you are in your knowledge and application of differentiation. It can also be used by a school to measure the entire staff's awareness of differentiation and set an agenda for professional development. As you take the survey, be as honest as you can in your responses. The more accurately you identify your understanding of differentiation, the more likely you are to move yourself and your school to greater levels of student achievement.

Visible Differentiation: Supporting Teachers Through Observation Practices

Differentiation is a complex process that requires practice, patience, and support. School leaders and coaches can help develop teachers' abilities to effectively differentiate curriculum and instruction but generally need guidance to do so. Many school districts and educational groups have found success using Charlotte Danielson's Framework for Teaching Evaluation Instrument[3] or Robert Marzano's Teacher Evaluation Model.[4] Based on empirical studies and theoretical research, Danielson and Marzano created comprehensive frameworks that identify aspects of effective teaching for evaluation.

That said, evaluating a developing practice may not be the most effective way to assist teachers with differentiation. Direct observation of a teacher in action may be better. By using the Danielson and Marzano models, I have identified four critical dimensions of a differentiated classroom that can be observed. Teacher leaders, instructional coaches, administrators, and others can use these ideas to help a teacher plan and prepare for differentiation, arrange the classroom environment, use effective management strategies, implement instructional practices and assessments that promote differentiation, and increase professional development focused on differentiation.

The indicators in each domain are suggested techniques or strategies that coaches can see in action in a differentiated classroom. Observing these indicators can help teachers reach greater success. I recommend that coaches use the Classroom Indicators of Differentiated Instruction form on pages 24–27 for three to four of the following observations:

Observation #1: Coach meets with the teacher prior to instruction. This meeting is intended to initiate a discussion about the teacher's knowledge of differentiation and how the teacher is considering the four key areas of differentiation: classroom *environment*, lesson *content*, learning activities (*process*), and ways for students to demonstrate learning (*product*). As the teacher discusses ideas, the coach listens for particulars cited in the left-hand column of the Classroom Indicators form. After the meeting, the coach reviews his or her notes to decide where the teacher is in developing a differentiation practice and shares with the teacher areas in which she or he is doing well and areas that may need developing.

Observation #2: Coach views teacher and students in classroom environment. This observation is intended to get a feel for the environment and the general strategies a teacher uses to manage the classroom. During this classroom visit, a coach watches for things such as how well the classroom is organized, the flow in the room, how students are developing self-regulation and independence, and so forth. The coach keeps an eye on the students and the classroom in general to assess how joyful the environment is. After the observation, the coach reviews and shares what he or she observed and suggests what the teacher might focus on to make the classroom environment more effective.

Observation #3: Coach reviews teacher's classroom instruction and assessment. After the coach has met with the teacher to share ideas for planning and environment, he or she directly observes the teacher's instructional practices of differentiation and assessment. While not all of the items listed in the left column of the Classroom Indicators form can be seen in one observation, the coach should be able to see or have represented items such as: clear objectives posted; "with-it-ness"; student uses of technology when appropriate; and so forth. The coach records observations and shares them with the teacher, asks if unseen items may be represented in other lessons or at other times, and makes recommendations for adjustments and additions.

---

3. Danielson, C. *The Framework for Teaching Evaluation Instrument, 2013 Edition.* Princeton, NJ: The Danielson Group, 2014.
4. Marzano, R. J. "The Marzano Teacher Evaluation Model." Englewood, CO: Marzano Research Laboratory (August 2011).

Observation #4 (optional): Coach and teacher discuss further professional development. After the coach has had three meetings with the teacher and has a better feel for where the teacher is at in the development of differentiation, he or she is ready to make suggestions for further professional development. The coach takes the entirety of the Classroom Indicators observation form into account when making suggestions for the teacher's development. The bullets in the left column of the form provide broad areas for development.

Differentiated instruction involves a teacher's proactive planning of instruction and curriculum meant to engage learners where they are in readiness levels, interests, and learning preferences.

Hallmarks of a Differentiated Classroom

- Clear and focused learning goals
- Alignment of learning goals, assessment, and instruction to standards
- Flexible grouping of students
- Flexible use of time, space, and materials
- Shared responsibility for learning
- Emphasis on individual growth
- Respectful work for all
- Focus on upward achievement for all
- High expectations for all
- Active partnerships with parents, other school resources, and community members
- Proactive planning to meet the needs of individual students

Technology Use in the Differentiated Classroom

As a teacher today, you likely employ many different forms of technology in your classroom to assist you in differentiating curriculum and instruction, ranging from tablets to electronic student response systems to one-to-one computers. These devices can be of great assistance in customizing lesson plans, tasks, activities, and assessments for students of diverse abilities and preferences. This book does not directly address technology use or computer literacy in today's classrooms; that topic is for another volume altogether (or, rather, multiple volumes). And yet the use of technology pervades nearly all of this book's contents. The tools and skills being used by you and your students to achieve the goals presented here are becoming more and more computer-based and technology-specific each year. Our goal for today's classrooms should go beyond the technology and skills of a global economy. We need to prepare our students for technologies that haven't been invented yet, to be employed in careers that don't exist yet, and to be able to deal with the exponential growth of knowledge and information. Our students must be ready to take on challenges never before encountered and be able to solve increasingly complex world problems. Technology is but one tool in our students' toolbox for building a better world.

Depending on your viewpoint, technology has made our lives either more efficient or more difficult. Technology has definitely improved our society and our schools, but in some cases, it may have caused our students to rely too much on it that they have become intellectually lazy or unimaginative. Other possible pros and cons of technology are highlighted in **Figure 1.1** on page 20.

Chances are, you've heard a student say, "If the calculator can figure it out for me, why should I learn how to do the equation?" or "Why do I have to study this information if all I have to do is an Internet search to find the answers?" This line of thought, while at times showing a student's resourcefulness, can also lead to chronic intellectual laziness. As teachers, we have a duty to prevent and cure this laziness through persistently and routinely infusing differentiation practices, rigorous tasks, and thinking skills into our daily classroom routines, lessons, and units, as well as into our own practices.

Above all, we must keep in mind that technology is only as effective as the person who has created it and the person who is using it. This book's focus is on the learning habits and the thoughts of those behind, and the students seated in front of, the computers. Our responsibility as teachers is to facilitate and coach our students to use thinking as a tool to enhance the efficiency of technology.

Figure 1.1 The Pros and Cons of Technology Use

PROS	CONS
Expands the possibilities of thought	May limit imagination
Allows ready access to multiple views and limitless information	Encourages instant gratification and information overload
Enables users to customize content to meet their individual needs	Reduces shared language and experience
Requires the use of thoughtful examination and filtering of information	Increases impulsivity and reduces perseverance
Enables virtual connections with people around the world from diverse backgrounds	Fosters working in isolation without physical human contact
Provides access to a greater degree of global information media	Media can be formulaic and passive, and present an inaccurate view of the world
Encourages the use of ethics and open-mindedness in dealing with diversity	Encourages an egocentric view of the world
Increases productivity	Wastes time
Produces highly trained workers with new and malleable skills	Reduces workforce by automating jobs
Increases profits through reduced waste and higher productivity	Is often costly to build and maintain
Provides ease of communication	Increases cyberbullying and security threats

10 Elements of a Differentiated Classroom

1. **Content goals** are defined.
   - Know: Factual Knowledge
   - Able to Do: Procedural Knowledge
   - Understand: Conceptual Knowledge

2. **Learning differences** are acknowledged.
   - Interests
   - Learning Preferences
   - Readiness

3. The three types of **assessment** are employed, analyzed, and used to adjust curriculum and instruction for student learning.
   - Preassessment
   - Formative Assessment
   - Summative Assessment

4. Curriculum and instruction foster **brain-compatible learning**.

5. The classroom environment respects **active learning**.

6. Learners develop **21st Century Skills**.
   - Higher Order Thinking Skills (HOTS)
   - Creative Thinking
   - Critical Reasoning
   - Self-Regulation
   - Communication and Collaboration

7. **Flexible grouping** is used to achieve optimal learning.

8. **Tiered and parallel assignments and activities** respond to learning needs and differences.

9. The learning environment is **interesting, enjoyable, challenging,** and **choice-filled** for all students.

10. Students develop **learning autonomy**.

From *Advancing Differentiation: Thinking and Learning for the 21st Century* by Richard M. Cash, Ed.D., copyright © 2017. This page may be reproduced for use within an individual school or district. For all other uses, contact Free Spirit Publishing Inc. at www.freespirit.com/permissions.

10 Elements of a Differentiated Classroom Survey

ELEMENT	EXAMPLE	(SELDOM)				(ALWAYS)
Content goals are defined at the beginning of each lesson and reviewed at the end of each lesson	Students will know the facts; Students will be able to do strategies/skills; Students will understand the concepts/principles/theories	1	2	3	4	5
Learning differences are acknowledged throughout instruction	Instruction, activities, and assessments are designed to integrate student interests, learning preferences, and readiness	1	2	3	4	5
The **three types of assessments** are employed, analyzed, and used to adjust curriculum and instruction for student learning	Teacher regularly analyzes and uses data from preassessments, formative assessments, and summative assessments to make adjustments	1	2	3	4	5
Curriculum and instruction foster **brain-compatible learning**	Teacher creates a safe and welcoming learning environment; provides stimulation of all five senses; offers opportunities for physical action; connects learners' prior experiences; and provides accurate, efficient, relevant, and timely feedback	1	2	3	4	5
The classroom environment respects **active learning**	Students are routinely involved in meaningful active learning experiences that require them to collaborate and communicate with others	1	2	3	4	5
Learners develop **21st Century Skills**	Teacher infuses higher order thinking, creative thinking, critical reasoning, self-regulation, and effective communication and collaboration strategies into every lesson and requires students to employ them	1	2	3	4	5

continued

From *Advancing Differentiation: Thinking and Learning for the 21st Century* by Richard M. Cash, Ed.D., copyright © 2017. This page may be reproduced for use within an individual school or district. For all other uses, contact Free Spirit Publishing Inc. at www.freespirit.com/permissions.

10 Elements of a Differentiated Classroom Survey (continued)

ELEMENT	EXAMPLE	(SELDOM)				(ALWAYS)
Flexible grouping is used to achieve optimal learning	Students are regularly grouped and regrouped based on interests, learning preferences, and/or readiness; curriculum and instruction are differentiated to meet the needs of the grouping type	1	2	3	4	5
Tiered and parallel assignments and activities respond to learning needs and differences	Teacher uses varied lesson activities and assignments that are respectful, meaningful, and relevant to each learner	1	2	3	4	5
The learning environment is **interesting, enjoyable, challenging, and choice-filled** for all students	Students are genuinely interested in the learning activities, enjoy the classroom, feel sufficiently challenged by the content, and have choices in how, what, where, and when they learn	1	2	3	4	5
Students develop **learning autonomy**	Teacher guides students toward being independent and intrinsically motivated to learn	1	2	3	4	5

Classroom Indicators of Differentiated Instruction

CLASSROOM INDICATORS OF DIFFERENTIATED INSTRUCTION	DEVELOPMENTAL STAGE	BASIC STAGE	PROFICIENT STAGE	DISTINGUISHED STAGE
Teacher Planning and Preparation				
Teacher conveys understanding of differentiated instruction through designed learning activities and instruction with an acceptance of and response to student learning needs and differences Teacher plans knowing prerequisite knowledge all students must possess Teacher demonstrates an understanding of and prepares for student cultural, linguistic, economic, and gender differences Teacher sets goals and develops learning activities that are connected to essential standards and assessment Teacher understands how to connect content across disciplines and engage students in authentic experiences Teacher plans activities that invoke inquiry, critical reasoning, creative thinking, problem solving, and collaboration between and among students Teacher prepares and utilizes a variety of resources to enhance course/class materials Teacher develops learning activities that are relevant and respectful and promote high expectations for all students Teacher finds ways to effectively incorporate technology in each lesson when appropriate Teacher prepares formats/templates (for example, rubrics, checklists) to provide descriptive feedback to students	Teacher displays *little understanding or knowledge of differentiated instruction with no planning of instruction*	Teacher displays *a basic or general knowledge of differentiated instruction with some suitable planning of instruction*	Teacher has *a thorough knowledge and understanding of differentiated instruction with purposeful planning of instruction*	Teacher has *a thorough knowledge and understanding of differentiated instruction with consistent purposeful planning of instruction*

continued

Adapted from Danielson, C. *Enhancing Professional Practice: A Framework for Teaching.* Alexandria, VA: ASCD, 2007; Heacox, D. *Making Differentiation a Habit: How to Ensure Success in Academically Diverse Classrooms.* Minneapolis: Free Spirit Publishing, 2009; Marzano, R. J. "The Marzano Teacher Evaluation Model." Englewood, CO: Marzano Research Laboratory (August 2011); Tomlinson, C. A. *Fulfilling the Promise of the Differentiated Classroom: Strategies and Tools for Responsive Teaching.* Alexandria, VA: ASCD, 2003. From *Advancing Differentiation: Thinking and Learning for the 21st Century* by Richard M. Cash, Ed.D., copyright © 2017. This page may be reproduced for use within an individual school or district. For all other uses, contact Free Spirit Publishing Inc. at www.freespirit.com/permissions.

Classroom Indicators of Differentiated Instruction (continued)

CLASSROOM INDICATORS OF DIFFERENTIATED INSTRUCTION	DEVELOPMENTAL STAGE	BASIC STAGE	PROFICIENT STAGE	DISTINGUISHED STAGE
Classroom Environment and Management				
Teacher has developed routines for flexible and efficient movement among groups (from whole group to small group to individual instruction)	Teacher displays *little or inefficient* strategies to create a challenging and respectful learning environment	Teacher displays *basic or generally appropriate* strategies to create a challenging and respectful learning environment	Teacher conveys a *consistent message of high expectations* for all students and *routinely provides* challenging and respectful work	Teacher and students convey an *extraordinary enthusiasm for high quality work* in an environment where all are *routinely provided* challenging and respectful work
Teacher uses multiple levels of instruction, such as learning centers, tiered activities, and independent study				
Students appropriately use technology to enhance and advance instruction				
Teacher creates and maintains an intellectually challenging and stimulating learning atmosphere				
Students are allowed to initiate and choose work				
Students are able to explain why they are working on projects that may vary from student to student				
Teacher's interactions and instruction create an environment of respect and mutual rapport				
Teacher and students project enthusiasm for learning				
Teacher has articulated high expectations and standards for all				
Teacher utilizes space in the classroom to maximize learning				

continued

Adapted from Danielson, C. *Enhancing Professional Practice: A Framework for Teaching.* Alexandria, VA: ASCD, 2007; Heacox, D. *Making Differentiation a Habit: How to Ensure Success in Academically Diverse Classrooms.* Minneapolis: Free Spirit Publishing, 2009; Marzano, R. J. "The Marzano Teacher Evaluation Model." Englewood, CO: Marzano Research Laboratory (August 2011); Tomlinson, C. A. *Fulfilling the Promise of the Differentiated Classroom: Strategies and Tools for Responsive Teaching.* Alexandria, VA: ASCD, 2003. From *Advancing Differentiation: Thinking and Learning for the 21st Century* by Richard M. Cash, Ed.D., copyright © 2017. This page may be reproduced for use within an individual school or district. For all other uses, contact Free Spirit Publishing Inc. at www.freespirit.com/permissions.

Classroom Indicators of Differentiated Instruction (continued)

CLASSROOM INDICATORS OF DIFFERENTIATED INSTRUCTION	DEVELOPMENTAL STAGE	BASIC STAGE	PROFICIENT STAGE	DISTINGUISHED STAGE
Instructional Practices and Assessment				
Teacher has accurately articulated clear goals and high standards for all students				
Teacher preassesses students for learning preferences, interests, and/or readiness				
Instruction reflects evidence-based practices that engage and motivate learners through their learning preferences, interests, and/or readiness levels				
Teacher demonstrates flexibility, multitasking, and "with-it-ness"				
Instruction reflects different levels of complexity, offering students multiple pathways to higher levels of thinking	Teacher displays *little or inefficient* strategies to develop higher level challenges and learning	Teacher displays *basic or generally appropriate* strategies to develop higher level challenges and learning	Teacher displays a consistent use of *higher level* challenges and learning	Teacher *and students* consistently engage in *higher level* challenges and learning
Students are engaged in activities/assessments related to and reflecting essential learning goals and standards				
Students are encouraged to use and apply technology whenever appropriate				
Teacher and students employ high quality questioning and discussion techniques				
Teacher frequently assesses students for acquisition of content knowledge and skills and uses the data to adapt instruction and inform students of progress				
Teacher provides descriptive feedback to students to promote continuous improvement and success in learning				

 continued

Adapted from Danielson, C. *Enhancing Professional Practice: A Framework for Teaching*. Alexandria, VA: ASCD, 2007; Heacox, D. *Making Differentiation a Habit: How to Ensure Success in Academically Diverse Classrooms*. Minneapolis: Free Spirit Publishing, 2009; Marzano, R. J. "The Marzano Teacher Evaluation Model." Englewood, CO: Marzano Research Laboratory (August 2011); Tomlinson, C. A. *Fulfilling the Promise of the Differentiated Classroom: Strategies and Tools for Responsive Teaching*. Alexandria, VA: ASCD, 2003. From *Advancing Differentiation: Thinking and Learning for the 21st Century* by Richard M. Cash, Ed.D., copyright © 2017. This page may be reproduced for use within an individual school or district. For all other uses, contact Free Spirit Publishing Inc. at www.freespirit.com/permissions.

Classroom Indicators of Differentiated Instruction (continued)

CLASSROOM INDICATORS OF DIFFERENTIATED INSTRUCTION	DEVELOPMENTAL STAGE	BASIC STAGE	PROFICIENT STAGE	DISTINGUISHED STAGE
Professional Responsibilities				
Teacher routinely reflects on instruction, student learning, and professional practice				
Teacher maintains records on student learning preferences, interests, and readiness levels that are used to inform instruction				
Teacher routinely communicates and collaborates with students and parents/guardians/caregivers to enhance student achievement/aptitude/engagement/development/success				
Teacher continually develops understanding of how to best meet "whole child" needs of every student regardless of academic ability, cultural background, social and emotional needs, or economic opportunities	Teacher makes little effort or has limited interest in differentiated instruction	Teacher is developing an awareness of the need for differentiated instruction		
Teacher is a leader in developing a school climate for differentiated instruction				
Teacher seeks out professional development in differentiated instruction			Teacher seeks out additional support for development of differentiated instruction	Teacher consistently initiates and participates in personal and schoolwide development of differentiated instruction
Teacher models ethical conduct and upholds professional standards of practice				
Teacher uses district/state/provincial/national standards or scope and sequence to build learning activities				
Teacher engages and collaborates with colleagues and community members to develop a culture of student success				
Teacher uses effective reporting systems to guide learning activities and gauge student achievement				

Comments:

Adapted from Danielson, C. *Enhancing Professional Practice: A Framework for Teaching.* Alexandria, VA: ASCD, 2007; Heacox, D. *Making Differentiation a Habit: How to Ensure Success in Academically Diverse Classrooms.* Minneapolis: Free Spirit Publishing, 2009; Marzano, R. J. "The Marzano Teacher Evaluation Model." Englewood, CO: Marzano Research Laboratory (August 2011); Tomlinson, C. A. *Fulfilling the Promise of the Differentiated Classroom: Strategies and Tools for Responsive Teaching.* Alexandria, VA: ASCD, 2003. From *Advancing Differentiation: Thinking and Learning for the 21st Century* by Richard M. Cash, Ed.D., copyright © 2017. This page may be reproduced for use within an individual school or district. For all other uses, contact Free Spirit Publishing Inc. at www.freespirit.com/permissions.

Chapter 2

Defining the Essentials of a Differentiated Curriculum

The principal goal of education is to create [people] who are capable of doing new things, not simply of repeating what other generations have done.

—Jean Piaget, cognitive psychologist

Skills for a New Century

The world has changed dramatically over the last 50 years. Advances in technology have altered both the educational and workforce landscapes. During the past two centuries, students could graduate from high school and expect to obtain a job that would sustain their own lives, and perhaps their families' lives, for decades. The workforce needs of the nineteenth and early twentieth centuries were based primarily on the lower-level skill of application, the ability to work with one's hands. Schooling, therefore, taught the skills of remembering and application.

Today's careers, however, demand more sophisticated skills beyond application. "Of all the big developed countries, America now has the smallest proportion of factory workers in its labor force."[1] In the twenty-first century, the growing need in the workforce—of the United States and of most developed countries—will be for knowledge workers: those who analyze, evaluate, and create new knowledge within and across fields of discipline **(Figure 2.1)**. The knowledge workers of tomorrow are the classroom students of today. We must have a curriculum that will prepare our students for their futures.

Essential to this curriculum development process is having a clear understanding of the content (what you expect students to learn) to ensure that you are addressing the wholeness of the goals and standards. Additionally, as discussed in Chapter 1, to effectively differentiate you must know **what** you are differentiating, **how** you intend to differentiate, and most importantly, **why** you need to differentiate at all. This chapter will help you identify those essential components of your curriculum.

According to the Partnership for 21st Century Learning and the Institute for the Future,[2] the 10 essential competencies of the new century are:

1. Sense-making for deeper understanding
2. Flexible and adaptive thinking

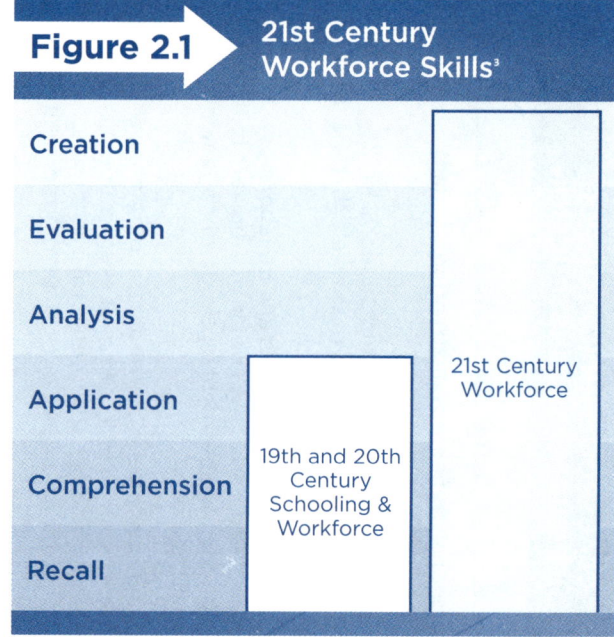

Figure 2.1 21st Century Workforce Skills[3]

---

1. Drucker, P. F. "The Next Workforce: Knowledge Workers Are the New Capitalists." *The Economist* (November 2001).
2. The Partnership for 21st Century Learning (p21.org); The Institute for the Future (iftf.org).
3. Based on Anderson, L. W., and D. R. Krathwohl (Eds.). *A Taxonomy for Learning, Teaching, and Assessing: A Revision of Bloom's Taxonomy of Educational Objectives*. New York: Longman, 2001.

3. Initiative, self-direction, and self-regulation
4. Social and cross-cultural communication skills
5. Multidisciplinary understanding
6. Evolving media literacy
7. Reasoning using data and abstract concepts
8. Productivity and accountability
9. Leadership and responsibility
10. Virtual collaboration

Today's curriculum and instruction must ensure that students are proficient in these competencies. Furthermore, the Institute for the Future cites six forces that are driving changes to the landscape of the workforce of 2020:

1. People are living and staying in the workforce longer, meaning students of today must compete with a larger employment base.
2. Machines and systems are "smarter" and have taken over automation, eliminating low-level repetitive jobs.
3. The increases in computers, sensors, and information processing have changed the way we deal with problems and manage information.
4. Ever-evolving media are expanding the ways we communicate, especially through visual formats.
5. "Superstructured" organizations are ones enormous in size and extreme in scale requiring greater productivity and creativity.
6. Global connectivity is diversifying the centers of operations away from North America and Europe to other parts of the world.

The Partnership for 21st Century Learning addresses these drivers of change by defining a framework for future curriculum and instruction that accomplishes the following:

- Teaches students thinking skills embedded within core subjects and twenty-first century interdisciplinary themes; these themes include:
  - global awareness
  - financial, economic, business, and entrepreneurial literacy
  - civic literacy
  - health literacy
  - environmental literacy
- Requires students to apply thinking skills across content domains through performance-based activities
- Demands the use of multiple medias to communicate broadly and accurately
- Allows students to utilize technology and resources beyond the classroom walls

A Hierarchy of Knowledge: Factual, Procedural, Conceptual

This new idea of curriculum is a design that concentrates on the essentials of what students should know, be able to do, and understand in the twenty-first century. With advances in neuroscience, it is clear that the brain learns most efficiently through the following three dimensions of knowledge: factual (knowing the facts), procedural (doing the tasks), and conceptual (understanding the concepts) knowledge. Based on this finding, we should develop curricular activities that emphasize these dimensions. The design laid out for you in this chapter will help you define what is essential for your students to know, be able to do, and understand. This design is grounded in brain research, reflecting the knowledge built from both cognitive science and motivational theory.

"If a student engages in a curriculum that is well beyond that student's level of readiness, stress results, and the brain overproduces key neurotransmitters that impede learning."[4] Conversely, if the curriculum is redundant for the child—beneath that student's level of readiness—the brain is not inclined to engage or respond and, consequently, does not release the levels of dopamine, noradrenalin, serotonin, and other neurochemicals needed for optimal learning. The result is apathy.[5] Understanding this hierarchy of knowledge construction provides teachers a more refined way of approaching the development of unit and lesson design.

But, in many classrooms, curriculum and instruction tend to be anchored in factual and procedural levels of knowledge. Most classroom assessments that measure student achievement are often regenerations of factual and lower-level procedural knowledge. However, assessments tied

---
4. Koob, G. F., et al. "Stress, Performance, and Arousal: Focus on CRF." *National Institute on Drug Abuse Research Monograph*, 97 (1990): 163–176.
5. Schultz, W., P. Dayan, and P. R. Montague. "A Neural Substrate of Prediction and Reward." *Science*, 275 (1997): 1593–1599.

to new generation standards are moving beyond factual knowledge to the more advanced procedural and conceptual knowledge levels of evaluation. Thus, there is an urgent need for teachers to have the curricular and instructional strategies to prepare students to do well on more sophisticated levels of assessment.

The essential twenty-first-century tool missing from many curriculum, instruction, and assessment equations is *conceptual* knowledge; specifically, the creative idea generation and critical reasoning that is grounded in conceptual levels of thinking. Experts think conceptually; they use creativity and critical analysis and make efficient use of facts and procedures when solving problems. For our students to be effective thinkers, we must ensure that our curriculum and instructional scaffolds move them toward conceptual levels of thinking.

As we review our curriculum and instructional practices for the twenty-first century, we must commit to the following goals:

1. Identify how standards reflect and specifically address factual, procedural, and conceptual levels of learning
2. Focus appropriate amounts of instructional attention on factual, procedural, and conceptual levels of thinking and learning
3. Guarantee that *all* our students are proficient in factual knowledge, procedural abilities, and conceptual understandings

Four Steps to Defining the Essentials of Curriculum

Step 1: Define the Key Components of Curriculum

The model in **Figure 2.2** illustrates how twenty-first-century curriculum is constructed. Curricular materials are developed with a broad foundation of factual knowledge, general to specific procedural abilities, and conceptual levels of thinking. This model is framed not only in the foundations of brain-compatible learning, but also in the taxonomy of educational objectives defined by Benjamin Bloom in 1956, with updates in 2001. (See Chapter 8 for an in-depth discussion of Bloom's Taxonomy.)

Factual Knowledge

At the foundation of all curricula is the factual level of knowledge. This level contains all of the basic elements of vocabulary or the language of the discipline, symbols, resources, and other components of indisputable evidence that students must know to be acquainted with a subject. Factual knowledge can most easily be represented and assessed using tests or quizzes centered on information recall and remembering.

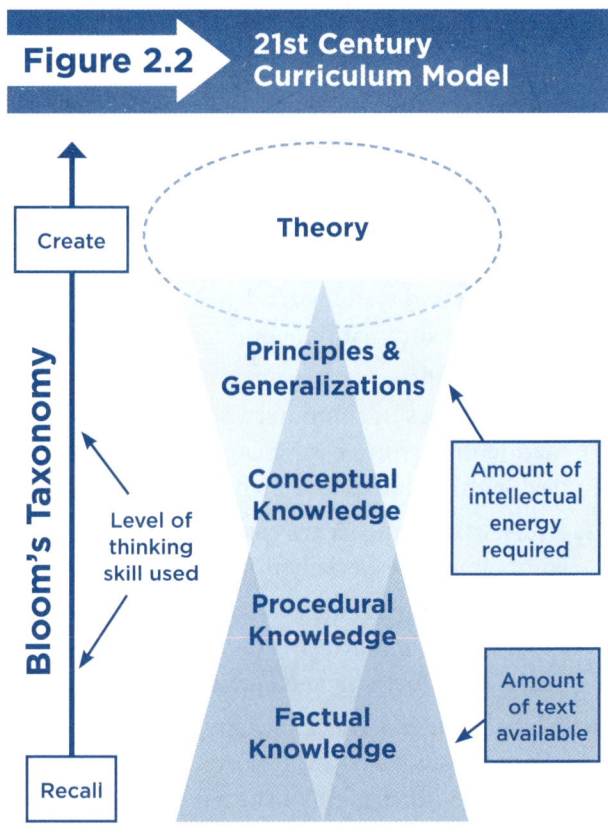

Figure 2.2 21st Century Curriculum Model

Procedural Knowledge

While acquiring factual knowledge, students begin to interact with procedural knowledge, or the "know-how" of a discipline. Procedural knowledge includes actions or tasks to be learned and carried out, such as thinking skills, writing processes, experiments, and rules of doing. Also, at this level students are introduced to the tools of the discipline, such as editing, calculating, research, measurement, or any of the other tools a disciplinarian would use to solve problems, create, or produce within a domain of study.

Procedural knowledge can be broken down into two identifiable categories:[6]

Strategies
- Discrete conscious actions
- Often step-by-step directions
  - Example: the scientific method
    - Step 1: Ask a question
    - Step 2: Do background research
    - Step 3: Create a hypothesis
    - Step 4: Test hypothesis by doing experiments
    - Step 5: Analyze data and draw a conclusion
    - Step 6: Report findings

Skills
- Acquired when a sufficient number of strategies have been amassed
- Skills emerge once strategies become automatic
  - Example: reading comprehension
    - Students employ a number of strategies to gain the skill of understanding increasingly complex text.

In other words, the acquisition and automatic employment of strategies leads to skill development. Teachers teach strategies while students develop skills.

Conceptual Knowledge

As students become more proficient in the areas of factual and procedural knowledge, they solidify their conceptual knowledge. Conceptual knowledge refers to the broad, overarching ideas, generalizations, principles, and theories that are found within and across disciplines. Concepts help students understand the deeper meanings within a discipline, as well as across a curriculum. Concepts offer avenues toward interdisciplinary study by helping students see the similarities and differences a single concept can possess in many different domains. Ultimately, concepts help students go more deeply into the subject matter by building connections and relationships between and across content areas. Concepts naturally inspire a sense of curiosity and provide students entries into the curriculum and ways to attach learning to their interests.

Conceptual knowledge can be divided into two general categories:
- **Concrete** (it can be seen, touched, heard, smelled, or tasted). Examples of concrete concepts are home, dog, music, sour, and sweet.
- **Abstract** (it cannot be seen, touched, heard, smelled, or tasted, and it is a public idea rather than a personal belief). Examples of abstract concepts include ideas such as freedom, history, change, and beauty. (See **Figure 2.3** on page 32 for more examples.)

Here are the three types of concepts that can be addressed in the curriculum:

Universal concepts. Extremely broad, applicable to any subject (particularly mathematics)
- Examples:
  - Adaptation
  - Change
  - Models
  - Systems

Content-based concepts. Specific to subject areas, not easily applied to other subject areas
- Examples:
  - Math (number sense, arithmetic, geometry, ratio and proportion)
  - English Language Arts (alienation, courage, fantasy, voice)
  - Science (classification, experimentation, form/function, state)
  - Social Studies (authority, government, rule, tradition)

Self-regulatory concepts. Meant to guide students toward being better learners
- Examples:
  - Autonomy
  - Individuality
  - Organization
  - Responsibility

The way in which you focus on the concept during the learning process will define the type. To assist you in defining the type of concept, note the asterisks (*) next to some of the concepts in Figure 2.3 denoting them as universal concepts. The

---

6. Afflerbach, P., P. Pearson, and S. G. Paris. "Clarifying Differences Between Reading Skills and Reading Strategies." *The Reading Teacher*, 61 (5) (2008): 364–373.

Figure 2.3 — 200 Abstract Concepts

1. Adaptation*
2. Alienation
3. Attitude
4. Authenticity
5. Authority
6. Autonomy
7. Awareness
8. Beauty*
9. Behavior
10. Being and becoming
11. Beliefs*
12. Caring
13. Cause & effect*
14. Certainty
15. Change*
16. Childhood
17. Civilization
18. Classification*
19. Commitment
20. Communication*
21. Community
22. Compassion
23. Conflict*
24. Conflict resolution
25. Conformity
26. Connectedness
27. Conscience
28. Consciousness
29. Conservation
30. Constancy
31. Consultation
32. Contemplation
33. Control
34. Cooperation
35. Courage
36. Creativity*
37. Crisis
38. Culture
39. Cycles*
40. Decision
41. Democracy
42. Destruction
43. Detachment
44. Development*
45. Discipline
46. Discovery
47. Dualism
48. Education
49. Emotion
50. Empathy
51. Energy
52. Engagement
53. Engineering
54. Environment
55. Equality
56. Essence
57. Eternity
58. Ethics
59. Evolution
60. Existence
61. Experience
62. Experimentation
63. Exploration
64. Extinction
65. Faith
66. Falsity
67. Family
68. Fantasy
69. Feelings
70. Free will
71. Freedom
72. Global
73. Good and evil
74. Goodness
75. Group
76. Growth*
77. Habit
78. Harmony
79. Having
80. Holism
81. Humankind
82. Human rights
83. Idea
84. Ideals
85. Identity
86. Imagination
87. Independence
88. Individuality
89. Indoctrination
90. Infinity
91. Information
92. Initiation
93. Insight
94. Instinct
95. Integrity
96. Intelligence
97. Interdependence
98. Intuition
99. Invention
100. Judgment
101. Justice
102. Justification*
103. Knowledge*
104. Language*
105. Learning
106. Life and death
107. Literature
108. Love
109. Loyalty
110. Man
111. Management
112. Materialism
113. Meaning*
114. Meditation
115. Memory
116. Metaphor
117. Method
118. Migration
119. Mind
120. Models
121. Moral
122. Morality
123. Mystery
124. Myth
125. Nature
126. Negotiation
127. Objectivity
128. Openness
129. Origins*
130. Ownership
131. Paradigm
132. Paradox
133. Participation
134. Patterns*
135. Peace
136. Perception
137. Personhood
138. Perspective*
139. Philosophy
140. Physical
141. Planning
142. Play
143. Poetry
144. Politics
145. Positivism
146. Potential
147. Power*
148. Principles*
149. Problem-solving
150. Qualitative
151. Qualities
152. Rationality
153. Reality
154. Reason*
155. Reductionism
156. Reflection
157. Rejection
158. Relationships
159. Religion
160. Resolution
161. Responsibility
162. Revolution
163. Rituals
164. Scale*
165. Science
166. Self
167. Self-esteem
168. Self-image
169. Self-knowledge
170. Sensitivity
171. Service
172. Socialization
173. Society
174. Soul
175. Spirituality
176. State*
177. Story
178. Subjectivity
179. Survival
180. Systems*
181. Teacher
182. Teamwork
183. Time*
184. Tolerance
185. Tradition
186. Training
187. Transformation*
188. Truth
189. Understanding*
190. Utilitarian
191. Validity
192. Value*
193. Violence
194. Vision
195. Voice
196. Wholeness
197. Will
198. Wisdom
199. Woman
200. Work

* = universal

concepts marked as universal are merely suggestions. Concepts not identified as universal can be considered content-based and/or self-regulatory. There are no absolutes regarding concept types and some concepts work well in multiple categories. You may find some concepts not identified as universal work well in your content area. If you can support the use and students can demonstrate their deeper learning, then it works!

Have you ever put together a jigsaw puzzle? If so, you probably looked at the box cover to see what the puzzle should look like when you finish. You use the box cover as a model to see the "big picture" of where you are going and how all of the pieces fit together. This is how learning should happen in the classroom. Starting a unit of study from the concept view can offer students the "big picture"; give them direction as to where they are headed; show them how the facts, strategies, and skills all link together; and provide them with a connection to their prior knowledge of the content area.

Generalizations

Within the dimension of conceptual knowledge are generalizations and principles. Both generalizations and principles are the "big ideas," or enduring beliefs, of a content area. Generalizations are formed from our personal experiences that we connect to the concepts. Generalized statements can be said to be either always true or almost always true, again, based on our personal experiences. Factual examples of the generalization are used in the content lessons to provide a common understanding. Teaching through generalizations gives students context to remember facts and procedures. Examples of generalizations include the following (notice the qualifiers: *often*, *may*, *can*):

- People are often willing to move to improve their lives.
- Animals and plants can be affected by their environment.
- Algebra can be used to solve problems.
- Literature often reflects culture.

Figure 2.4 on pages 34–35 presents a sample lesson plan for helping you and your students first make connections between concepts and then develop generalizations. When students make connections to the concepts, they find *relevance* in a concept, which makes the curriculum pertinent and meaningful to their lives. In creating generalizations from these concepts, students form a *relationship* to the unit of study—a sense of personal ownership of the content. This now supports your development of a *rigorous* curriculum, because students have formed relevance to the concept and a relationship with the content; in other words, you've provided "sense-making for deeper understanding" for the students (see **Figure 2.5** on page 36).

The model in Figure 2.4 involves both inductive and deductive reasoning processes. Used as a beginning lesson in the unit, the model focuses on the creation of generalizations from a student-derived list of created concepts and essential questions. This lesson is comprised of six steps and involves student participation at every step. Students begin with a broad concept, determine specific examples and non-examples, create appropriate categorization systems, establish a generalization from those categories, and then create either an individual or group essential question that will be the focus of the unit of study. (See page 38 for rules that help create quality essential questions.) This activity works best by dividing the class into small groups for initial work, followed by whole-class discussion after each stage of the process. Figure 2.4 illustrates the use of the model around the concept of change.

A Concept Development Worksheet is provided on page 49, and an example worksheet is presented in **Figure 2.6** on page 36. Students should keep the resulting question in a notebook throughout the unit of study and continue to try to answer the question until the end of the unit. Alternately, you can take one essential question and display it on a bulletin board or in an electronic file for the entire class to try to answer throughout the unit. Encourage students to post answer ideas and bring in news articles or website links that help answer the question. This also acts as a reminder to you to focus all activities and lessons on providing students with information to answer their own essential question or the class essential question. If you develop a class essential question, inform students at the beginning of the unit that it will be included on the final exam and that they should be continuously looking for information to answer the question to prepare for the exam.

Figure 2.4 — Concept Development Lesson Sample[7]

Concept: **Change**

Materials:

- Concept Development Worksheet
- Different color highlighters for each group of students
- Bulletin board or individual notebooks for the unit

	BEHAVIORAL OBJECTIVES	FOCUSING QUESTIONS
Step 1	Students generate examples and non-examples of change derived from their own understanding and experiences with changes in the world.	What examples of change have you read about or experienced? Why do these things change? Now list examples of things that do not change. Why do these things *not* change?
Step 2	Students group words that are alike.	Think about what the words in your lists have in common. Group words that are alike. *Note:* You might not use all of the words, and you may use some words twice if they fit into more than one category.
Step 3	Students label the categories.	Create a label for each category you created.
Step 4	Students write generalizations.	Review all of the categories you have created. Write at least three statements or generalizations about change. Plan to share with your group.
Step 5	Students create essential questions.	Using at least one of the generalizations you have created, turn that statement into a good question. Remember, good questions are open-ended and have more than just one right answer.
Step 6	Students post their generalizations and essential questions.	As a group, decide which of your generalizations and essential questions your team would like to investigate and attempt to answer throughout this unit.

7. Based on the curriculum model in Taba, H. *Curriculum Development: Theory and Practice*. New York: Harcourt Brace and World, 1962.

NOTE: The final step can be done as a class. Instead of each student having their own essential question, the class decides upon one question they would like to answer as a team. This generalization and corresponding question are then posted on a bulletin board. Throughout the unit, students can post notes, ideas, suggestions, websites, and news or magazine articles on the bulletin board to help answer the question. This question is then used as the final question on the unit summative assessment.

SUPPORT PROCEDURES

Have students form groups and generate at least 15 examples. These words are placed on the **+** side of the Concept Development Worksheet.

Encourage students to think carefully about non-examples of the concept of change. Each group should list five to six non-examples. These words are placed on the **−** side of the Concept Development Worksheet.

Have students explain their reasoning for assigning categories and seek clarification from each other as a class. Ensure that students have accounted for all (or most) of their items through the categories established.

Students categorize the words on their Concept Development Worksheet by circling or highlighting with different colors. Have students look for categories that can be combined with other categories to make bigger or more general categories.

Have students work in groups to create generalizations. To advance this activity, have students write their own generalizations. If students struggle, assist them by offering some examples of generalizations about change:
- *Change is everywhere.*
- *Change may happen naturally or be caused by people.*
- *Change may be perceived as orderly or random.*
- *Change can be positive or negative.*
- *Change is linked to identity.*
- *Change influences identity.*

In their groups, students decide on at least one of the generalization statements to turn into an essential question. Examples include:
- *In what ways is change linked to time?*
- *Why is it important that we understand change is everywhere?*
- *In what ways is change orderly and/or random?*
- *In what ways does change happen naturally or with the help of humans?*

Student groups decide on one generalization and the corresponding essential question to answer during the unit. Students either post the generalization and question on a bulletin board or write it in their unit notebooks. Throughout the unit, students take notes to supply an answer to their essential question.

Remind students that their essential question will be the final question on the summative assessment for the unit. They will be allowed to use their notes to answer the question, so they should be encouraged to take succinct notes during every class period and after every major activity.

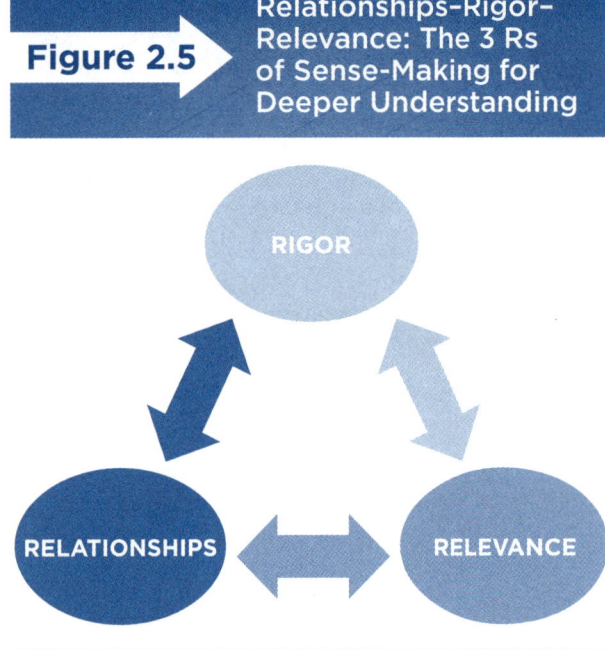

Figure 2.5 Relationships-Rigor-Relevance: The 3 Rs of Sense-Making for Deeper Understanding

Principles

Principles, like generalizations, are derived from the content area's concepts. Whereas generalizations are broad, principles are mostly specific in nature and usually refer to the rules, laws, codes, truths, or assumptions within a content domain. Examples of principles include the following (notice the lack of qualifiers such as *sometimes, generally, almost always, usually, mostly,* etc.):

- Science seeks to understand the natural world through experimentation and observation.
- The law of supply states that supply increases as prices increase and decreases as prices decrease.
- The rules of the English language require a sentence to include a verb.
- When there are m ways of doing one thing and n ways of doing another, and m and n are independent of each other, then there are $m \times n$ ways of doing both (Example: $m = 2$, $n = 3$, $2 \times 3 = 6$).

Theories

Out of generalizations and principles comes theory. A theory is an abstract idea that has been evaluated and supported by experts within the field. Theories explain, in relatively simple terms, ideals or abstract thoughts structured from the content area. Theories are not often developed or created in the K–12 setting but are used as guides to the larger intent of the curriculum. Here are some examples of theories:

- The theory of relativity
- Number theory
- Direct reference theory
- Social distance theory
- Music composition theory
- The theory of aesthetics

At each level of the 21st Century Curriculum Model (Figure 2.2)—from factual knowledge to theory—learners go through a thought process that requires intellectual energy. At the lowest level of this design, very little intellectual energy is expended to recall information. As learners progress upward toward conceptual knowledge into generalizations and principles, they are required to use more areas of their brain and engage in deeper levels of thought.

Most curriculum materials do not provide for this advanced level of thinking. Therefore, it is up to you as the teacher to develop activities and performances that engage your students in more sophisticated levels of thinking. This can be accomplished through an awareness of how content standards are structured. When you are able to define what students should know, be able to do,

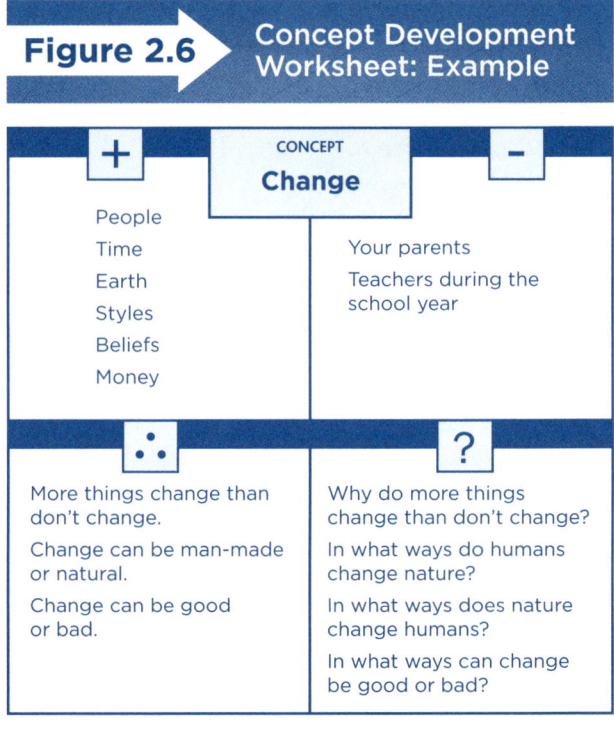

Figure 2.6 Concept Development Worksheet: Example

and understand, you can more easily guide them toward high levels of thinking.

Step 2: Form Objectives for What Students Will *Know, Be Able to Do,* and *Understand*

To Know

To know something is to be able to directly recognize it, recite it, or tell it to others in concrete language. In the classroom, what we want students to know are the facts, terms (language of the discipline), symbols, and specific factual details of the domain of study. These are "Students will know…" objectives within content standards. Here are some examples:

- Students will know the multiplication tables 0 through 9.
- Students will know the capital cities of each state in the United States.
- Students will know all of the elements in the periodic table.
- Students will know the elements of art (form, shape, line, color).

To Be Able to Do

This objective involves using the procedures and processes, tools, or techniques of the subject. Procedural strategies are those step-by-step actions a student takes to solve a problem. Processes are the thinking skills a student uses to solve or think through a problem such as specific problem-solving strategies of the content area. Procedural skills are built by the actions that students participate in and can demonstrate. These are the "Students will be able to do…" objectives within standards. Here are some examples (note the action verb in each statement):

- Students will be able to write a five-paragraph essay.
- Students will be able to do an experiment.
- Students will be able to multiply fractions.
- Students will be able to use graphs and charts to solve problems and identify trends.
- Students will be able to design a map using a compass, key, and symbols.
- Students will be able to analyze information to identify trends.

To Understand

Concepts, as stated previously, are those big ideas that students will understand through the content delivery. When students understand a concept, they have grasped the meaning and significance of the content area, as well as the interrelationship between disciplines. Understanding is an abstract intellectual process built on the foundation of factual knowledge and procedural abilities. These are the "Students will understand…" objectives. Here are some examples:

- Students will understand the concept of change.
- Students will understand the theory of relativity.
- Students will understand why mathematics is an essential tool in today's world.
- Students will understand the impact of language on culture.

Figure 2.7 illustrates the three levels of the Pyramid of Knowledge. **Figure 2.8** (page 38) shows how a math standard has been broken down into the concepts, procedures, and facts. Note that many new generation standards have been refined to focus attention on the conceptual and procedural levels of knowledge, with little emphasis on factual regeneration. When breaking down the standards, be sure to look for the factual knowledge that may be required to successfully achieve

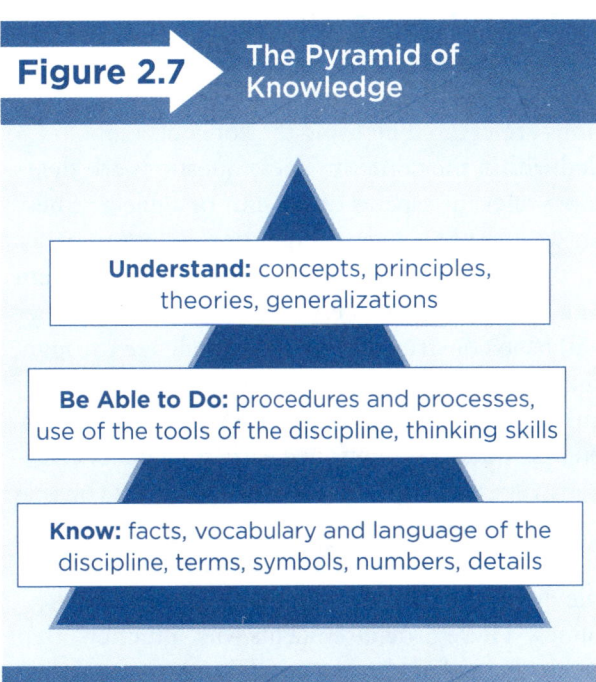

Figure 2.7 The Pyramid of Knowledge

Understand: concepts, principles, theories, generalizations

Be Able to Do: procedures and processes, use of the tools of the discipline, thinking skills

Know: facts, vocabulary and language of the discipline, terms, symbols, numbers, details

> **Figure 2.8** Breaking Down the Essentials: Example Math Standard
>
> **CONTENT STANDARD:**
> *Understand* the **place value system**.[8]
>
> **BENCHMARKS:**
> 1. **Recognize that in a multi-digit number, a digit in one place represents 10 times as much as it represents in the place to its right and 1/10 of what it represents in the place to its left.**
> 2. *Explain patterns in the number of zeroes of the product when multiplying* a number by powers of 10, and *explain patterns in the* placement of the decimal point *when a decimal is multiplied or divided by a power of 10. Use* whole-number exponents *to denote powers of 10.*
> 3. *Read, write, and compare* decimals to thousandths.
> 4. *Read and write decimals to thousandths using* base-ten numerals, number names, and expanded form, for example, 347.392 = 3 × 100 + 4 × 10 + 7 × 1 + 3 × (1/10) + 9 × (1/100) + 2 × (1/1000).
> 5. *Compare two* decimals to thousandths based on meanings of the digits in each place, *using* >, =, and < symbols *to record the results of comparisons.*
> 6. *Use* place value *understanding to* round decimals *to any place.*
>
> **KEY:**
> **Concept**
> *Procedure*
> Facts
>
> 8. Adapted from Common Core State Standards for Mathematics, Grade 5: Number & Operations in Base Ten, corestandards.org/Math/Content/5/NBT.

the standard. In the example (Figure 2.8), students must know the terms used in the standard, powers of 10, decimal placement, decimals to thousandths, and so forth. Having this critical factual knowledge prior to performing the procedural aspects of the standard can ensure student success.

Step 3: Create Essential Questions

From here you can now construct the essential questions related to the learning. Essential questions are created by using the concepts embedded within the content. These questions are the most relevant aspects of the unit or subject. The answering of an essential question is a journey through the curriculum. Students may never come to a conclusion on an essential question, but they will have constructed content knowledge through the exploration of various answers. Remember, answering an essential question is a process, *not* an end product. As mentioned earlier, students can construct their own essential questions or you may construct them as a teacher.

Essential questions help students transcend the discipline and connect it with other disciplines. These provide students with a framework of reference within the content. Ultimately, essential questions should cause students to generate more questions than answers. The technique of constructing quality essential questions is predicated on the design of a well-formed question. Writing an effective question can engage students in higher levels of thinking, as well as problem solving and decision making. Also, well-formed questions can illicit deeper levels of conversation about the content, thus making it relevant to the learner.

We all know the categories of questions: Who? What? When? Where? Why? Which? and How? (6 Ws and H). Unfortunately, in many cases, the 6 Ws and H questions can produce a single response from students when ill formed. Here are some examples:

- Who is the leader of the United States?
- What is photosynthesis?
- When did the industrial revolution occur?
- Where is the continent of Africa?
- Why are there 60 minutes in an hour?
- Which flavor of ice cream is the most popular?
- How do animals adapt to various climates?

Well-crafted essential questions should be written open-ended and in ways that challenge and intrigue the students in discourse. They should also be uncluttered: straightforward and containing only one question. To form quality essential questions, keep the following rules in mind:

- *Who* questions should engage the students in making choices.
- *What* questions should involve students in hypothesizing.
- *When* questions should require students to predict.
- *Where* questions should have students developing plans.
- *Why* questions should use the students' skill of analysis.
- *Which* questions should provoke students to use criteria and evidence to make decisions and reason arguments.
- *How* questions should compel students to synthesize meaning by gathering information on the manner or method of solving problems.

Using the math standard example provided in Figure 2.8, well-formed essential questions for this unit of study would be:

- Why are number (place value) systems used?
- How do patterns in numbers help define place value?
- Why would the process of rounding numbers be used today?

Here are the previous ill-formed questions rewritten as well-formed ones:

Ill-Formed Question	Well-Formed Question
Who is the leader of the United States?	Who do we depend upon to lead the United States and for what reasons?
What is photosynthesis?	What could occur if one step in the photosynthesis process were changed?
When did the industrial revolution occur?	When might we encounter another industrial revolution?
Where is the continent of Africa?	Where is the heart of Africa?
Why are there 60 minutes in an hour?	Why do we use the units of minutes and hours to define a day?

Ill-Formed Question	Well-Formed Question
Which flavor of ice cream is the most popular?	Which flavor of ice cream is predicted to remain popular into the next decade?
How do animals adapt to various climates?	How might animals adapt to natural or man-made disasters?

As stated earlier, essential questions get to the heart of the learning, giving the lessons meaning. Questioning is a critical tool in the classroom used to stimulate discussion, encourage deeper thinking, and engage students in the richness of the content. We can inspire student engagement through various types of essential questions. Following are two types of essential questions that focus on the content of the learning:

Universal Essential Questions (UEQ)

- Represent the broadest form of questioning
- Are devoid of personification (she/we/us/people)
- Are interdisciplinary in nature, not specific to one content area
- Most often begin with "Why..."

Example: Why do systems function or dysfunction?

Content-Based Essential Questions (CEQ)

- Focus on one content area
- Link multiple topics or units together
- Most often begin with "How..."

Example: How do systems of government function or dysfunction interdependently?

Finally, essential questions should spark curiosity, provoke wonder, require multidisciplinary approaches to answering, and use the skills of inference and interpretation. Here are some more examples:

- Why might conflict be positive and/or negative?
- Why do patterns occur?
- Why is it important to understand the causes and effects of change?
- Why does prejudice exist?
- How does community form?

- How do systems break down?
- How can causes have multiple effects?

Step 4: Develop Unit Questions

Unit questions are formed as subordinate questions to the essential questions, nested within the essential question. Unit questions build an understanding of the content and support the approaches to the essential question. They are used as the framework for the activities that demonstrate understanding of the content and concepts.

Unit questions are specific to the lesson or unit of study and use the vocabulary of the discipline. They often provide the guiding questions for a particular activity or expected outcome of the lesson or unit. Using the math standard example in Figure 2.8 and the sample essential questions in the figure below, here are some sample unit questions. Note that these questions begin with "In what ways..." Other question starters include "How might...," "Where might...," "Who might...," "What might...," and so on.

- In what ways can you define place value in a multi-digit number?

Figure 2.9 — Breaking Down the Essentials: Math Example (Lower Grades)

CONTENT STANDARD

Understand the place value system. Recognize that in a multi-digit number, a digit in one place represents 10 times as much as it represents in the place to its right and 1/10 of what it represents in the place to its left.[9]

ESSENTIAL QUESTIONS	FACTUAL KNOWLEDGE

■ Why are number systems used?
■ How do patterns in numbers help define place value?
■ Why would rounding numbers be used today?
	Students will know:
	■ Place value
	■ Multi-digit numbers
	■ Whole number exponents
	■ Decimals to thousandths, notated by:
	  ▸ Base-ten numbers
	  ▸ Number name
	  ▸ Expanded form
	■ Meaning of >, =, and < symbols
	■ Round numbers

CONCEPTUAL KNOWLEDGE	
Students will understand: ■ Place value system	
PROCEDURAL KNOWLEDGE	
Students will be able to: ■ Explain patterns of numbers ■ Use whole number exponents to denote powers of 10 ■ Read, write, and compare decimals to thousandths ■ Use proper notation and symbols to record comparisons ■ Round decimals to any place	

UNIT QUESTIONS

- What is the value of the last digit in the number 444,444,444.444?
- What is the expanded form of 453.567?
- Write the fractions 2/10, 15/100, and 3/1000 as decimals.
- If a number (.57) is written as .5w7000, does it change its value?
- Define the symbols <, >, =, ≠

---

9. Adapted from Common Core State Standards for Mathematics, Grade 5: Number & Operations in Base Ten, corestandards.org/Math/Content/5/NBT.

- In what ways can you explain the pattern of zeroes when multiplying by powers of 10 to represent a number's value?
- In what ways can you represent decimals to thousandths?

In completing these four steps in defining the essentials of the curriculum, you are constructing lessons and activities that are meaningful to your students. Your curriculum design provides a roadmap for the teaching of skills, processes, and concepts through an interdisciplinary approach; it is infused with authentic experiences and assessments; and it enables students to think innovatively, critically, and thoughtfully. In essence, a twenty-first century curriculum design blends thinking skills with content knowledge so that your students are well prepared for future success.

The Breaking Down the Essentials template (**Figures 2.9** and **2.10** show examples and page 50 is a blank form) can be used as a course or unit guide for you and your students. For younger

Figure 2.10 Breaking Down the Essentials: English Language Arts Example (Upper Grades)

CONTENT STANDARDS
Reading, writing, speaking, and listening standards relating to literature about slavery and the American Civil War.[10]

ESSENTIAL QUESTIONS	FACTUAL KNOWLEDGE
■ How does resilience influence success? ■ In what ways are relationships connected to resilience?	Students will know: Facts and vocabulary related to racism, slavery, and the Civil War, including: ■ The Middle Passage ■ Three-Fifths Compromise ■ Slave trade ■ Plantation life for slaves ■ Slave resistance (sabotage, shutdowns, escapes, rebellions) ■ Underground railroad ■ Fugitive Slave Law

CONCEPTUAL KNOWLEDGE	
Students will understand: ■ Racism ■ Fiction versus memoir ■ Unreliable narrators ■ Writing for an audience	

PROCEDURAL KNOWLEDGE	
Students will be able to: ■ Analyze both the content and structure of *Incidents in the Life of a Slave Girl* and *A River Between Us* ■ Identify plot, character, conflict, setting, theme, and authorial purpose ■ Demonstrate understanding of reading by supporting opinions with source material ■ Discuss ideas in Socratic Seminar-type situations ■ Write skillful responses and/or critiques addressing one or more issues from the novels	

UNIT QUESTIONS
- Why has racism been such a historically complex and divisive issue?
- How do relationships give people strength to endure hardships?
- What is an unreliable narrator?
- How does a reader evaluate a writer's purpose and persuasive strategies?

10. Adapted from Common Core State Standards for English Language Arts, Grade 8: Reading: Literature, corestandards.org/ELA-Literacy/RL/8; Writing, corestandards.org/ELA-Literacy/W/8; Speaking & Listening, corestandards.org/ELA-Literacy/SL/8.

students, this may be sent home to share with the family exactly what will be covered in the unit. For intermediate-level students, the form can be used to keep students attentive to each part of the unit of study, highlighting the levels of knowledge as they go along. For older students, the form can be used as the unit syllabus and as a way to prepare for formative and summative assessments.

Designing this roadmap means that you are able to identify and define what is essential for our students to know, be able to do, and understand. In the process of differentiating, you must have solid knowledge of these essentials of the curriculum. In my experience, teachers have been trained to deliver curriculum but not necessarily taught how to develop curriculum. Understanding these basic components of the curriculum will make differentiation more doable.

Mapping a Concept-Based Plan of Curriculum

Now that you have developed a greater understanding of the parts of your curriculum, you are ready to take it to an advanced level. One of best ways to advance the level of your curriculum for all students is to design concept-based learning experiences. Concept-based learning is learning through big ideas and using factual knowledge and procedural skills to connect ideas and solve problems. H. Lynn Erickson, a leading expert in the field of concept-based teaching and learning, states that concept-based curriculum and instruction requires students to transfer knowledge between subject domains, use advanced levels of thinking, and construct new knowledge[11]—all essential skills for solving complex problems in today's world.

Developing a concept-based framework for your classroom requires a solid understanding of what you want your students to know, be able to do, and understand at the end of each lesson. Through the process of breaking down the curriculum essentials (see Figures 2.8, 2.9, and 2.10) you have the foundation for building a concept-based model. Upon reviewing your entire year of content, identify the major concepts that flow throughout the curriculum. Narrow the number of concepts to a manageable level (I suggest no more than five in a school year), so students have time to learn the concepts in-depth. Using too many concepts can overwhelm students and reduce the amount of time they spend investigating the big ideas, resulting in "shallow" levels of investigation.

Once you have defined the year-long concepts, select one to be an overarching thematic concept. This concept will unite and focus the entire school year's curriculum. It's best to select an interdisciplinary or universal concept for the thematic concept, so it will transcend all content areas and be less limiting in its application. For secondary teachers, this may require grade-level teachers to come together to agree on the concepts.

The other concepts you identified are supporting concepts you can use term-by-term or for shorter periods of time throughout the school year. **Figure 2.11** shows a four-term interconnected concept model constructed by a team of seventh-grade teachers in Washoe County School District in Nevada. The thematic concept is *interactions*, and the supporting concepts are *hierarchy*, *transformation*, *exploration*, and *relationships*.

Once you have decided upon the interconnected concepts, you can then frame intersecting essential questions to focus instruction and learning. Here are some examples from **Figure 2.12**:

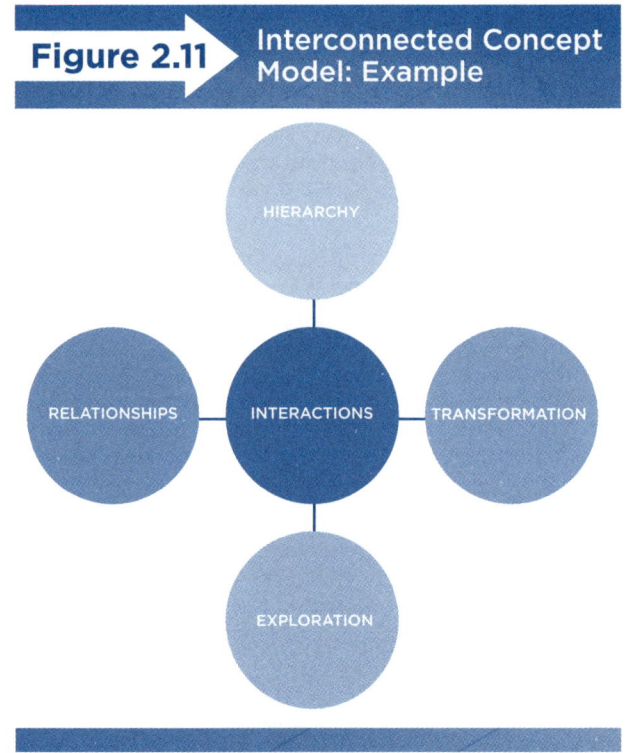

Figure 2.11 Interconnected Concept Model: Example

Created in collaboration with teachers in Washoe County School District, Nevada.

---

11. Erickson, H. L. *Concept-Based Curriculum and Instruction for the Thinking Classroom*. Thousand Oaks, CA: Corwin Press, 2007.

Universal Essential Question:
- Why is it important to understand interactions?

Content-Based Essential Questions:
- How do hierarchies influence interactions?
- How can interactions be transformative?
- How does exploration affect interactions?
- How do interactions affect relationships?

Now you are ready to frame your units of study around the interconnected concepts. Using the Concept-Based Curriculum Map (**Figures 2.12** and **2.13** on page 44) you can plan your entire year of study around concept-based learning. The form can be adjusted from two to four columns to fit your school calendar and instructional needs. Figures 2.12 and 2.13 show four-term and three-term examples; page 51 shows the template for the four-term map. The digital content includes blank templates of two-, three-, and four-term curriculum maps.

Building Concept-Based Unit Plans

Once you have crafted a Concept-Based Curriculum Map, you are ready to begin building unit plans using the concept-based development model. Unit plans keep instruction focused on what you want students to know, be able to do, and understand, as well as on the essential and content-based questions. The form on pages 52–54 (and the example in **Figure 2.14** on pages 46–48) puts all your instructional information in one place.

Key to Using the Unit Plan
Concepts
The unit plan has spaces for the overarching thematic concept and the supporting concepts for the duration of the unit.

Essential Questions (EQ)
The unit plan has spaces for the universal essential question (UEQ) as well as the content-based essential questions (CEQ).

Figure 2.12 — Concept-Based Curriculum Map (Four-Term Example)

Grade: 7 Year: 2017–2018

Thematic Concept: Interactions
Universal Essential Question (UEQ): Why is it important to understand interactions?

Supporting Concept 1: Hierarchy
Content-Based EQ: How do hierarchies influence interactions?

Supporting Concept 2: Transformation
Content-Based EQ: How can interactions be transformative?

Supporting Concept 3: Exploration
Content-Based EQ: How does exploration affect interactions?

Supporting Concept 4: Relationships
Content-Based EQ: How do interactions affect relationships?

ELA Unit: *Flowers for Algernon*	ELA Unit: *Chains*	ELA Unit: *Undaunted Courage Captain's Dog*	ELA Unit: *The Red Pony* *The Pearl*
SS Unit: Colonies	SS Unit: Revolution	SS Unit: Westward Expansion	SS Unit: Antebellum America and the Civil War
SC Unit: Energy + Force and Motion	SC Unit: Energy + Force and Motion	SC Unit: Matter and Its Interactions	SC Unit: Waves and Their Application in Technology for Information Transfer
Math Unit: Integers and Rational Numbers	Math Unit: Proportions and Percent	Math Unit: Exponents and Radicals	Math Unit: Counting and Probability

Figure 2.13 — Concept-Based Curriculum Map (Three-Term Example)

Grade: 3 **Year:** 2017–2018

Thematic Concept: Connectedness
Universal Essential Question (UEQ): Why is connectedness influential?

Supporting Concept 1: Community
Content-Based EQ: How does connectedness strengthen/weaken community?

Supporting Concept 2: Attitude
Content-Based EQ: How does attitude affect connectedness?

Supporting Concept 3: Reflection
Content-Based EQ: Why is reflection essential to connectedness?

Supporting Concept 1	Supporting Concept 2	Supporting Concept 3
ELA Unit: Socialization Through Writing and Literature	ELA Unit: Nonfiction Reading and Writing	ELA Unit: Government
SS Unit: *Sarah Plain and Tall*	SS Unit: Ohlone Indians	SS Unit: Local Redwood City History
SC Unit: Astronomy	SC Unit: Matter and Energy	SC Unit: Plant and Animal Adaptation
Math Unit: Number Sense	Math Unit: Geometry and Measurement & Data	Math Unit: Time and Fractions

Created in collaboration with teachers at North Star Academy in Redwood City, California.

Generalizations

Generalizations, also known as universal understandings, are broad statements or ideas students will gain from the tasks, activities, information, and experiences of the unit. These statements are most often true, however, sometimes a generalization won't apply. Students will need time to gather supporting facts, work through several examples, pull from prior experiences, and use logic and reasoning to understand a valid generalization. Knowing how to generalize is an important skill, because it can help students identify commonalities across content and situations. Generalizing extends thinking and reasoning beyond the subject area. Generalizations can either be universal (applying across the content areas) or content-specific. Determine generalizations prior to the lessons to keep students focused on what you want them to learn. See the following examples.

Universal Generalizations

- Systems are made up of subsystems.
- Power impacts systems.
- Change can be positive and/or negative.
- Force may contribute to conflict.
- Conflict may perpetuate order or chaos.

Content-Specific Generalizations

Math:

- When counting by 5, every other number in the ones place is the same. In the tens place, the digit stays the same twice after the first number (for example: 5, 10, 15, 20, 25, 30, 35, 40 or 9, 14, 19, 24, 29, 34, 39, 44, 49, and so on).
- Given a set of consecutive numbers, subtracting the first number from the second number always leaves 1.
- Adding the first and last number in a list of consecutive numbers always results in an odd sum.

Science:

- Magnetic attraction is stronger the closer magnets get to each other.
- Solids dissolve faster if they are smaller and the solution is warmer.
- Evaporation will increase as the surface area, air movement, and temperature of the liquid increases.

Social Studies:

- People explore to expand knowledge, gain resources, or find new products.

- If we don't understand our history, we are doomed to repeat it.
- Culture affects language and language affects culture.

Standard(s)
All good instruction must have standards to support the practice. In this box, you can simply list the standard numbers. Keeping a log of where and when you are addressing the standards will help you ensure units of study are focused on students' college and career readiness.

Unit Outcomes
Unit outcomes are what you expect students to learn from the unit as a whole. The outcomes should be listed broadly, while the specifics of what students will know, be able to do, and understand are listed later. In the Concept-Based Unit Plan example in Figure 2.14, the activities in the unit are linked to what students should understand. The outcomes are listed as products in which understanding is being developed.

Unit Description
Describe the unit of study as succinctly as possible. Brevity is important, since this is how you encapsulate what you want students to learn. In most cases, the unit description will highlight the conceptual level of knowledge and learning.

Knowledge Levels
In these spaces, detail a list of what you want students to understand, be able to do, and know. The example in Figure 2.14 presents the levels of knowledge (conceptual, procedural, and factual) as the objectives for the unit outcomes. Be as thorough as possible when creating these three items. Clearly stating each knowledge level and objective will help ensure all students have prior mastery of the factual and procedural levels. If students haven't fully acquired all the facts or procedures, you can craft pre-lessons or background experiences. If you see many repetitions in the factual and procedural levels, you can compact those items or offer shorter lessons to bring students up to speed.

For the conceptual knowledge level, make sure students have prior experience with the concepts or provide sufficient background knowledge early in the unit. In Figure 2.14, many of the conceptual level items are written abstractly, whereas the procedural and factual items are specific.

Knowledge Level Assessments
This element ensures that all levels of knowledge are being assessed through both formative and summative processes. In Figure 2.14, activities, rather than specific measures, are used for the formative assessments. This is because, as a teacher, you need to allow yourself the flexibility to incorporate unstructured formative assessments, such as observations, exit tickets, individual or small group questioning for understanding, and so forth. You will, however, want to list the more structured formative assessments on the form as a reminder throughout the unit to guide instruction and student mastery.

The summative assessments should be specific in nature, since they are your unit endpoints. In Figure 2.14, individual parts of the conceptual, procedural, and factual knowledge levels are listed to show they are being evaluated within the particular summative assessment. Summative assessment requires specificity to guarantee all the components of the knowledge levels are evaluated.

Self-Regulatory Strategies
Many schools and districts are incorporating social and emotional learning (SEL) into the classroom. Social and emotional learning is a process through which students build skills to manage emotional responses, set and achieve goals, demonstrate empathy toward others, develop positive relationships, and make good decisions. In some cases, SEL lessons are stand-alone lessons, isolated from the curriculum. Social and emotional learning can also be described as the development of self-regulation.

An effective way to assist students in developing self-regulation for learning is by infusing activities and strategies into lessons and units of study. The Concept-Based Unit Plan breaks down self-regulation into three dimensions: *affect* (how we manage our emotional responses), *behavior* (how we manage ourselves during learning), and *cognition* (how we manage our thinking while learning). Addressing each dimension in coordination with each other helps students learn to balance their own self-regulatory abilities. In Figure 2.14, various attributes are identified that students will develop during the unit. See Chapter 5 for additional information about self-regulatory development.[12]

Resources and Materials
This space is where the different texts, resources, materials, and supplies for the unit can be listed.

---

12. See also Cash, R. M. *Self-Regulation in the Classroom: Helping Students Learn How to Learn*. Minneapolis: Free Spirit Publishing, 2016.

Figure 2.14 Concept-Based Unit Plan: Example

Unit: Energy, Forces, and Motion
Grade: 7   **Subject:** Physical Science   **Year/Term:** 2017, terms 1 & 2

Thematic Concept:
Interactions

Universal EQ:
Why is it important to understand interactions?

Supporting Concepts:
Hierarchy
Transformation

Content-Based EQ:
How do hierarchies influence interactions?
How can interactions be transformative?

Generalizations:
Energy is all around us; energy is required for existence; there is no life without energy.
Force is an imbalance in power; force attracts, repels, or holds.
Motion is movement; motion is constant unless acted upon by an outside force.

Standard(s):
- MS-PS3: 1, 2, 4 (Roller Coasters)
- MS-PS2: 1, 2, 4 (Motion Activities; Newton's Laws of Motion/Rocketry)
- MS-PS3: 3, 4, 5 (Thermal Energy Transfer)
- MS-PS2: 3, 5 (Electricity and Magnetism)[13]

Unit Outcomes:
- Describe the relationships of kinetic energy to the mass and speed of an object.
- Construct a rocket and present arguments, using evidence, to support claims of how Newton's Three Laws of Motion affect the rocket's flight.
- Research, identify, argue, and provide evidence supporting the optimal energy-generating sources for the state of Nevada.
- Identify electric and magnetic interactions and how forces impact these interactions.

Unit Description:
This unit focuses on the two categories of energy—potential and kinetic—and how energy is conserved and transferred.

Conceptual Knowledge
Students will **understand:**
- Proportional relationships (speed, distance, time, scale, and quantity) as they relate to energy
- The causes and effects of relationships between kinetic and potential energy

Procedural Knowledge
Students will **be able to:**
- Implement safety procedures
- Convert measurements using the KHDBDCM chart
- Take measurements using different lab equipment

Factual Knowledge
Students will **know:**
- Laboratory safety procedures
- Metric conversion chart
- SI units for volume, mass, distance, and temperature
- Scientific method of inquiry

Chapter 2: Defining the Essentials of a Differentiated Curriculum **47**

- Why the motion of an object is determined by the sum of the forces acting on it
- Why energy is conserved within a system
- The environmental and financial impacts of various energy sources on a society
- The interactions between electric and magnetic forces
- The strengths of attractive and repulsive forces are dependent on the magnitude of the currents, magnetic strength, and distance between interacting objects

- Construct a model and observe relationships between potential and kinetic energy
- Measure the motion (speed, velocity, and acceleration) of an object
- Use mathematical calculations to show the relationships of an object's motion
- Collect, analyze, and graph data based on a series of experiments related to motion
- Carry out various investigations related to the net force exerted on an object
- Design a rocket and apply Newton's Laws of Motion to maximize the flight of the rocket
- Obtain, evaluate, and communicate information
- Research Nevada's various energy sources and propose a solution to meet the state's future energy needs
- Create an electromagnet

- Vocabulary related to motion, force, and energy
- Mathematical formulas for calculating quantities related to motion, force, and energy
- How to collect, record, and analyze data
- Vocabulary for magnetism and electricity

Conceptual Formative Assessments:
- Roller Coaster Challenge
- Speed Challenge
- Acceleration Lab
- Friction Lab
- Volume Lab
- Density Lab
- Magnetism activities/labs/notes
- Electricity activities/labs/notes
- Electromagnet Challenge

Procedural Formative Assessments:
- Roller Coaster Challenge
- Speed Challenge
- Acceleration Lab
- Friction Lab
- Volume Lab
- Density Lab
- Magnetism activities/labs/notes
- Electricity activities/labs/notes
- Electromagnet Challenge

Factual Formative Assessments:
- Roller Coaster Challenge
- Speed Challenge
- Acceleration Lab
- Friction Lab
- Volume Lab
- Density Lab
- Metric Conversions
- Magnetism activities/labs/notes
- Electricity activities/labs/notes
- Electromagnet Challenge

NOTE: The assessments in the above columns are nearly identical, since it's difficult in science to separate the conceptual, procedural, and factual elements into separate assessments.

continued →

Figure 2.14 ▶ Concept-Based Unit Plan: Example (continued)

Conceptual Summative Assessments:
- Rocketry—Apply Newton's Three Laws of Motion to flight
- Thermal Energy—Conduct an experiment that shows how energy is conserved
- Electromagnet Challenge and Write Up

Procedural Summative Assessments:
- Rocketry—Collect and interpret data with respect to the rocket's flight
- Thermal Energy—Collect and interpret data to support the Law of Conservation of Energy
- Energy Source Poster—Explain the process of energy transformation from source to resource (for example, battery/chemical energy for example, flashlight/light energy)
- Electromagnet Challenge—Design an electromagnet and discuss design procedure and findings in a write-up

Factual Summative Assessments:
- Energy Source Poster—Explain the efficiency of various energy sources
- Unit exams on motion, force, energy, and electricity/magnetism

Affective Self-Regulatory Strategies:
- Build confidence through collaboration

Behavioral Self-Regulatory Strategies:
- Follow science safety procedures
- Use scientific method

Cognitive Self-Regulatory Strategies:
- Reflect on daily collaboration

Resources/Materials:
- Probes and software
- Roller coaster supplies: PVC insulation tubing, various marbles of different densities, stop watches, tape, meter stick
- Friction blocks
- Spring scales
- Water bottle rocket challenge kit and launcher
- Hot and cold water
- Styrofoam cups
- Calculator
- Paper, computers
- Metric conversion chart
- Laboratory equipment for measurements
- Electrical circuits (Snap kits)
- Magnets, iron filings
- Electromagnet supplies

13. Adapted from the Next Generation Science Standards, MS-PS3 Energy, nextgenscience.org/dci-arrangement/ms-ps3-energy; and MS-PS2 Motion and Stability: Forces and Interactions, nextgenscience.org/dci-arrangement/ms-ps2-motion-and-stability-forces-and-interactions.

Concept Development Worksheet

Instructions:

1. Write the concept in the concept square.
2. In the **+** (plus) box, list words or simple statements that represent or define the concept.
3. In the **−** (minus) box, list words or simple statements that do *not* represent or define the concept.
4. Review the list and categorize the words or statements in both boxes.
5. In the ∴ (therefore) box, create statements that explain your categorizations. (These are called *generalizations*: statements that are always or almost always true.)
6. In the **?** (question) box, turn each of your generalizations into an open-ended question. These questions are your *essential questions*.

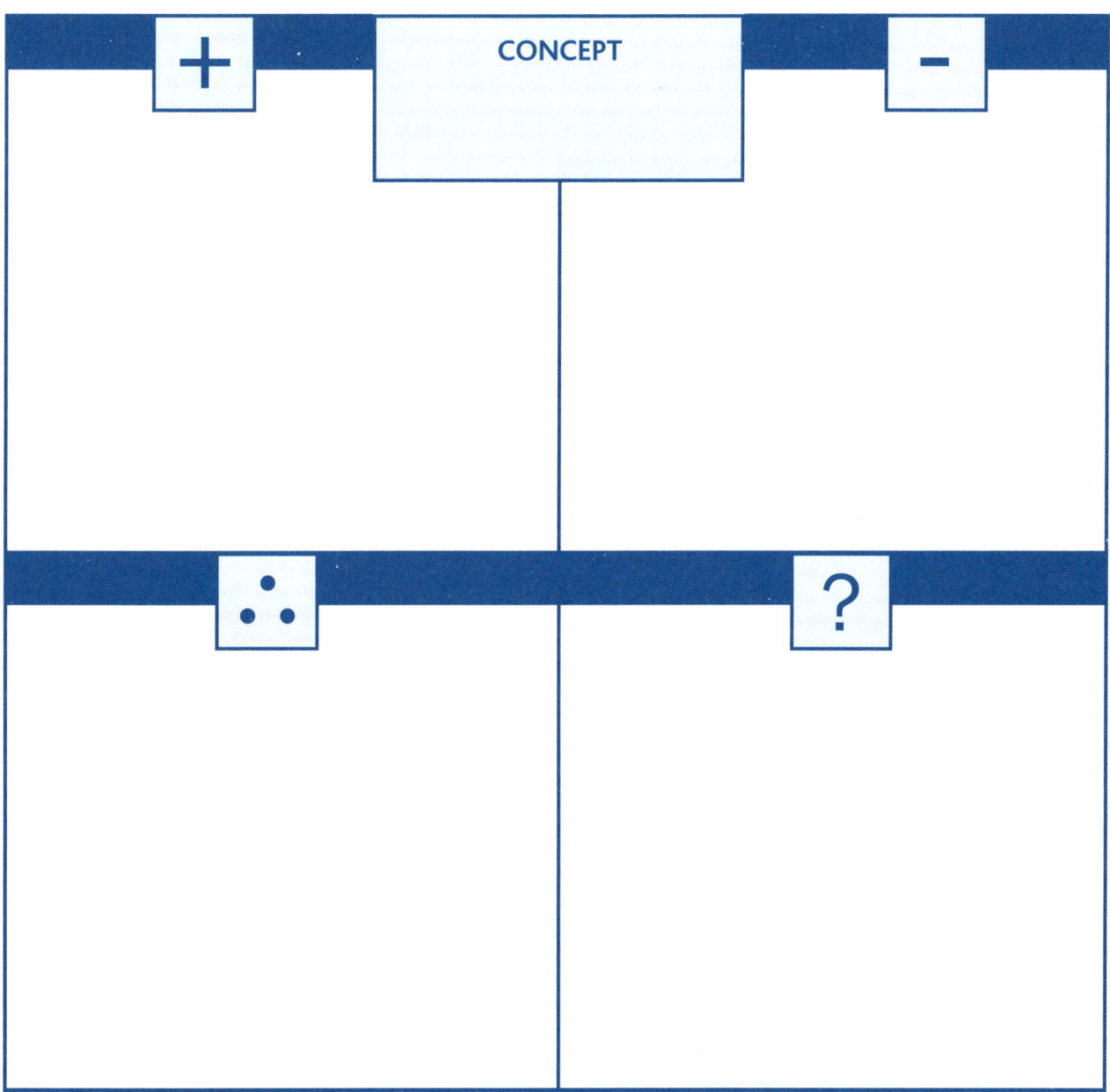

Based on the curriculum model in *Curriculum Development: Theory and Practice* by Hilda Taba. New York: Harcourt Brace and World, 1962.

From *Advancing Differentiation: Thinking and Learning for the 21st Century* by Richard M. Cash, Ed.D., copyright © 2017. This page may be reproduced for use within an individual school or district. For all other uses, contact Free Spirit Publishing Inc. at www.freespirit.com/permissions.

Breaking Down the Essentials

CONTENT STANDARD

ESSENTIAL QUESTIONS

FACTUAL KNOWLEDGE

CONCEPTUAL KNOWLEDGE

PROCEDURAL KNOWLEDGE

UNIT QUESTIONS

From *Advancing Differentiation: Thinking and Learning for the 21st Century* by Richard M. Cash, Ed.D., copyright © 2017. This page may be reproduced for use within an individual school or district. For all other uses, contact Free Spirit Publishing Inc. at www.freespirit.com/permissions.

Concept-Based Curriculum Map (Four-Term)

Grade: **Year:**

Thematic Concept:

Universal Essential Question (UEQ):

Supporting Concept 1:	Supporting Concept 2:	Supporting Concept 3:	Supporting Concept 4:
Content-Based EQ:	Content-Based EQ:	Content-Based EQ:	Content-Based EQ:
ELA Unit:	ELA Unit:	ELA Unit:	ELA Unit:
SS Unit:	SS Unit:	SS Unit:	SS Unit:
SC Unit:	SC Unit:	SC Unit:	SC Unit:
Math Unit:	Math Unit:	Math Unit:	Math Unit:

From *Advancing Differentiation: Thinking and Learning for the 21st Century* by Richard M. Cash, Ed.D., copyright © 2017. This page may be reproduced for use within an individual school or district. For all other uses, contact Free Spirit Publishing Inc. at www.freespirit.com/permissions.

Concept-Based Unit Plan

Grade:　　　　Subject:　　　　Year/Term:

Thematic Concept:	Universal EQ:
Supporting Concepts:	Content-Based EQ:
Generalizations:	
Standard(s):	
Unit Outcomes:	
Unit Description:	

continued →

From *Advancing Differentiation: Thinking and Learning for the 21st Century* by Richard M. Cash, Ed.D., copyright © 2017. This page may be reproduced for use within an individual school or district. For all other uses, contact Free Spirit Publishing Inc. at www.freespirit.com/permissions.

Concept-Based Unit Plan (continued)

Conceptual Knowledge **Students will understand:**	*Procedural Knowledge* **Students will be able to:**	*Factual Knowledge* **Students will know:**
Conceptual Formative Assessments:	**Procedural Formative Assessments:**	**Factual Formative Assessments:**

continued

Concept-Based Unit Plan (continued)

Conceptual Summative Assessments:	Procedural Summative Assessments:	Factual Summative Assessments:
Affective Self-Regulatory Strategies:	Behavioral Self-Regulatory Strategies:	Cognitive Self-Regulatory Strategies:
Resources/Materials:		

Chapter 3

Advancing Differentiation to New Levels Through a Rigorous Curriculum

*What we want is to see the child in pursuit of knowledge,
and not knowledge in pursuit of the child.*

—George Bernard Shaw, playwright

With advancing technologies, greater globalization, and competition for highly talented employees, the landscape for the future workforce continues to evolve. Our students' college and career readiness now depends upon a more sophisticated level of knowledge and abilities. To prepare students for the rigors and complexity of this new world, teachers must examine what is taught and why. The first step is for you to know the essentials of the curriculum and how they are connected to what your students are expected to know, be able to do, and understand. Then, to better equip yourself for meaningful differentiation, you must also ensure that all students are challenged, engaged, and motivated to reach high expectations. This is achieved by articulating a rigorous curriculum that prepares your students for success in today's world.

Differentiation expert Carol Ann Tomlinson has often said that you can't differentiate garbage. If a curriculum is not solid with clearly defined goals, standards, expectations, and outcomes, it won't matter how many different ways you offer the information; it will not be effectively learned. Quality differentiation can only be achieved when we can clearly articulate what we want students to know, be able to do, and understand, and build a curriculum that is coherent with a focus on our students' future success. This is why teachers should understand the essence of a rigorous curriculum, know how to define it, and be able to construct activities that guide students toward deep levels of learning.

What Is a Rigorous Curriculum?

What exactly is a "rigorous" curriculum? Answer: One that stretches each learner to grow intellectually, through engaging and challenging activities, to a point where the learner is self-directed, autonomous, and able to contribute successfully to society. See Figure 2.2 on page 30.

A rigorous curriculum:

- is inquiry based
- relies less on facts, more on concepts
- involves critical reasoning
- infuses creative idea generation
- requires problem finding and solving
- employs authentic tasks and products
- necessitates the application of knowledge
- encourages reflection
- integrates assessment *for* and *of* learning

Building a rigorous curriculum requires teachers to have:

- a thorough knowledge of the content
- a complete understanding of the concepts that underlie the content
- a solid grasp of instructional skills
- autonomy to make judgments of what is taught and how

- quality assessment practices to identify where and when learners need support or extensions
- a deep comprehension of how students learn

Hallmarks of a Rigorous Curriculum: Effective, Engaging, Exciting, Enriching (E⁴)

Russian psychologist Lev Vygotsky defined intellectual growth as a process that moves the learner from observation, to mimicking, and ultimately to independence of thought. Vygotsky's theory of the "zone of proximal development" (ZPD) suggests that learning happens when a person is challenged to stretch beyond what is comfortable to that which is difficult. For students to be challenged, they must be provided instruction that levels support from *guidance* to *autonomy*, and curriculum that scaffolds information from *basic* to *complex*. This scaffolding of information can be accomplished through four main traits: complex, ambiguous, provocative, and personally or emotionally challenging.[1] Curriculum can be varied in degree of rigor by increasing any or all of the four traits just listed, which could also be described as: **effective** (complex), **engaging** (personally or emotionally challenging), and **exciting** (provocative and ambiguous), as well as **enriching** (authentic and substantive).

Effective—Create Complexity Through Concept-Based Learning

For curriculum to be effective, it must offer students a variety of complex activities. Complex activities are those that go deeply into the content, allow students to explore content through different learning preferences, or expose students to new ways of thinking and doing. This is best achieved when curriculum is organized around complex and interrelated *concepts*. Concepts are those universal thoughts or ideas that transcend and unite disciplines. They might be discipline specific or content-based (such as multiplication and sums in math, transportation and government in social studies, temperature and gravity in science, or vowels and folktales in language arts); interdisciplinary general or universal (such as change, systems, models, or loyalty); or even self-regulatory (such as responsibility, organization, empathy, or commitment). Concepts help students organize ideas and categorize information in a coherent fashion. You can increase curriculum rigor by using multifaceted concepts that require a greater understanding of content principles.

Example of Simple to Multifaceted Concepts

- Self
- Family
- Friends
- Community
- City
- State
- Nation

Conceptual development and design is explored in greater detail in Chapter 2.

Engaging—Challenge Students Personally and Emotionally

Emotional engagement drives attention; attention drives learning. Research suggests that engagement is a multifaceted construct.[2] To motivate and engage students in learning, we must consider their affective, behavioral, and cognitive needs. Students will not engage in a learning situation unless the content has some personal or emotional relevance to them, they find the learning activities meaningful to their future success, and they are cognitively challenged. Getting students emotionally engaged in learning begins with focusing on student interests and passions. Using these interests, you can motivate learners to find new connections to old information and to make information personally relevant and worthwhile. This emotional engagement piques students' desires to go deeper into topics or areas of study. The more emotionally charged a topic is, or the more the student feels personally connected to it, the more rigorous and engaging that topic becomes for the student.

---

1. Strong, R. W., H. F. Silver, and M. J. Perini. *Teaching What Matters Most: Standards and Strategies for Raising Student Achievement*. Alexandria, VA: ASCD, 2001.
2. Fredricks, J. A., P. C. Blumenfeld, and A. H. Paris. "School Engagement: Potential of the Concept, State of the Evidence." *Review of Educational Research*, 74 (1) (Spring 2004): 59–109.

> **Strategies to Engage Students**
>
> - Conduct an interest survey at the beginning of a major unit.
> - Preview the topic with students. Have them look through the text and flag pages or pictures that pique their interest.
> - Provide students with choices and options within the learning.
> - Foster students' confidence through emotional support.
> - Offer specific descriptive feedback on what students are doing well and where they should focus their efforts.
> - Give clear directions to achieve success.
> - Build strong caring relationships with students.
> - Allow students to work collaboratively with others.
> - Share your own interest in the topic.
> - Have students bring in items from their personal lives that connect to the topic.
> - Create a joyful learning environment where intellectual risk taking is encouraged.

Exciting—Choose Ambiguous and Provocative Topics

Ambiguity is an exceptional learning tool. When material, issues, or solutions are less obvious, the learner must invest greater amounts of mental energy to develop knowledge. Curriculum that allows for ambiguity forces students to look for multiple meanings within the context of the information. When students deal with ambiguity they learn how to deal with uncertainty, develop perseverance, make personal sense of the information, rationalize debates, and form solid independent opinions. Curriculum that infuses greater ambiguity, such as focusing on symbols and images full of multiple meanings, raises the level of rigor. Dealing with ambiguity helps students understand the richness and intricacy of the world around us.

Ambiguous topics are often also provocative. A provocative curriculum centers on problems within and across disciplines, and it challenges students' beliefs, understandings, and prior knowledge. These issues elicit responses from students, evoke feelings, and excite students to find solutions or resolutions. See the chart on page 58 for examples of topics.

Enriching—Create Authentic Tasks and Substantive Conversations

Another way to ensure curriculum rigor is to have students practice operations and skills in authentic ways and engage in meaningful discussions.

Create Authentic Tasks

Tasks are authentic when students are using content skills and knowledge in real-world applications found outside of the classroom walls, such as at home or in the workplace. An authentic task is most often constructed so that there is no one right way to complete the task, nor one right answer. These tasks require students to use the content skills and knowledge holistically and in interdisciplinary context. Students are motivated to persevere and put forth greater effort.

A hallmark of quality authentic tasks is *student collaboration*. When students collaborate they build community by working together toward a common goal. Interactions between diverse learners (whether the diversity be academic, social, or cultural) provide new opportunities for ideas to blossom and grow. Collaborative efforts in authentic tasks require students to use higher order thinking skills, critical reasoning, and problem-solving strategies.

The real problems presented in authentic tasks require more careful attention to finding real solutions, thus forcing students to employ *valid research strategies*. Students are challenged to plan initiatives, organize materials, develop new ideas, assess while learning, and evaluate outcomes. Students build ownership, foster a sense of community, and develop an entrepreneurial spirit in learning. There is a greater chance that learning developed through authentic tasks will transfer outside of the content area, as well as beyond the classroom walls.

Authentic learning tasks for the twenty-first century, or learning-by-doing, are generally considered the most effective way to learn. In today's world, authentic tasks must take into account the use of technology, experimentation, inquiry, and problem solving. Students develop "portable skills" that are transferable to all content areas, including:

- judgment about the reliability of information
- persistence, patience, and perseverance
- creative and critical thinking

Authentic tasks also employ the use of *expert sources*, from materials to individuals. For students to solve real problems they must use materials that reflect the causes and effects of the problem. For instance, for students to understand how to represent data they must work with actual charts and graphs that hold meaning for them, such as those found in the newspaper or on the Internet.

Examples of Provocative Discussion Topics

- abortion rights
- advertising in schools
- affirmative action
- allowance
- alternative medicine
- animal rights
- artificial intelligence
- bioethics
- biological weapons
- bullying/cyberbullying
- capital punishment
- cell phones in school
- censorship
- chores
- children's rights
- citizenship
- cloning
- conflict vs. cooperation
- consumerism
- cosmetic surgery
- curfews
- death penalty
- drug legalization
- drug testing
- eating disorders
- environment
- euthanasia
- evolution
- family
- fast food in schools
- foreign policy
- friendship
- gambling
- genetic engineering
- genocide
- gender identity
- global warming
- grief and loss
- gun control
- hairstyles/clothing
- hate crimes
- healthcare
- helmet laws
- HIV/AIDS
- homelessness
- homeschooling
- homework
- immigration
- Internet use in school
- legal age for driving, alcohol consumption, voting
- marriage equality
- nuclear energy
- nuclear weapons
- obesity
- parental consent/supervision
- performance-enhancing drugs
- piercings/tattoos
- piracy of music and other media
- prayer in school
- prisoner rights
- punishment at home/school
- racism
- ratings for movies, TV shows, games
- reality TV
- rules for classroom/school
- school uniforms
- school violence
- single-sex classrooms/schools
- sex education
- sexual harassment
- smoking bans
- stay-at-home parenting
- stem-cell research
- steroid use
- suicide
- teamwork vs. independence
- teenage pregnancy
- terrorism
- video games
- welfare
- women's rights

Examples of Authentic Tasks

- project-based or problem-based learning
- student-designed experiments, questions, or problems
- service learning projects
- science experiments
- WebQuests
- robotics
- simulations
- debates
- inquiry-based learning

10 DESIGN ELEMENTS FOR AUTHENTIC LEARNING TASKS

When designing authentic learning experiences, incorporate these elements to make any subject more effective, engaging, exciting, and enriching:[3]

1. **Real-world problems:** Activities are actual problems that professionals would tackle.
2. **Ill-defined problems:** Tasks have multiple levels of problems and complex issues where solutions are not easily found.
3. **Long-term investigations:** Problems go beyond being solved in minutes or even a few hours. Students will need to spend significant time investigating, collecting data, forming hypotheses, and coming up with solutions.

---

3. Reeves, T. C., J. Herrington, and R. Oliver. "Authentic Activities and Online Learning." In *Research and Development in Higher Education: Quality Conversations Vol. 25*. T. Herrington (Ed.). Perth, Australia: Higher Education Research and Development Society of Australasia, 2002.

4. **Multiple sources and perspectives:** Solving an authentic problem will require students to use a variety of sources and encourage them to obtain the perspective of others.
5. **Collaboration:** Complex problems require many minds to come to good/workable solutions.
6. **Reflection:** Authentic tasks encourage learners to think about and plan appropriately for quality solutions.
7. **Interdisciplinary perspective:** Real-world problems are not contained to one topic or subject area—they require the use of multiple disciplines.
8. **Integrated assessment:** Assessments are ongoing and woven throughout the solving of authentic problems.
9. **Authentic products:** Authentic problems require the creation of authentic products that have value to others.
10. **Multiple outcomes:** Authentic problems will go beyond one right answer and will produce different types of interpretations and outcomes.

Ignite Substantive Conversations

Students crave the chance to discuss, debate, and challenge each other's ideas. In a rigorous curriculum, students put new information to work and engage in exchanges of ideas that build on prior knowledge. Taking part in substantive conversations with peers as well as with experts in the field helps students clarify ideas, form opinions based on fact or experience, and grasp a deeper understanding of and connection to issues in the real world. At the center of a rigorous curriculum are those issues that provoke students to wrestle with real problems that challenge their ideas, beliefs, and prior knowledge.

For students to engage in substantive conversations, the content must be emotionally enlivened enough for students to interact with the information. Enlivening content requires the use of relevant and current issues that relate to what is being taught. Students will converse when they feel ownership of the issue, so making a topic relevant to students will engage them in discussion. By taking stories from the news, students' daily lives, or general social issues and weaving the content through these stories, you are helping students emotionally engage in discussions.

Strategies to Incorporate Substantive Conversations

- **Debate** controversial issues in your discipline; *for lower elementary students*: Debate the actions of a character in a story.
- **Discuss** alternative/risky solutions that characters/individuals might have considered; *for lower elementary students*: Discuss alternative observations made during a science experiment by asking, "What else can account for the outcome of this experiment?"
- **Question** methods/ulterior motives of famous figures; *for lower elementary students*: Question a famous person from history about why they did what they did, using role play or writing a letter to the person.
- **Mediate** the pros and cons of political decisions; *for lower elementary students*: Mediate an argument between two characters from a story using role play.

Keywords to Ignite Conversation

Debate	Interrogate
Ponder	Arbitrate
Argue	Mediate
Dispute	Reconcile
Contend	Deduce
Deliberate	Reason
Confer	Interpret
Discuss	Infer
Question	Construct
Inquire	

Infusing Rigor Into Your Curriculum

Many teachers believe their curriculum is the textbook. While the textbook is one source within a curriculum, it is *not* the only source. Textbooks rely on providing a broad general sweep of a content area. A curriculum is more than just the textbook. It includes the standards of the discipline, knowledge within and around the content, and skills and practices used within the subject matter. Curriculum is also the teacher's content expertise and knowledge that is infused to excite students to pursue deeper understanding of the subject. All of the strategies and ideas listed in this section are ways teachers can excite students. Rigor is achieved when students have identified relevance to the topic and then can form a relationship to the learning.

To help in creating a school culture of rigor, I've created the principles of curriculum and instruction that advance learning (page 61), and classroom practices that advance learning (page 62). These lists can be used by a site team to define how content is delivered beyond the textbook or by individual teachers as a reminder of ways to ensure rigor. I suggest these lists be publicly posted throughout the school or classroom so students and families are also aware of the implementation of principles and practices of a rigorous school culture.

Also included is a Walkthrough Checklist of Differentiation for Advancing Learning on page 63. This can be used by school administrators, peer coaches, or content specialists when doing brief classroom walkthroughs. Walkthroughs are a powerful tool educational leaders use to assist and guide teachers toward fidelity of implementation of a rigorous curriculum and instructional practices.

Strategies to Develop a Rigorous (E4) Curriculum

- Engage students in the learning by piquing their interests in the topic of study. This can uncover hidden talents or undiscovered areas of interests.
- Anchor enrichment activities to the regular curriculum through either concept or process.
- Unite content through the use of interdisciplinary topics or a single theme.
- Allow students to wrestle with ambiguous case studies or authentic issues that require them to use higher level thinking skills and creativity.
- Encourage students to better know themselves as scholars by assessing their learning preferences.
- Establish an open environment within your classroom where students are encouraged to take risks, voice opinions, debate ideas, and tackle controversial issues.
- Orchestrate flexible instructional groups in the classroom allowing students to work both with peers who are alike and peers who are different.
- Offer respectful tasks that you can scaffold for those who need additional support and stretch for those who need additional challenge (see a Guide to Tiering Assignments and Activities on pages 64–65).
- Teach using multiple learning modes to encourage students to reach beyond their comfort zones and seek sources of information.
- Use humor in your classroom to create a more enjoyable learning setting and to relieve stress.

Principles of Curriculum and Instruction for Advancing Learning

- Present content that is related to broad-based issues, themes, or problems.

- Integrate multiple disciplines into the area of study.

- Present comprehensive, related, mutually reinforcing experiences within an area of study.

- Allow for the in-depth learning of a self-selected topic within an area of study.

- Develop independent or self-directed study skills.

- Develop productive, complex, abstract, or higher order thinking skills.

- Focus on open-ended tasks.

- Develop research skills and methods.

- Integrate basic skills and higher level thinking skills into the curriculum.

- Encourage the development of products that challenge existing ideas and produce "new" ideas.

- Encourage the development of products that use new techniques, materials, and forms.

- Encourage the development of self-understanding (i.e., recognizing and using one's abilities, becoming self-directed, appreciating likenesses and differences between oneself and others).

- Evaluate student outcomes by using appropriate and specific criteria through self-appraisal, criterion referenced, or standardized instruments.

Classroom Practices for Advancing Learning

- Create an open environment.
- Use flexible instructional groups.
- Include multiple approaches to information.
- Use multiple learning modes.
- Be aware of student strengths.
- Use humor (not sarcasm).
- Draw on multiple and varied resources.
- Build an inquisitive atmosphere.
- Encourage acceptance of diversity (in people and ideas).
- Provide independent and small group instruction.
- Teach and use research skills.

Walkthrough Checklist of Differentiation for Advancing Learning

CONTENT	PROCESS	PRODUCT
☐ Content is linked to broad issues, themes, or problems	☐ Teacher knows and uses advanced levels of Bloom's Taxonomy	☐ Students are encouraged to create new products and ideas
☐ Content reinforces interdisciplinary study	☐ Students are offered in-depth learning opportunities	☐ Students create products that incorporate techniques, materials, and forms taught throughout the unit of study
☐ Content is linked to fields of study or discipline	☐ Students are guided toward higher levels of thought through open-ended questions	
☐ Students are provided choices in topics within an area of study	☐ Students problem find and solve issues that are relevant and worth solving	☐ Students are allowed choices to work on projects collaboratively or independently, depending on the requirements of the project
☐ Students have the opportunity to pursue independent or self-directed studies	☐ Students know and employ research skills	☐ Assignments are tiered by the readiness, interest, or learning preference of the students
☐ The content has direct relevant links to students' experiences and lives	☐ Students know and employ creative thinking skills	
☐ The curriculum is grounded in conceptual, procedural, and factual knowledge	☐ Students know and employ critical reasoning tools	☐ Students are given choices in how to represent knowledge acquisition
☐ The teacher knows and focuses student attention on conceptual, procedural, and factual knowledge	☐ Students make connections between self and the curriculum	☐ Students use technology in the creation and presentation of projects
☐ The curriculum is directly linked to state or national standards	☐ The classroom environment is welcoming and accepting of all students	☐ Student products represent an accumulation of knowledge rather than a regeneration of facts
☐ Formative assessment is utilized to guide students toward success	☐ Flexible instructional grouping practices are used	☐ Students are encouraged to act as scholars
☐ Summative assessment is used to inform achievement	☐ Multiple instructional strategies are used to engage students in understanding	☐ Student products are authentic, valuable to others, and presented to an authentic audience
	☐ A variety of resources are available to and used by students	
	☐ Teacher acts as guide in learning and discovery	

From *Advancing Differentiation: Thinking and Learning for the 21st Century* by Richard M. Cash, Ed.D., copyright © 2017. This page may be reproduced for use within an individual school or district. For all other uses, contact Free Spirit Publishing Inc. at www.freespirit.com/permissions.

Guide to Tiering Assignments and Activities

What Do I Tier?
Tiered assignments/activities should:
- be different work, not simply more or less work
- offer equal amount of interest and engagement
- be respectable tasks for all
- take roughly the same amount of time to accomplish the task
- develop conceptual, procedural, and/or factual knowledge

How Do I Tier?
Tiered assignments/activities can be structured by:

- **Challenge Level (depth of content)**—from shallow to deep levels within the content. *Examples:*

  ### Social Studies
  Shallow: Define acts that lead up to the war.
  Deep: Define the tenants of a revolution and how they impact people, economics, politics, or social structures.

  ### Science
  Shallow: Name the parts of a cell.
  Deep: Analyze the interrelationship between the parts of a cell and describe their common elements.

  ### Math
  Shallow: Name the factors of 100.
  Deep: Create a graphic to assist in converting decimals to fractions.

  ### Literature
  Shallow: Summarize the chapter.
  Deep: Interpret the actions of the main character in the chapter and predict how his/her actions may affect the movement of the plot in future chapters.

- **Complexity Level (degree of thinking/process)**—from basic to sophisticated levels of thinking. *Examples:*

  ### Social Studies
  Basic: List important dates of the war on a timeline.
  Sophisticated: Analyze the various arguments each party had against the oppressor and explain which argument was most valid.

  ### Science
  Basic: Define how each part of the cell operates within the system.
  Sophisticated: Define how a cellular system operates like a manufacturing plant or factory.

  ### Math
  Basic: List the steps needed to complete the equation.
  Sophisticated: Create a new method to correctly solve the equation.

  ### Literature
  Basic: Create a character map that links all characters together.
  Sophisticated: Create a new character who could move the plot in a different direction but who would still work within the framework of the story.

continued

Guide to Tiering Assignments and Activities (continued)

- **Interest/Preference/Readiness**—with awareness of interest, learning preference, or readiness. *Examples:*

    Social Studies
    Interest (sports): Research the games that were played by a person your age during the American Revolution. What does this research tell you about a young person living at that time?
    Learning Preference (musical): Compose a song that summarizes the outcome of the American Revolution.
    Readiness (lower reading level): Using the highlighted text, summarize the main points made by the colonists.

    Science
    Interest (music): Describe how the cellular system is like an orchestra.
    Learning Preference (visual): Create a poster that demonstrates the interdependence of elements within the cellular system.
    Readiness (advanced science knowledge): Investigate how a cellular system can become dysfunctional and how its development can be arrested.

    Math
    Interest (theater): Diagram the angles formed by various types of stage lighting.
    Learning Preference (interpersonal): In a group, discuss the angles and come to consensus on the most efficient method of solving the problem.
    Readiness (basic math skills): Using a toy construction system, show each angle as listed.

    Literature
    Interest (adventure): Choose an adventure novel that uses the theme of rebellion.
    Learning Preference (auditory): After you have read each chapter, listen to the audio version to reinforce your memory.
    Readiness (previously read the assigned novel): Read *Moll Flanders* while the rest of the class reads *The Color Purple.* During class discussion, offer responses using examples from both novels you have read.

    Note: Differences in outcomes can also be considered within any of the options listed above.

Why Should I Tier?
Tiered assignments/activities work well when:
- students are found to need varied amounts of time to learn information
- students have varied degrees of motivation or engagement
- students are at different levels within the content

Other Considerations
Develop an efficient method for giving directions.
- work cards that clearly define the activity
- work stations with all the necessary materials

Develop an efficient method for moving students into groups.
- work stations
- desk clusters
- tables

Use a consistent grading format.
- rubric criteria that assess the same content regardless of the product
- criteria is well-defined and clear to all students
- grade reflects the learning

From *Advancing Differentiation: Thinking and Learning for the 21st Century* by Richard M. Cash, Ed.D., copyright © 2017. This page may be reproduced for use within an individual school or district. For all other uses, contact Free Spirit Publishing Inc. at www.freespirit.com/permissions.

Chapter 4

Motivating and Engaging Learners

There is a brilliant child locked inside every student.
—Marva Collins, educator

In today's classroom, students come with differing complexities, experiences, interests, and learning abilities. As a teacher, you must be prepared to meet the needs of each learner with a variety of strategies and techniques to differentiate the curriculum and instructional activities so that all your students are successful. This chapter defines some of the varied learning preferences students possess and offers valuable differentiation strategies that motivate and engage learners.

Think back to a time when you were required to attend a workshop or staff meeting. List all the reasons why you did not want to be in that workshop or meeting. Now list all the reasons why you wanted to be there. It's likely that many of the reasons why you did *not* want to be there included these:

- You were forced to be there.
- You knew you had someplace more important to be.
- You'd rather be doing something else.
- You felt that you already knew the information being presented.
- You were tired, hungry, angry, or upset.

And perhaps the reasons why you *did* want to attend the workshop or meeting included these:

- You thought you would gain new knowledge or skills.
- You wanted to meet new friends or connect with colleagues.
- You hoped the presenter would be engaging and interesting.
- You were hoping for some inspiration and encouragement.

These are the same reasons our students do or don't want to be in our classrooms. How often do you ask your students, "Who *doesn't* want to be here today and why?" or "Who *does* want to be here and why?" If you asked this more often of your students, you may be surprised how similar their responses are to your own. Also, if you ask your students to honestly tell you *why* they don't want to be in your classroom, you may then be able to address their needs so they can spend more of their mental energy on learning, rather than on resisting learning.

Emotion ➡ Attention ➡ Learning

A fundamental of brain-compatible learning is that emotion drives attention, and attention drives learning. Students underachieve or underperform for a variety of reasons. They may:

- perceive a lack of challenge in the content
- be uninterested in the content
- lack self-efficacy
- lack key skills
- not have practice in perseverance or the ability to control it
- be unable or unwilling to see the purpose of learning the content
- have too much or too little self-confidence
- be overinvolved with other activities
- have difficulty getting product-oriented
- lack task follow-through
- have a fear of failure
- tend to procrastinate
- be overly focused on personal difficulties

- depend too much on others to do things for them
- be highly distractible
- be experiencing distress in their personal or family lives

What this all comes down to is students' lack of *focused motivational drive*. In my work with teachers around the world, I hear this over and over again: "I just can't get my students motivated to learn!" Many teachers, administrators, and parents are frustrated by the lack of commitment that some students have toward learning and producing. All people are motivated in one way or another, whether it be from the outside or the inside. Each type of motivational drive has benefits, depending on the situation. So how do we get our kids to use the right motivational drive to learn what we need them to learn? How do we motivate them to do well on the products, performances, and those ever-present tests? Students' motivational drive to learn and perform to the highest levels of their potential has puzzled researchers for years. Understanding what motivates and engages individuals and why is a very complex issue.

What Is Motivation?

If you break down the word *motivation*, you get *motive + action*. A *motive* is "something that causes a person to act in a certain way or do a certain thing." In other words, it is an incentive to perform. *Action* is "doing." So *motivation* is "a desire to do or a drive to complete," in other words, motivational drive. In the classroom, we want our students to be motivated to achieve, to be "achievement motivated." Achievement motivation is about striving for competence. To attain achievement motivation, students must feel and recognize their own competence.

Two highly regarded experts in the study of motivation, Andrew Elliott and Carol Dweck, state that competence is "a condition or quality of effectiveness, ability, sufficiency, or success."[1] All people want to be competent at meaningful tasks—it's part of being human. We naturally aspire to competence at meaningful tasks, because it defines who we are, promotes self-esteem, and makes us valuable to others. Achievement motivation occurs when the learner feels a sense of ownership of the learning, has a level of skill development to expand upon, desires the incentive offered, and feels good about the accomplishment. Knowing this reality, you might think differently about why your students may or may not be motivated to learn what you want them to learn.

Motivational Drives: Extrinsic and Intrinsic

Generally, we can divide motivation into two types of drives that propel us to action: *extrinsic* and *intrinsic*.

Extrinsic motivation comes from outside the learner in the form of such things as stickers, money, rewards/awards, grades, trophies, and diplomas. These types of external incentives, or drives, can help learners acquire self-regulating strategies, and they can support the development of intrinsic motivation. Whereas extrinsic rewards may be beneficial in changing behaviors, research suggests that there is little long-term retention of learning through the extensive use of extrinsic motivation.[2]

Intrinsic motivation is the internal drive to perform regardless of the external reward. All people are naturally intrinsically motivated (or "self-motivated") to do things they find interesting, fun, personally meaningful, or relevant. Intrinsic motivation can assist people in overcoming difficult situations or tasks, or provide the extra effort required to complete a task. Research also suggests that when the learner has the intrinsic desire to learn, there is greater longer-term retention of the learning.[3] Although motivational drives can be categorized as either extrinsic or intrinsic, both types are dependent upon each other. A person usually cannot be intrinsically motivated without some form of extrinsic motivation. For example, even though you may love the art of teaching, would you be willing to come to work every day if you were not paid? Realizing the cyclical effect of both types of motivational drive can help you understand how to move your students from purely extrinsic motivation ("I'm only doing it for the grade") to more intrinsic motivation ("I'm learning this because I want to be better at this skill"). See **Figure 4.1** on page 68.

---

1. Elliot, A. J., and C. S. Dweck (Eds.). *Handbook of Competence and Motivation.* New York: Guilford Press, 2005.
2. National Research Council. *How People Learn: Brain, Mind, Experience, and School (Expanded Edition).* Washington, DC: National Academy Press, 2000.
3. Ibid.

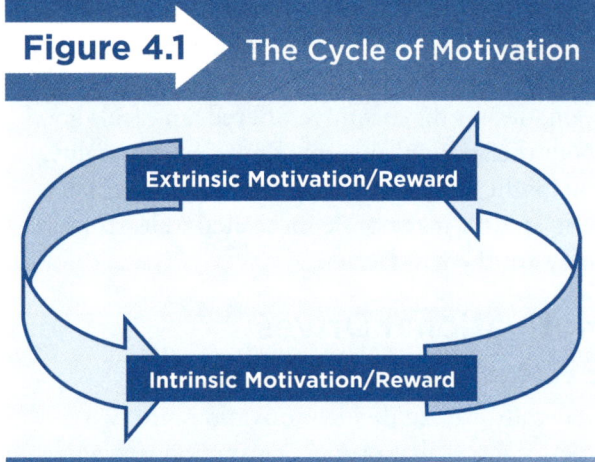

Figure 4.1 The Cycle of Motivation

Understanding How the Brain Learns

You can assist students in building intrinsic achievement motivation by providing a classroom environment that addresses the students' basic human needs and offers engaging, relevant, and meaningful tasks. To fully understand basic human needs, you must have a rudimentary understanding of how the brain works. In general, all brains are *organized* in the same way, but not all brains *learn* in the same way. Research findings support that a person's environment can actually change his or her brain.[4] Therefore, your job as a teacher is to create learning experiences and opportunities for your students to develop talent and achieve success; in short, you must provide your students with *brain-compatible learning*.

Note: The following section is a general overview of the human brain and is not intended to be comprehensive, nor is it complete. The intent is to point out a few highlights of how the brain is organized and the significance of how the parts work together.

The Three Brain Domains

In the most general of terms, the brain can be divided into three domains: the cerebral cortex, the midbrain, and the hindbrain (see **Figure 4.2**). Each area has significance to the learning process working in tandem with the other areas. What follows is a broad representation of how the brain is organized. Having this knowledge will help you attune your learning environment and instructional practices to address the workings of the brain, so your students will be more motivated and engaged to find greater success in the classroom.

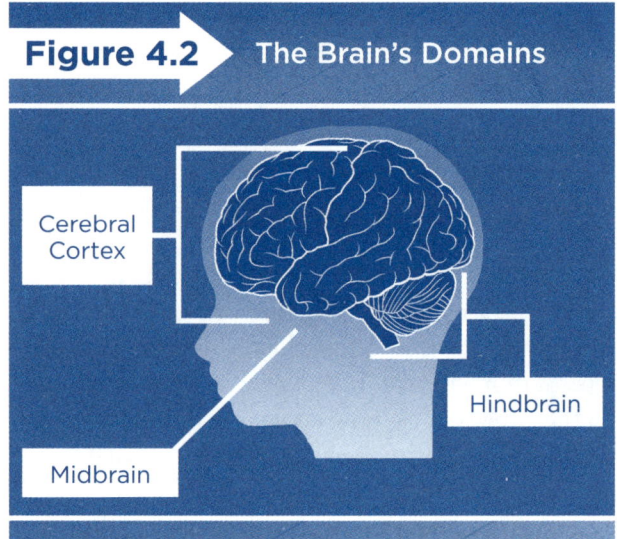

Figure 4.2 The Brain's Domains

The Hindbrain

Starting in the back of the brain coming up out of the spinal column is the brain stem (see **Figure 4.3**). The oldest and most primitive part of the organ, the brain stem controls and organizes the autonomic systems of our body (circulatory, digestive, respiratory, nervous, and so forth). While the brain stem is the smallest part of your brain, it performs an extremely important function: keeping your body alive so the rest of your brain can keep working. Motor and sensory information coming into and out of the brain pass through this area. The information corresponding to attention, arousal, and consciousness is evaluated at this point for the purposes of survival. If the information is deemed to be threatening to the body, the brain stem will pull energy away from the other parts of the brain to protect itself and the body as a whole. When students enter your classrooms lacking the basic survival needs of food, shelter, and water, their brains are likely to be paying attention to those needs rather than to lessons on nouns, fractions, or chemical compounds.

The cerebellum, two fist-shaped bundles of brain matter at the back of your brain, controls your body's movements, balance, and coordination. It is also important to the procedural memories

---

4. Nussbaum, P. D., and W. R. Daggett. *What Brain Research Teaches About Rigor, Relevance, and Relationships: And What It Teaches About Keeping Your Own Brain Healthy.* Rexford, NY: International Center for Leadership in Education, 2008.

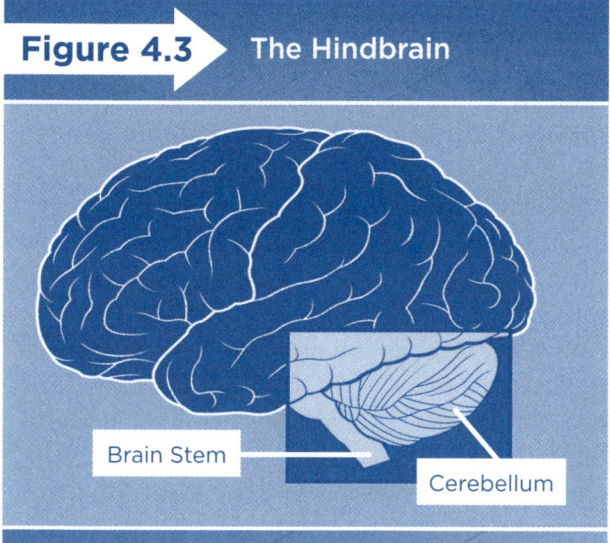

Figure 4.3 The Hindbrain

(Brain Stem, Cerebellum)

you develop by practicing movements or actions. For instance, take the act of driving a car. Have you ever said, "My car just *knows* the way to work"? Actually, it's your cerebellum that knows the way to work. It processes the information of how much pressure to put on the gas or brake pedal, when to turn your signal on, how to move your arms to turn the steering wheel, and so forth. This type of automatic brain processing allows the other more conscious parts of your brain to perform more advanced levels of thinking and doing, such as listening to songs on the radio, thinking about your plans for the day, or processing a fight you had with your friend.

Therefore, the cerebellum is a significant component to the thinking and learning process. It regulates the rote parts of process and actions, while allocating energy to the upper areas of the brain to process high-level thoughts and actions. For students in your classroom, this means that they require sufficient practice to develop *automaticity* of the skills and strategies learned, so they can reserve brain energy for more advanced levels of thinking. If students have deficits in what is considered basic knowledge, they will spend precious brain energy processing low-level skills, such as multiplication facts.

The Midbrain

Also called the limbic system, the midbrain is a set of structures that play a critical role in learning, memory, and emotion. This very complicated interrelated system spans across to your sensory system and motor system. The limbic system also has an influence on the executive functioning of the prefrontal cortex. The two areas of the limbic system that are most involved in learning, memory, and emotion are the hippocampus and the amygdala (see **Figure 4.4**).

The *hippocampus* plays an important role in the process of long-term memory and spatial orientation. In fact, it is one of the first areas of the brain that is affected by Alzheimer's disease. It has densely packed layers of neurons, the underlying cellular structure of learning and memory. The female brain is believed to have a larger hippocampus, which means that girls have a greater advantage in school-based learning, especially in the language arts.[5]

The *amygdala* provides the emotional coloring of your experiences. As information passes through the midbrain, the amygdala stimulates a chemical reaction within the brain to affect an emotional state. The amygdala also plays a role in regulating attention, forming perceptions, and recalling specific memories, possibly through the interplay of emotional memories. When you feel good about an experience, you are more likely to repeat the experience or attempt a variation of the experience. During adolescence, emotional responses may be considered irrational or impulsive. That may be due to the fact that the prefrontal cortex (which forms reasoned responses to emotion) is not well developed in the adolescent brain, so the amygdala is in action instead.

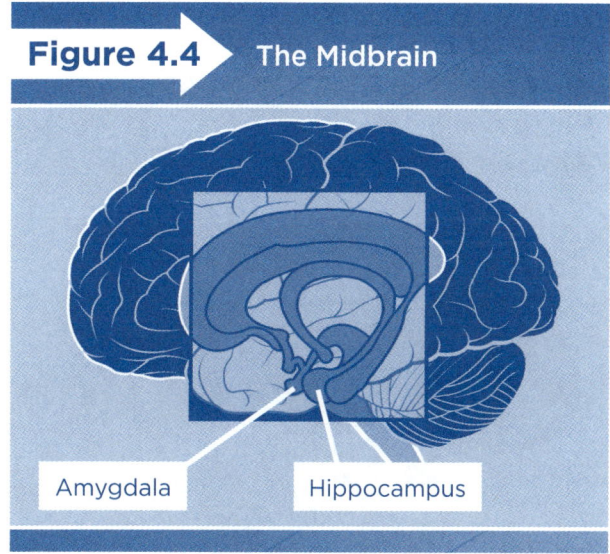

Figure 4.4 The Midbrain

(Amygdala, Hippocampus)

---

[5]. Gurian, M., and K. Stevens. *The Minds of Boys: Saving Our Sons from Falling Behind in School and Life.* San Francisco, CA: Jossey-Bass, 2005.

Safety and Survival: The Reptilian Brain

In a very general sense, the lower parts of the brain (brain stem, cerebellum, and limbic system) can be considered the reptilian brain (see **Figure 4.5**). These older and smaller regions of the brain are the least evolved, and they resemble and function similar to the brains of present-day reptiles. The processes mediated in these regions lack language and are impulsive, instinctual, and ritualistic. The reptilian brain is concerned with the fundamental needs of survival, protection, and mating. When needs within the reptilian brain are not being met or are challenged, a person naturally goes into what is called a "downshift." Energy is pulled away from the more conscious or thinking parts of your brain and directed toward the lower parts of the brain in a "fight or flight" action. Think about the last time someone confronted you. You more than likely said something that you should not have said, and it wasn't until later that you thought of a more articulate response. This is the process of downshifting; you responded from a relatively unevolved part of your brain, and after your brain had time to reorganize the energy back to the thinking part of the brain, you were able to think more clearly and "smarter."

To avoid the downshifted response in an argument or a difficult situation:

- Take a deep breath (this floods your brain with oxygen-rich blood for better processing).
- Count to 10 (this gives your brain time to upshift and send energy to the cerebral cortex and gives the limbic system time to process the chemical reaction of emotion).
- Then, respond.

The Cerebral Cortex

The cerebral cortex (*cerebral = brain; cortex = bark*) is the outer mantel of cells encasing the two hemispheres of the brain (see **Figure 4.6**). The cortex ranges in thickness from between one and four millimeters. The elaboration of the cortex is the most distinguishing characteristic of the human brain. The specific functions of the various areas of the cerebral cortex allow us to use language, have conscious thoughts and movements, think through difficult situations, understand emotions, remember past experiences, learn new ideas, and perform other higher-order cognitive operations. These abilities are what make our brain unique from any other animal.

The cerebral cortex is divided into four major interrelated lobes (see **Figure 4.7**). Understanding the functions of each of these lobes can help you better meet the needs of your students.

The **frontal lobe** is our primary motor cortex. This area is responsible for our planning, initiating, and follow-through of our movements, as well as higher-level cognitive functioning. This high-level cognitive functioning, or "executive functioning," is carried out in a part of the frontal lobe called the *prefrontal cortex*. The prefrontal cortex acts as your brain's CFO (chief functioning operator) in that it:

- controls your planning and organization
- is the seat of your working memory
- modulates your moods
- inhibits your behavior (impulse control)
- controls empathy, insight, reason, and introspection

Figure 4.5 The Reptilian Brain

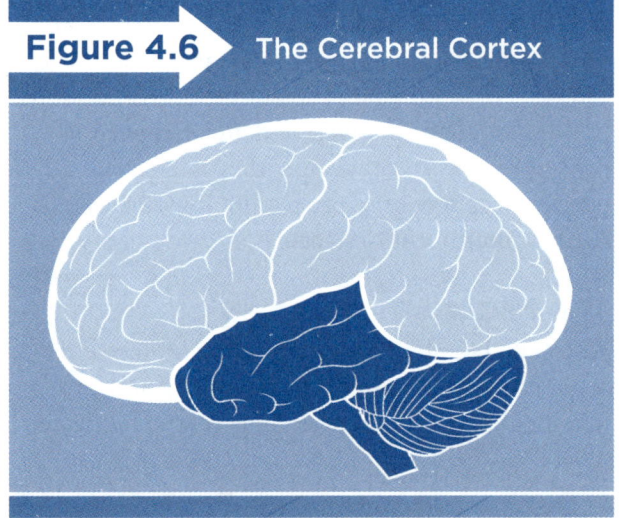

Figure 4.6 The Cerebral Cortex

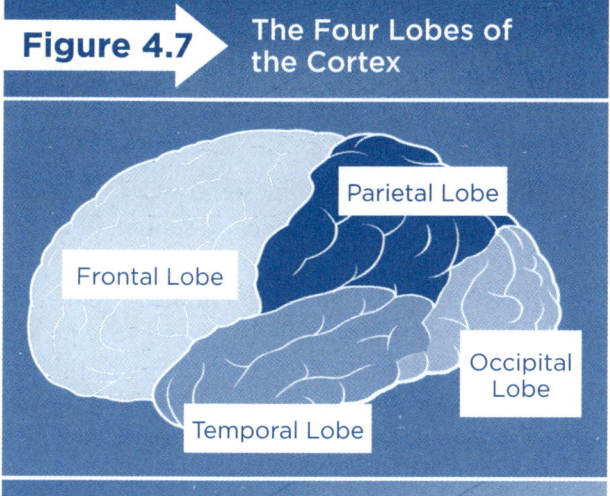

Figure 4.7 The Four Lobes of the Cortex

This area of the brain is under a great deal of development during the adolescent years. Therefore, it is essential that you provide opportunities in your classroom for students to develop these skills.

The **parietal lobe** runs across the top of your brain. This area is responsible for the processing of:

- sensory information that comes in from the body (touch, pain, the feel of your body in space)
- written language (this is critical to the acts of reading and writing)

The **occipital lobe**'s primary function is visual. You process visual stimuli in this area of the brain.

The **temporal lobe** is primarily responsible for processing auditory information. The understanding of language and facial recognition are also functions of the temporal lobe. Learning and memory are greatly enhanced because of the temporal lobe's direct connection to the hippocampus.

The brain is a fascinating and complex organ that forms the seat of all learning, and yet it is first and foremost concerned with safety and survival. When you want to ensure that students feel they can survive in your classroom, you must first pay attention to their basic needs for food, water, shelter, and safety. Students who are well nourished and hydrated, have a home or feel at home in your classroom, and feel safe in and around school are ready to learn. In addition, students need to feel safe within the content of what they are learning. Consider, for example, a girl who is math phobic, or a boy who has repeatedly been told he can't read. These children are less ready to learn new information because they have downshifted, fearing for their academic survival. When students feel safe and have a sense of belonging, they are ready to take on learning tasks.

Gender Differences in Learning

Human beings are very social animals. When students can make social connections in the school environment, they have a greater chance for learning and understanding. Making personal connections with both the content and the community of learners helps students build responsibility for their own learning, as well as engage the midbrain process of memory and emotional connection. However, making connections to the learning community and the content can mean different things for male students and female students.

Recent brain research has found that generally girls' brains develop differently from boys' brains.[6] This developmental difference may have significant implications for how we teach girls and boys. What follows are some significant discoveries from recent studies on brain development. Keep in mind that the connections between the research and educational practices have not been fully validated. Also, the generalizations about girls versus boys are just that: generalizations. There will always be exceptions to the rules.

In general, girls have a greater advantage in school because of the way their brains are organized. Girls are believed to have stronger neural connectors in the temporal lobe, which may be why they typically have better listening skills, provide greater detail in their writing, and often are able to remember information more holistically, especially sensually. Girls also have a more active prefrontal cortex that can assist in making fewer impulsive decisions. And they use more of the cortical areas of the brain for verbal and emotional functioning, which may explain why girls often use words and emotions to connect with or hurt others. On the other hand, girls' learning is inhibited by the stress of competition, while boys' learning is enhanced by it. This may help explain why girls' achievement often falls off and boys' achievement rises at the high school level, where the stress of competition becomes greater.

---

6. Eliot, L. "The Truth About Boys and Girls." *Scientific American Mind* (May/June 2010).

Boys are thought to have a more sophisticated occipital lobe. The occipital lobe is primarily responsible for visual processing. This makes sense, as prehistorically, the male's job was to hunt and gather food. Hence, males relied on their vision not only for protection, but also survival. Males are therefore more visually stimulated, which may explain why explicit magazines, websites, and video games are more attractive to boys than to girls. Because of this need for greater visual stimulation, it is recommended that teachers provide boys with visual images of directions and graphic organizers to visualize their thoughts.

Boys lateralize brain activity with less blood flow extending across the entire brain, meaning that they are often poor multitaskers, have a shorter attention span, and find it difficult to quickly transition from one activity to another. Boys also use more of their cortical areas for spatial understanding, meaning that they move objects three-dimensionally in their head. In addition, boys have lower levels of serotonin and oxytocin (the human bonding chemicals) in their brains, which may explain why they are more physically impulsive and less likely to bond with others through language and emotions.

Due to the way boys' brains are organized, we may be disadvantaging them in school because of the way we teach. Using high levels of auditory information with limited amounts of visual stimuli may inadvertently disengage the boy brain. (See pages 81–82: 25 Strategies for Developing a Boy-Friendly Classroom.)

The Impact of Race, Ethnicity, and Culture on Learning

The biological systems of the brain develop and change based on the influences of the social, cultural, and familial world. All kids have varying degrees and types of opportunities prior to starting school. This may be due to economic status or cultural backgrounds. These experiences or lack of experiences may affect the way students' brains are processing information, how they prefer to learn, their interests, and ultimately how they personally connect or interact with the curriculum and other learners.

Students who perceive themselves to be chronic targets of others' discrimination or mistreatment often lose confidence in themselves and in their self-efficacy. Students who are part of a cultural or linguistic minority often experience such adverse effects from the stereotyping and social isolation that can happen in school. Their loss of confidence can contribute to academic disengagement and other problem behaviors at school. In effect, these students' brains may be in perpetual downshift during the majority of their school day, which prevents them from thinking or acting at higher levels.

Those students who have formed a positive racial identity are more likely to have higher academic achievement than their counterparts with negative racial identity. They may have developed strategies to upshift their thinking.[7] The key to success in school for culturally or linguistically diverse students appears to be the development of a strong bicultural or bilingual competence, or the ability to function effectively in the dominant culture while retaining a primary ethnic identity. Always keep in mind that the number one factor in increasing achievement motivation is a caring adult who can guide, coach, and encourage the learner—no matter the learner's gender, race, ethnicity, or cultural background.

The Effects of Poverty on Learning

According to the National Center for Education Statistics, more than 15 million children under the age of 18 in the United States in 2014—approximately 20 percent of school-age children—were in families living in poverty. Low income students, those living below and just above the poverty line, make up a majority of all students in U.S. public schools.[8] These numbers are staggering and expected to climb. In other nations, these numbers are even higher.

Being raised in poverty is the single greatest threat to a child's well-being. Children living in poverty are less prepared for primary schooling, possess a greater number of developmental delays or learning disabilities, are more likely to be behind their classmates in learning, have higher rates of

---

[7]. Graham, S., and C. Hudley. "Race and Ethnicity in the Study of Motivation and Competence." In *Handbook of Competence and Motivation*. A. J. Elliot and C. S. Dweck (Eds.). New York: Guilford Press, 2005.
[8]. National Center for Education Statistics. "Family Characteristics of School-Age Children." *The Condition of Education 2016* (nces.ed.gov/programs/coe/pdf/coe_cce.pdf).

absenteeism, change schools more often, have higher drop-out rates, and are less likely to enroll and graduate from post-secondary institutions.[9] Poverty puts a huge strain on the education system, as well as other social systems.

Eric Jensen, author and brain-compatible learning expert, notes that students being raised in poverty may exhibit behaviors, learning attitudes, and social skills perceived as negative or different from children of middle- to upper-class families. He also states that children in poverty have emotional and social challenges, acute and chronic stress-related issues, and greater health and safety concerns.[10] Therefore, it is extremely important for teachers to have ready tools to differentiate for and address the needs of children living in poverty (see **Figure 4.8**).

Pathway to a Motivating and Engaging Classroom

Taking into account all that has been stated about how the brain learns, how boys and girls learn differently, how race and ethnicity impacts learning, and how poverty can affect achievement, I have developed a pathway to building a motivating and engaging classroom (see **Figure 4.9** on page 74).

First, students must feel **competent** in the content and know that you, their teacher, are competent in instructing and guiding them through the content. While you may not have all the answers, you must be able to help learners find the answers.

Closely aligned with competence is the need for the learner to feel **connected** to the content and find relevance in it. If learners can't attach themselves to the information, or if you're unable to assist them in making those connections, it is highly likely that your students will not engage in future learning.

As students begin the process of learning, they must feel **supported** and allowed to make mistakes. Taking intellectual risks should be expected and nurtured as part of the learning process. Students must have the support through all phases of learning, from you and from others in the learning community.

When they feel competent, connected, and supported, your students can start to feel **responsible** for their learning. This includes initiating their own learning as well as being accountable for what they have learned. Responsible learners hone the skills

Figure 4.8 Students' Needs, Wants, and Requirements

Students need reliable relationships in the classroom, including:
- a safe, secure, and respectful learning environment
- predictable classroom procedures and processes
- long-term relationships with adults, such as having a teacher for more than one year
- a community where networks and connections abound
- consistent modeling of appropriate behaviors and interactions
- a sense of empowerment gained through ownership, responsibility, and connections

Students want strong peer relationships in which each person:
- is accepted, empowered, respected, and supported
- understands clear boundaries and norms
- expects and respects diversity
- feels included
- uses inclusive language (example "our classroom" rather than "my classroom")

Students require a chance to be an important individual through:
- encouragement of their unique qualities
- an understanding of their individual differences
- development of their talents
- building upon their interests
- being good at something
- celebration of their successes

of being prepared every day for learning, sharing in the operations of the classroom procedures, and developing independence and organizational techniques for success.

Next, learners become able to take **control** of their learning. Control in learning is about setting goals, managing the process to reach the goal, and monitoring and evaluating goal attainment. As the "guide on the side," you must allow for **choices** in what the students learn, where they learn it, and how they learn it. Students build self-efficacy,

---

9. Dosomething.org. "11 Facts About Education and Poverty in America" (dosomething.org/us/facts/11-facts-about-education-and-poverty-america).
10. Jensen, E. *Teaching with Poverty in Mind: What Being Poor Does to Kids' Brains and What Schools Can Do About It*. Alexandria, VA: ASCD, 2009.

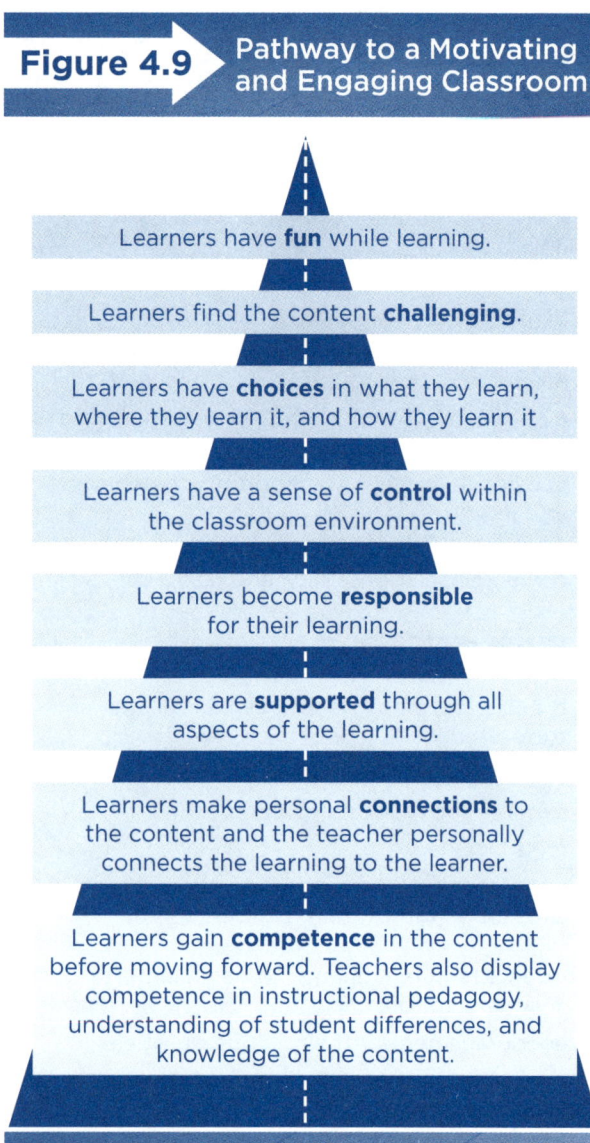

Figure 4.9 — Pathway to a Motivating and Engaging Classroom

- Learners have **fun** while learning.
- Learners find the content **challenging**.
- Learners have **choices** in what they learn, where they learn it, and how they learn it.
- Learners have a sense of **control** within the classroom environment.
- Learners become **responsible** for their learning.
- Learners are **supported** through all aspects of the learning.
- Learners make personal **connections** to the content and the teacher personally connects the learning to the learner.
- Learners gain **competence** in the content before moving forward. Teachers also display competence in instructional pedagogy, understanding of student differences, and knowledge of the content.

self-esteem, and confidence in their capabilities when they engage in **challenging** activities. Your role becomes one of improving learners' capacity for self-guided learning. (See Chapter 6 for more on developing learner autonomy.)

Finally, learning should be **fun**! As students build their competence and confidence in learning, they experience greater feelings of intrinsic motivation. Learning becomes fun because the students have committed themselves to studies they are interested in.

Strategies to Motivate and Engage Students

As stated earlier, when students are emotionally engaged they are more likely to pay attention to the learning tasks. Also, all students want to be competent at meaningful tasks. Therefore, taking into account how the brain learns best, we should:

- use the students' interests to engage them in the learning process
- use the students' learning preferences to teach new information and confirm preexisting knowledge
- routinely use assessment to motivate students to achieve at the highest level possible

Use Student Interests to Motivate and Engage

Critical to the learning process is getting students interested in what you have to offer. Find out what will hook learners about the topic or the concepts being presented. Integrating student interest in the classroom is a way to add personal meaning and relevance to the content. Additionally, you can help students make connections between what they already know to the new information being generated.

Surveys

Find out what students are interested in and how that can connect to the curriculum. One way to do this is to administer an interest survey or inventory. Many surveys and inventories exist to assist you in fine-tuning curriculum and instruction to address student interests. If you choose to use surveys or inventories, make sure you are willing to change instruction to either address or incorporate the students' responses. Keep the survey results handy, use them often in your planning process, and allow students to adjust their responses at any time. Try to give students the survey or inventory at least two times throughout the year.

Topic Previews

Another way to motivate and engage learners is to get them interested in the topic. This can be done through a preview of a textbook or other source material (see page 86).

KIQ Charts

Another strategy is using a KIQ chart: what I *Know*, find *Interesting*, and have *Questions* about (see page 87). A KIQ chart is similar to a KWI chart (what I *Know*, *Want* to know, find *Interesting*) or a KWL chart (what I *Know*, *Want* to know, *Learned*), but the final box is changed to solicit students' questions about a topic. This strategy helps students recognize that they don't know everything about a topic and that nobody *can* know everything there is to know about any topic. Even medical students take courses in "what I don't know about medicine." This form can also generate topics for independent research or group projects.

Rank Your Interests Forms

In some cases, you may want students to become "experts" in a certain part of a unit. Using the Rank Your Interests form (page 88) can help guide this practice. Steps to using this form are as follows:

1. Organize the unit around specific concepts, themes, or categories.

2. Offer a mini-lesson (a brief two-minute explanation) of the unit components.

3. Have students rank their preferred topics from high to low.

4. Group students using the ranking. (Tell students you will try hard to give them their first choice, but if too many students are in one group or you feel some students won't/can't work well together, you may need to go to their second choice. Tell them you will try very hard not to give them their third choice and will almost never give them their fourth choice.)

5. Students work in collaborative groups to build a project that represents their knowledge and research of the topic. The project/presentation must include connections to other content/curricular areas and use students' creative talents.

6. Students present the projects either throughout the unit of study or at the end as a wrap-up to the unit.

An example is provided in **Figure 4.10**.

You may find that you already have "experts" in your classroom. One strategy to acknowledge these experts is by doing a "passion project" (see passion project guidelines and rubric on pages 89–90). Passion projects can be used as tools to encourage students to share their passions with others or to enhance a unit of study where students have already gained some valuable working

Figure 4.10 Rank Your Interests: Example—The Nervous System

UNIT TOPICS
Rank the topics below: 1 (your least favorite) through 5 (your favorite).

_____ Topic: Cerebrum
_____ Topic: Autonomic nervous system
_____ Topic: Peripheral nervous system
_____ Topic: Pons, medulla oblongata, and spinal cord
_____ Topic: Midbrain and diencephalons

ASSIGNMENT
You will team up with others who have similar interests. Your team will decide on a topic and create a project to present the topic. Your team must connect the project to music, art, literature, math, sports, family life, or the life of a person like you. You must also incorporate the following learning objectives:

- **Know:** how the parts of a system work together to maintain homeostasis.

- **Be able to:** explain how the anatomy of a structure is related to its physiology.

- **Understand:** the human body systems.

Be creative, think outside the box!

knowledge. Offering students a chance to do a passion project can:

- allow gifted students to share an interest they have spent time studying on their own

- give other students ideas of talent areas and extensions from subjects being learned in school

- give students who may not get the opportunity to share much about themselves a chance to shine

A passion project can be used with every student in your class as a year-long anchoring assignment, or on an individual basis. The project can replace another unit project, be a stand-alone assignment, or be used for extra credit purposes. You will note that when the student makes a presentation about their passion, they are encouraged not to relay everything they know about the topic so as to encourage others to do their own research. Students should give just enough information to pique their audience's interest and offer lists of resources, websites, books, or other materials that another student could use to start their own investigation.

On page 91 is a list of additional strategies to motivate and engage students based on their interests.

Use Student Learning Preferences to Motivate and Engage

Dr. Robert Sternberg, one of the world's leading cognitive psychologists, has theorized a balance of intellectual abilities that he calls "successful intelligence." According to Sternberg, when people are aware of their strengths and abilities they are more likely to use those strengths to compensate or correct their limitations.[11] Also, when people are able to best use those strengths in effective ways, they are more likely to be successful in life. Successful individuals have figured out how to adapt to, shape, or select environments where their abilities and strengths are best used.

Sternberg's design of successful intelligence has three ability dimensions: **creative, analytical,** and **practical.** While we all have each of these abilities, we have varying degrees of them. And since we tend to have learning preferences that match our abilities, we also vary in our learning preferences across the three dimensions. Based on their abilities, most people will prefer one or two of the dimensions when learning, but those individuals who understand all three dimensions collectively can more effectively use them in combination to be more successful.

Creative Dimension

Individuals with creative ability often:
- think outside the box
- generate new and interesting ideas
- make connections between seemingly disjointed information
- may not perform well in school on standardized tests or follow directions well
- come up with novel ways to represent information

Learning activities preferred by creative individuals:
- creating
- inventing
- discovering
- exploring
- imagining
- pretending
- hypothesizing
- postulating
- theorizing
- designing

Assessment or questioning techniques suitable for creative individuals:
- open-ended
- active
- conceptual
- unusual or novel
- techniques that elaborate on information beyond the facts

Analytical Dimension

Individuals with analytical ability often:
- do well in school, especially on standardized tests, and follow directions well
- are book smart
- may recognize flaws in lines of thought or reasoning
- prefer to follow directions rather than come up with their own way of doing things

Learning activities preferred by analytical individuals:
- analyzing
- evaluating
- judging
- critiquing
- comparing/contrasting
- testing
- examining
- studying
- investigating
- questioning

Assessment or questioning techniques suitable for analytical individuals:
- structured
- individually focused

---

11. Sternberg, R. J., and E. L. Grigorenko. *Teaching for Successful Intelligence: To Increase Student Learning and Achievement.* Thousand Oaks, CA: Corwin Press, 2007.

- factual or information rich
- logical
- organized

Practical Dimension

Individuals with practical ability often:

- do moderately well in school
- have an abundance of common sense
- are resilient and easily adapt to social situations
- are considered social leaders

Learning activities preferred by practical individuals:

- applying
- using
- implementing
- collaborating
- working with their hands or tools
- operating
- manipulating
- managing
- practicing
- authenticating

Assessment or questioning techniques suitable for practical individuals:

- group process
- authentic application
- process-oriented
- demonstrating feasibility of product
- displaying information in an "everyday" useful manner

Again, to some degree, everyone has all three of these abilities. How we recognize the need for each ability and then use the abilities within a given setting is what determines our success. We must give students a chance to safely explore each of the ability dimensions—not only the ones they are strong in and prefer—through learning activities so they build awareness of how to best employ the skills involved.

One way to help students understand the three dimensions of successful intelligence is through the activity on pages 92–93. Share with students a list of people both famous and not-so-famous who possess strengths in each of the three dimensions. Then have students develop a list of individuals whom they believe to have strengths in the three dimensions. Also, have students recognize when to rely on each of the different dimensions and when using a combination of the dimensions would be most beneficial. Students who are flexible in shifting their thinking depending on the situation will find greater success.

Following on page 94 is a list of additional strategies for motivating based on student learning preferences.

Using Assessment to Motivate and Engage

In the past, assessment and evaluation were often used to rank students or to keep some students in or out of certain programs, especially gifted programs. Today, assessment has three primary uses: to gather information about how students are learning; to determine where students are in the learning process; and to provide feedback to the teacher on the success of methodology and practice, which then guides changes needed in the instruction. A fourth use for assessment that is sometimes overlooked is to motivate and stimulate students to learn. When students are aware of how they're doing and what new knowledge they're acquiring at all points in the learning process, they are more likely to engage in and take ownership of the learning, as well as experience several other benefits. See **Figure 4.11** on page 78.

Assessment should be used to inform students how close they came to meeting the learning goal. It should also represent a valuation of the students' application, demonstration, and understandings of newly acquired knowledge. Above all, assessment should be *flexible* (it is implemented differently for different students), *meaningful* (both the student and teacher can use the information to make changes), and *customizable* (some may need more assessments and some may need fewer).

Three Types of Assessment

Three main types of assessment are used in the classroom: **preassessment** (also called diagnostic), **formative** assessment, and **summative** assessment. Preassessment, as the name suggests, is used prior to the learning process. Formative assessment occurs during the learning process. Summative assessment

Figure 4.11 Using Assessment as Feedback to Students

- Enhances motivation to learn
- Builds ownership of learning
- Effort equals achievement
- Produces significant learning gains
- Encourages peer collaboration
- Develops an awareness of learning gaps

(All feeding into: Formative Assessment as Feedback)

Figure 4.12 Four Square Concept Map: Example

Concept: Independence

Definition	Looks Like
Being separate from authority; being your own authority	
Examples	**Nonexamples**
People who have a job and live on their own Adult animals	Children People who do not have jobs and need to live with their parents

---

is a summation of what the learner has learned and is used at the end of the learning process.

When teachers are fully aware of where their students are in the learning process, how they are learning, and what strategies and techniques are working, they are better able to meet the learners' needs. Many strategies exist for assessing student learning. Following is a review of a few of those ideas that determine if your students are ready for instruction and also motivate students to engage in new learning.

Preassessment

Using assessment *before* the learning helps you find out what students know and don't know, recognize their strengths and limitations, detect errors or holes in their learning, and gather data for remediation, enrichment, and extensions. Preassessments are also wonderful for piquing students' interest in the topic.

Preassessments are generally not graded. When students have the burden of a grade lifted in the assessment process they are more likely to show you what they do and don't know.

Examples of Preassessments
- Pretests
- Open-ended discussions
- KIQ charts (see page 87)
- Four square concept maps (page 95 and **Figure 4.12**)

The four square concept map uses multiple forms of representation, so you can assess learners' understanding of conceptual knowledge. Students should keep this preassessment throughout the learning and do another map at the end of the learning to compare their growth and advancing sophistication.

Formative Assessment

Formative assessment is assessment *for* learning. This includes strategies for finding out where students are in the learning process and in what ways the learner is approaching the goal. It provides the student with an understanding of his or her own proficiency regarding the benchmarks of a learning goal. This ongoing assessment also gives teachers guidance on adjusting and modifying instruction to move the learner closer to the benchmark and goal.

Grades on formative assessments are generally used to inform learners of individual progress. You may sometimes use these assessments to inform both students and parents about the learner's effort or attention to detail. Formative assessment grades should not be combined or averaged with a final evaluation grade; practice should be practice *only* and should not affect the final grade. If necessary, separate out the formative assessment grade as a stand-alone grade to inform parents and the student how much effort they put forth during the practice and to show growth during the learning process.

Formative assessment should also be descriptive in nature; it should tell students what they are doing well and what they need to do to improve. In John Hattie's groundbreaking book *Visible Learning*, he states that formative assessment, especially if descriptive in nature, has one of the most positive influences on student learning and achievement.[12] Descriptive feedback can also move your students from being extrinsically driven to being intrinsically motivated to perform with quality.

Examples of Formative Assessment

- Student reflection log
- Quizzes
- Homework
- Teacher/peer/parent observations
- Descriptive notes on student work by teacher, peer, or parent
- Daily work
- Discussion
- Read-Write-Pair-Share and Think-Pair-Share (see **Figure 4.13**)
- 3-2-1 Exit Slip/Entrance Ticket (see page 96)
- 1- to 3-Minute Coaching/Consultation (see **Figure 4.14**)

Figure 4.13 Read-Write-Pair-Share and Think-Pair-Share

Read-Write-Pair-Share

Directions:

1. Have students individually read a passage of written text. The entire class can read the same passage, or members can all read different passages.
2. Ask students to write about their passage, either answering guiding questions or summarizing what they read.
3. Have students work with partners to share their written work and discuss the guiding questions.
4. Have each pair or selected pairs share with the class what they discussed and the outcome. Post responses from all groups for the class to view.

Think-Pair-Share

Directions:

1. Ask students a provocative question, present information requiring discussion, or suggest a scenario worth pondering.
2. Use a guided thinking question (see Chapter 7, page 131) to frame the students' think time.
3. Allow students to spend no more than two minutes thinking about how they might respond to the guiding question.
4. Have students pair with another student to discuss and compare each of their answers to the guiding question. During this time students should decide which of their answers is most convincing or answers the question most completely. Or they may decide to form a new answer based on the shared discussion.
5. Have each pair or selected pairs share what they discussed and the outcome. Post responses from all groups for the class to view.

Figure 4.14 1- to 3-Minute Coaching/Consultation

Directions:

- Select a different small number of students with whom you will meet individually each day. You should be able to cover your entire class within one to two weeks of instruction.
- Near the end of class or during work time, invite individual students to meet with you for a few minutes to discuss how the learning is going.
- Coach the learner on strategies or techniques to improve learning, or praise the student on specific achievements in the learning.
- Invite the student to consult with you on individual learning matters, such as extended projects, enrichment, needs for remediation, or on other matters related to teacher-student relationships.

---

12. Hattie, J. *Visible Learning*. New York: Routledge, 2009.

- Tiered Review/Practice (see **Figure 4.15**)
- Roundtable Review (see pages 97–98)

Summative Assessment

Summative assessment, or assessment *of* learning, is conducted after a unit of instruction to determine where the learners are relative to the goal. Summative assessment gathers information on the students' factual knowledge, provides a way for students to demonstrate proficiency in skill development, and shows the students' ability to transfer their understanding of concepts. It is a culmination of the entire learning process.

Grading a summative assessment generally defines a learner's proficiency and goal attainment. It can also inform where and how to begin the next unit of study. In this way, summative assessment can be used as a preassessment of an upcoming unit, for example, does the student have enough prior knowledge from the previous unit? It can also be used as formative assessment, for example, what do I need to reteach or enrich so the students are engaged and successful in the next unit?

Examples of Summative Assessment
- Final exams
- Authentic projects
- Self/peer assessments
- Standardized tests

Figure 4.15 Tiered Review/Practice

Directions:
One way to ensure your students have addressed the three levels of objectives for a unit of study is to create a tiered system of review. Divide students into three groups (factual, procedural, and conceptual). Base groups on students' levels of readiness in each of the three domains, or use mixed-ability groups. Have groups spend up to 10 minutes at each of the tables to complete the activities. Then, groups either move to another table or present to the class what they created at each table. If students rotate between tables without reporting to the class, be sure you have created three separate activities at each table and that groups leave behind what they created so the other groups can review, assess, or interpret preceding groups' work.

Table One
Factual Knowledge
Students will *list (recall)* significant dates, times, elements, vocabulary involved in the unit of study. Use mirrored* questions or expectations to assist students in the review of factual knowledge.

Table Two
Procedural Knowledge
Students will *demonstrate (application)* the skills and/or strategies used in the unit of study. Provide mirrored processes used on the unit exam.

Table Three
Conceptual Knowledge
Students will *discuss/debate/examine/argue/interpret/offer new ideas for (analysis, synthesis, and evaluation)* related major concepts or topics covered in the unit. Provide mirrored essay questions that will appear on the unit exam.

*Mirrored: questions, examples, or processes that are similar to those that will appear on the exam. Providing students with mirrored examples will tune them in to the language of the exam and allow them to test their answering abilities without the risk of failure.

25 Strategies for Developing a Boy-Friendly Classroom*

1. **Create a "Success Team"** for each boy to act as a support system that can intervene when issues arise. Boys work best in a team mentality. The team can be made up of family, friends, relatives, religious leaders, teachers, counselors, and peers.

2. **Find successful, well-adjusted male role models** who can mentor boys in school and in life.

3. **Provide physical activities, games, and competitions** to develop resiliency and give boys chances to bond with others. Boys who are involved in organized sports or other team activities are more likely to be healthy, well adjusted, and resistant to adversity and delinquent activities (such as gangs, graffiti, and other unlawful behavior).

4. **Use the "talk while walking or driving" method of counseling.** Don't expect boys to maintain eye contact when dealing with stressful issues or concerns.

5. **Celebrate "rites of passage"** as a way to motivate boys and build their self-esteem. These rites could be anything from graduating from elementary school to getting a driver's license and beyond.

6. **Use "brain breaks" and "fidgets"** (such as squeeze balls). Boys can use these while at school or while doing a task that requires long periods of attention.

7. **Provide intricate activities** such as beadwork that can help develop fine motor skills.

8. **Provide experiential and kinesthetic outings.** These outings should be with specific groups to build social interaction, self-esteem, and a sense of belonging.

9. **Reduce verbal instructions,** or repeat the verbal directions several times and then have boys repeat the directions back to you. Another idea is to give boys a list of directions along with the verbal instructions.

10. **Lower the tone and pitch of your voice** so that boys are better able to hear you.

11. **Increase a sense of attachment** by allowing boys to personalize their own spaces.

12. **Encourage healthy eating habits.** Well-balanced, low-sugar, low-caffeine diets are crucial for many boys.

13. **Ask parents to become "homework coaches."** Homework for boys can be tedious and laborious. Show boys' parents how they can spend this time with their sons, keeping their sons focused and supported throughout the work.

continued

*Gurian, M., and K. Stevens. *The Minds of Boys: Saving Our Sons from Falling Behind in School and Life.* San Francisco, CA: Jossey-Bass, 2005; Eliot, L. "The Truth About Boys and Girls." *Scientific American Mind,* May/June 2010; Neu, T., and R. Weinfeld. *Helping Boys Succeed in School: A Practical Guide for Parents and Teachers.* Waco, TX: Prufrock Press, 2007.

From *Advancing Differentiation: Thinking and Learning for the 21st Century* by Richard M. Cash, Ed.D., copyright © 2017. This page may be reproduced for use within an individual school or district. For all other uses, contact Free Spirit Publishing Inc. at www.freespirit.com/permissions.

25 Strategies for Developing a Boy-Friendly Classroom (continued)

14. **Consider brain injury** when faced with a learning disability. During rough play at an early age, some boys may have experienced a brain injury, which may not have been diagnosed and could lead to later learning problems.

15. **Place books around the classroom** to encourage boys to read.

16. **Set up "Boys Only" book clubs** to bridge the gap in academic language acquisition and break down the stigma of reading being a feminine activity. Use literature as a way of shaping identity and forming social groups.

17. **Offer boy-friendly reading choices,** which may include action, gore, fun, and purposeful adventures. These types of choices can often be found in comic books, graphic novels, magazines, cartoon anthologies, or "How Things Work" books.

18. **Provide plenty of technological outlets** to stimulate creativity. Computer graphics and screen animations are excellent ways to engage boys in research and investigations.

19. **Limit screen time.** While computer time is highly beneficial for boys, it must be monitored and used in moderation. Also encourage parents to limit the amount of television or other media their boys consume.

20. **Focus curriculum and instruction on the self.** Adolescence, particularly for boys, is a period of egocentric development. Focusing the content on how boys fit within the topics will engage and encourage them to participate more completely.

21. **Make learning experiences meaningful, rigorous, and active.** Boys are often more physically active than girls. Therefore, by making the learning more authentic and active, boys will have a better chance of engaging in the tasks.

22. **Provide opportunities for safe risk taking.** The competitive nature of boys may stunt their intellectual risk taking. Ensure that your classroom is free of intimidation and is supportive when mistakes happen.

23. **Allow for choices.** When boys (particularly adolescent boys) don't have power within a situation, they will often rebel and are less likely to participate in the learning activities.

24. **Use bright natural light** for reading. Boys are generally more visually stimulated than girls.

25. **Use stories** to encourage social cohesion, build empathy, transmit knowledge, persuade, challenge, and develop boys' social acumen.

*Gurian, M., and K. Stevens. *The Minds of Boys: Saving Our Sons from Falling Behind in School and Life.* San Francisco, CA: Jossey-Bass, 2005; Eliot, L. "The Truth About Boys and Girls." *Scientific American Mind*, May/June 2010; Neu, T., and R. Weinfeld. *Helping Boys Succeed in School: A Practical Guide for Parents and Teachers.* Waco, TX: Prufrock Press, 2007.

From *Advancing Differentiation: Thinking and Learning for the 21st Century* by Richard M. Cash, Ed.D., copyright © 2017. This page may be reproduced for use within an individual school or district. For all other uses, contact Free Spirit Publishing Inc. at www.freespirit.com/permissions.

Strategies for Creating a Brain-Compatible Learning Environment

1. **Create a safe and nonthreatening atmosphere.**
   - Get to know each student as an individual.
   - Ensure the learning environment is free of intimidation, threats, bullying, sarcasm, stereotyping, and fear.
   - Let students know it is okay to be many different things, such as smart, athletic, attractive, quirky, popular, introverted, *and* funny.
   - Avoid the "pop quiz." Let students know what they will be assessed on and when.
   - Use a "fist to five" ranking method to assess understanding (for example, "If you don't understand show me a fist. If you totally get it show me five.")

2. **Provide stimulation of all five senses and allow for various learning preferences.**
   - Teach using varied learning preferences and techniques.
   - Use authentic learning experiences, mentors, role models, and field trips.
   - Make sure to offer students three ways of acquiring the information by seeing it, then saying it, and ultimately doing it.
   - Introduce content that encourages discussions and debates and challenges beliefs.
   - Allow students to do projects creatively and think outside the box.
   - Emphasize student independence rather than dependence on the teacher to always lead the learning.

3. **Offer opportunities for physical action and connections to the learners' prior experiences.**
   - Get students up and moving. Use activities such as "four corners."
   - Use "essential questions" to connect learning to students' interests.
   - Relate material to the learner.
   - Use graphic organizers to help learners attach new information to prior knowledge.
   - Use service learning approaches, role plays, and case studies.

4. **Provide accurate, efficient, relevant, and timely feedback.**
   - Use authentic assessments.
   - Teach students self-regulating strategies such as setting goals, monitoring those goals, and evaluating personal growth.
   - Provide specific descriptive feedback focused on positive growth.
   - Provide frequent "coaching conferences" as a way to give regular feedback.
   - Show students how effort is the major contributor to achievement.

From *Advancing Differentiation: Thinking and Learning for the 21st Century* by Richard M. Cash, Ed.D., copyright © 2017. This page may be reproduced for use within an individual school or district. For all other uses, contact Free Spirit Publishing Inc. at www.freespirit.com/permissions.

Brain Breaks

The brain works and learns best when it has time to process information and shift gears when you move from activity to activity. The following strategies can be helpful in giving the brain time to think and shift between activities.

- Use an "I Chart" to help students process information during instructional time.
- Use word puzzles, cartoons, jokes, and riddles to help relieve stress, transition between topics, or create an enjoyable learning climate.
- Use the 10:2/20:2 Rule (as seen in Figure 5.4) to ensure that students have time to think.
- Use creative thinking activities to help students think more broadly.
- Use physical activity to stimulate blood flow such as doing a quick set of jumping jacks, stretching, bending over to touch toes, taking three deep breaths, walking around the room, or singing the song: "Head, Shoulders, Knees, and Toes."
- Have students do facial stretching and relaxing to relieve tension in the head and neck.
- Use cross-lateral brain activity to stimulate the entire brain. Have students do the following activities:
  - Cross your right arm over your left arm and intertwine your fingers. Now, roll your clasped hands toward your body and wiggle your right index finger.
  - Hold up your right index finger and left thumb. Then, switch them back and forth quickly (right thumb/left index, right index/left thumb).
  - Touch your right hand to your left knee and then your left hand to your right knee. Repeat several times while singing a song.
  - Raise your right hand and cross it behind your head to touch your left shoulder. Do the same thing with your left hand and right shoulder. Repeat while counting backward by 3s from 52.

Benefits of Brain Breaks
- Relieve stress
- Provide physical activity
- Stimulate blood flow
- Energize the students
- "Wake up" students' brains and get them in gear for learning
- Make students more comfortable in the classroom
- Prepare students for presentations
- Help students stay focused
- Help students retain information
- Give students time to think

I Chart

I wonder	I discovered
I think	I question
I believe	I plan
I connected	I learned

From *Advancing Differentiation: Thinking and Learning for the 21st Century* by Richard M. Cash, Ed.D., copyright © 2017. This page may be reproduced for use within an individual school or district. For all other uses, contact Free Spirit Publishing Inc. at www.freespirit.com/permissions.

What Interests Me: Topic Preview

1. Write the title of the textbook or other source material here: _____

2. What do you think this title means OR what are your thoughts about the title?
   _____
   _____
   _____
   _____

3. Look over the contents. List at least three headings that jump out at you.
   - _____
   - _____
   - _____

4. Preview the entire textbook or other source material. Pick out three chapters or sections that seem interesting to you.
   - Interesting chapter/section title: _____
   - Why I think it's interesting: _____
   - Questions I have about this chapter/section: _____
     _____
     _____

   - Interesting chapter/section title: _____
   - Why I think it's interesting: _____
   - Questions I have about this chapter/section: _____
     _____
     _____

   - Interesting chapter/section title: _____
   - Why I think it's interesting: _____
   - Questions I have about this chapter/section: _____
     _____
     _____

5. Find a textbook, a website, or another resource that is similar or may deal with the same topic. If possible, bring it in to share with the class. Write the source below:
   _____
   _____

From *Advancing Differentiation: Thinking and Learning for the 21st Century* by Richard M. Cash, Ed.D., copyright © 2017. This page may be reproduced for use within an individual school or district. For all other uses, contact Free Spirit Publishing Inc. at www.freespirit.com/permissions.

KIQ Chart

What I KNOW about this topic	What I find INTERESTING about this topic	What I QUESTION or don't know about this topic

From *Advancing Differentiation: Thinking and Learning for the 21st Century* by Richard M. Cash, Ed.D., copyright © 2017. This page may be reproduced for use within an individual school or district. For all other uses, contact Free Spirit Publishing Inc. at www.freespirit.com/permissions.

Rank Your Interests

UNIT TOPICS
Rank the topics below: 1 (your least favorite) through 5 (your favorite).

_____ Topic: _____

_____ Topic: _____

_____ Topic: _____

_____ Topic: _____

_____ Topic: _____

ASSIGNMENT
You will team up with others who have similar interests. Your team will decide on a topic and create a project to present the topic. Your team must connect the project to music, art, literature, math, sports, family life, or the life of a person like you. You must also incorporate the following learning objectives:

- Know: _____
_____
_____
_____
_____
_____

- Be able to: _____
_____
_____
_____
_____
_____

- Understand: _____
_____
_____
_____
_____
_____

Be creative, think outside the box!

Guidelines for Creating a Passion Project

1. Passions are those things you love, greatly enjoy doing, and have a good storehouse of knowledge about. Clearly explain your passion and why others would want to know about this topic:

   _____
   _____
   _____
   _____
   _____
   _____
   _____
   _____
   _____

2. Meet with the teacher to find an appropriate unit project that can be replaced by your passion project.

   Teacher meeting date: _____

   Unit project to be replaced by the passion project: _____

   Due date for the passion project: _____

   Signature of teacher: _____

   Signature of student: _____

3. Construct your passion project for presentation to the class.
   - Think of an interesting way to present your passion project (computer slideshow presentation, speech, role play, charts/posters, etc.).
   - In your presentation, tell the class:
     ▸ How you became involved with the topic
     ▸ How you came to know your topic
     ▸ Why you enjoy your topic
     ▸ What makes your topic interesting
   - Provide classmates with information that could stimulate them to investigate this topic.
   - Offer the class a list of resources, websites, books, or other materials that could get other students started on your topic.

4. Your passion project will be graded based on the rubric attached. Your grade on the passion project will replace the grade on the unit project.

continued

Guidelines for Creating a Passion Project (continued)

Rubric for Passion Project

CATEGORY	4	3	2	1
Preparedness	Student is completely prepared and has obviously rehearsed.	Student seems fairly prepared but might have needed a couple more rehearsals.	Student is somewhat prepared, but it is clear that rehearsal was lacking.	Student does not seem prepared to present.
Enthusiasm	Student's facial expressions and body language generate a strong interest and enthusiasm about the topic in the audience.	Student's facial expressions and body language sometimes generate a strong interest and enthusiasm about the topic in the audience.	Student's facial expressions and body language are used to try to generate enthusiasm, but seem somewhat faked.	Student makes very little use of facial expressions or body language and did not generate much interest in the topic in the audience.
Content	Student shows a full understanding of the topic.	Student shows a good understanding of the topic.	Student shows a good understanding of parts of the topic.	Student does not seem to understand the topic very well.
Resources	Student provides a wide range of resources (at least 10) including websites, text, and artifacts.	Student provides a range of resources (at least 8) including websites, text, and artifacts.	Student provides some resources (at least 5) including websites and text.	Student provides few resources (less than 5), which include websites and text.
Connection to Content	Student makes exceptional connections to content including math, science, social studies, language arts, the arts, physical education, and/or other areas of study.	Student makes some connections to content including math, science, social studies, language arts, the arts, physical education and/or other areas of study.	Student makes few connections to content including math, science, social studies, language arts, the arts, physical education, and/or other areas of study.	Student makes no connections to content.

Motivation Strategies Based on Student Interests

The following activities stimulate students' curiosity and motivation and promote collaboration.

- **Group students by interest,** then jigsaw the material from alike to mixed groups. Students who have deep interest in content areas can be grouped with other like-minded learners, allowing them the opportunity to go into advanced levels of knowledge. The students should then share their interest-based learning with other students.

- **Allow students to opt out of assigned work** by doing a "passion project" that focuses on a complex issue related to the course of study. Students develop passion projects based on personal interests or hobbies. Through this project, students discover the skills required and developed by career possibilities within their interest or hobby.

- **Use interest surveys** to develop lessons and projects that require multiple interests to be included, as well as interdisciplinary subjects that encompass the arts, sports, family life, and social and civic issues. Interest surveys can help students define their level of engagement in a topic, specify what they like in learning, and identify assets they bring to their learning environment.

- **Allow students to design units, lessons, or projects** based on a meaningful question. This requires investigation that is semi-structured with articulated benchmarks, produces tangible end products that are presented to an authentic audience, and includes reflection on learning. Students complete the work based on an interest contract developed in concert with you and their parents.

- **Allow independent projects** that require students to use inquiry and discovery that expands and extends the classroom curriculum.

- **Incorporate authentic mentors and coaches** from the wider community within the content areas. Connect students to these adults to explore their areas of interest.

- **Develop community or service projects** based on student interests. Expose the students to the social and civic issues that involve their interests. Engage students in solving an authentic problem through community service or volunteerism.

- **Have students construct an online "wiki" to share information** on a particular topic of study or to assist other learners in gaining the necessary knowledge of a course of instruction.

- **Develop "Special Interest Groups" (SIGs)** that meet throughout the school year to discuss topics, work on tasks, network, create products, and find solutions to authentic student issues. Students learn to collaborate, define problems that are common to a greater number of individuals, share resources, plan and work toward solutions, and develop leadership skills within a community.

Sternberg Model of Abilities: Learning Preferences Activity

Activity
Learning preferences

Objectives
- Students will know the characteristics of analytical, practical, and creative abilities.
- Students will be able to define their preferred ways of thinking and doing.
- Students will understand the differences people bring to every situation and how those differences benefit the learning setting.

Concepts
- Learning differences, strengths, limitations

Procedure

1. Ask students what they believe "success" to be.
   List ideas.

2. Ask students what it takes to be successful.
   List ideas.

3. Discuss with students how each person comes to a learning setting with a different set of attributes that can be used for success. How we use those abilities to our benefit is what makes us successful. Refer to the list students made of "What it takes to be successful."

4. Explain Robert Sternberg's model of Successful Intelligence, which involves:
   - a set of three abilities needed to attain success
   - a person's ability to recognize and make the most of his or her strengths (everyone is good at something)
   - a person's ability to recognize and compensate for or correct his or her limitations (no one is good at everything)
   - utilizing individual strengths and limitations; successful people are able to either adapt to, shape, or select environments that best fit their learning preferences

5. On the Sternberg diagram, fill in as a class the descriptions of each of the three abilities.

6. Using the Sternberg diagram, have students place an X on the line of the triangle that represents their preferred areas of strength. Remind them that the lines between lettered corners are a continuum between the different abilities. For example, if a student feels more creative than analytical, she or he would place the X closer to the C corner than the A corner. If the student feels more practical than analytical, he or she would place the X closer to the P than the A. If the student feels an equal balance between creative and practical, she or he would place the X on the line midway between P and C.

7. Define three areas of your classroom to be A (analytical), C (creative), and P (practical) areas. Ask students to move to the part of the room that would best represent their area of strength. If students have balances between areas, they should choose one area over the others.

Discussion
Have the students discuss the similarities and differences between the three groups. Ask: Which groups have more students? Why? Which groups have fewer students? Why? Why do you think some people have balances or imbalances between the three areas? How might we use the strengths of the (A, C, or P) group to assist us in the classroom? How could we organize the classroom setting to best meet the learning needs of each of the three groups? How might we do group work differently now that we've identified these abilities? How could someone with a different (or similar) learning preference help you work on a project?

Closure
Have students write or draw a reflection on the need for all students to work with differing ways of learning. Or make suggestions for classroom arrangements, group work, or project assignments.

continued

From *Advancing Differentiation: Thinking and Learning for the 21st Century* by Richard M. Cash, Ed.D., copyright © 2017. This page may be reproduced for use within an individual school or district. For all other uses, contact Free Spirit Publishing Inc. at www.freespirit.com/permissions.

Sternberg Model of Abilities: Learning Preferences Activity (continued)

People with **analytical** ability can:

People with **practical** ability can:

ANALYTICAL

CREATIVE

PRACTICAL

People with **creative** ability can:

Motivation Strategies Based on Student Learning Preferences

The following activities engage and stretch students in both their preferred and nonpreferred domains of learning.

- **Present information in multiple ways,** including kinesthetic, to encourage learners to branch out of their learning preferences. Many learners tend to prefer specific domains of learning information—often verbal/linguistic for girls and visual/spatial for boys.
- **Use student models and examples** when introducing the learning to be accomplished. Seeing the work of other students who are like them will encourage students to explore beyond their comfort zones to master new subjects and materials.
- **Use wait-time** to allow students to process, connect, and reflect on information. Some learners are deep introspective thinkers and thus will take longer to respond to in-class questions.
- **Use journaling** as a method of reflection on and development of content knowledge. Having students record each day something new they have learned or something at which they excelled helps them recognize their learning growth. Metacognition may be difficult for some learners who have not been stretched to think beyond the basics.
- **Provide multiple options for students to complete assignments,** ranging from artistic representations to three-dimensional constructions to physical performances. Some learners think outside the box and prefer to do things their own way.
- **Ensure ample opportunities for learners to work in balanced groups as well as individually.** Some students are strong independent learners and need assistance in developing collaboration skills. A developed process to move them from individualistic (possessing only some of the skills needed to accomplish a task) to group-oriented (where a collection of individual skills creates a better product) will assist them in building positive social skills. You might also allow students to develop social networking accounts to network with other learners of like skill or preference.
- **Have students take a variety of learning preference instruments** to help them understand all their unique abilities and ways of thinking and doing. Many students have a good understanding of their abilities and learning preferences based on Howard Gardner's Theory of Multiple Intelligences, but may not be familiar with others, such as Anthony Gregorc's Model (Concrete, Abstract, Random, Sequential), Hemispheric Dominance Theory, VARK (Visual, Aural, Read/Write, Kinesthetic), and Sternberg's Successful Intelligence Theory (Analytical, Creative, Practical), to name a few. A simple Internet search of "learning preferences" will produce numerous websites of inventories and instruments. Be clear on your purpose and which preferences you are willing to work with and through.
- **Use elaborate rehearsal.** Elaborate rehearsal (ER) is the active process of relating new material to something the learner already knows. ER focuses on the meaning of information through authentic practice and blurring the lines between content areas. When using ER, students are required to actively use all of their senses to encode information into long-term memory. Activities that are considered elaborative rehearsals are:
    - clustering a series of numbers to resemble a phone number (1.8422384943 = 1-842-238-4943)
    - using acronyms or mnemonics to remember sequential or serial information (red, orange, yellow, green, blue, indigo, violet = ROY G BIV)
    - creating analogies, metaphors, or similes to summarize information
    - using mind maps, graphic organizers, or other diagrammatic representations of the information
    - engaging in a reenactment of an event, a role play, or simulations

Four Square Concept Map

Directions:

1. Write the concept in the middle circle.
2. In the upper left box, write a definition of the concept.
3. In the upper right box, draw a picture of what the concept looks like.
4. In the lower left box, give examples of the concept.
5. In the lower right box, write or draw examples of what the concept is *not*.

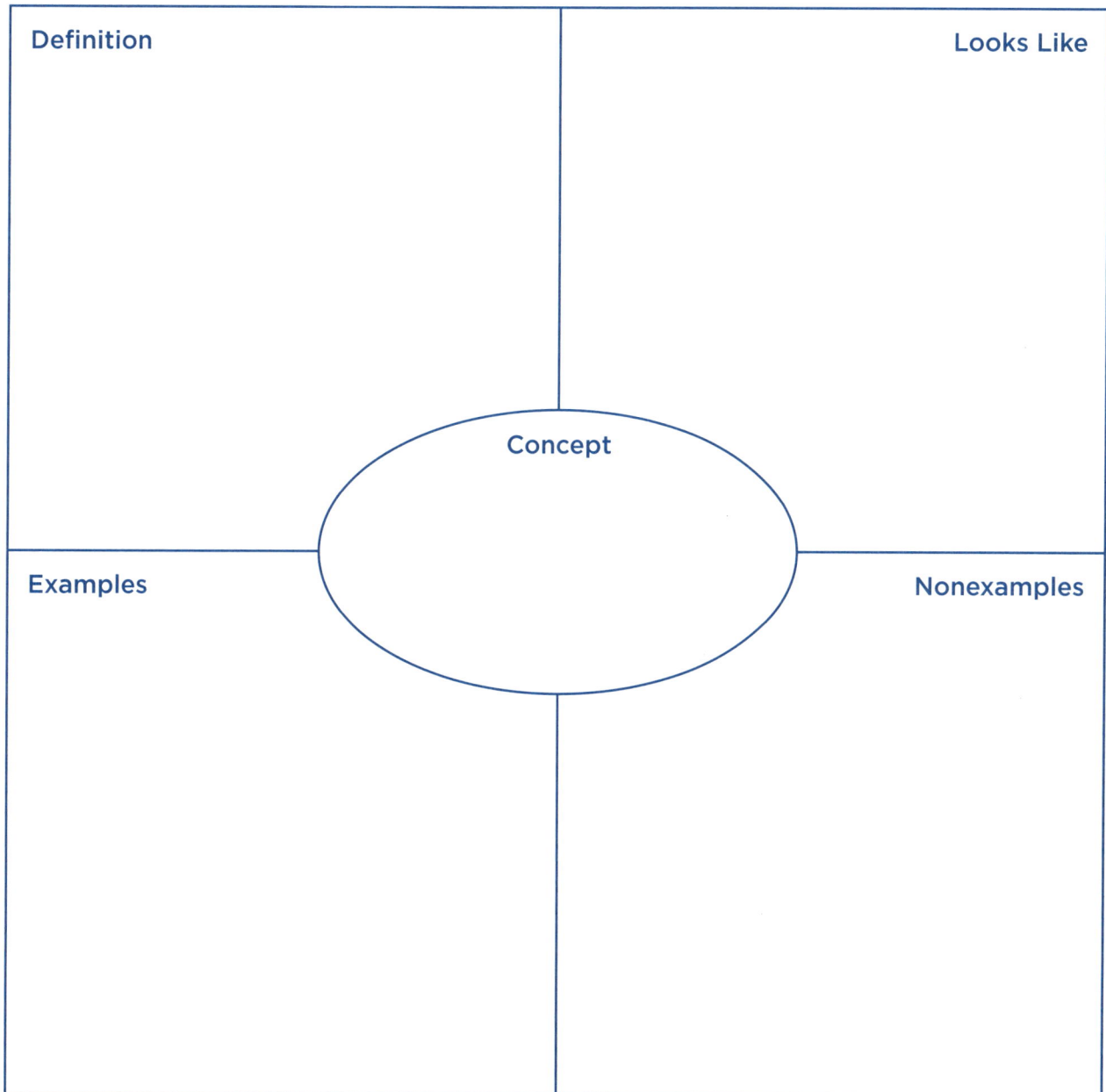

3-2-1 Exit Slip/Entrance Ticket

Directions:
Write in the boxes:
3 ideas or things you know or remember from the class session
2 connections you can make to other subject areas or topics you know something about
1 question that you still have or would like to ask in the next class session

3 Things you know about this topic

2 Ways this topic connects to other topics

1 Question you have about this topic

Roundtable Review

Directions:

1. On selected days throughout the unit or at the end of a unit of study, rearrange the classroom in table groupings. There should be as many tables as major topics in the unit of study.

2. At each table, place a placard with the topic listed. Choose discussion topics students either know a lot about or need to review. You may also want to put highlighted notes or important bits of information that students must know, be able to do, and understand at each table.

3. Students select at least four tables to visit throughout the class period.

4. Students will visit each table for up to five minutes to share information about the table's topic.

5. After each round, students spend two minutes debriefing, writing notes, and finding answers. (Use the attached Roundtable Reflection form.)

6. At the end of the four cycles, do a walk-through with students of all the topics covered.

Topics Covered in This Unit

continued

From *Advancing Differentiation: Thinking and Learning for the 21st Century* by Richard M. Cash, Ed.D., copyright © 2017. This page may be reproduced for use within an individual school or district. For all other uses, contact Free Spirit Publishing Inc. at www.freespirit.com/permissions.

Roundtable Review (continued)

Roundtable Reflection

TOPIC	WHAT I REMEMBER	WHAT I LEARNED

Additional Thoughts:

_____
_____
_____
_____

From *Advancing Differentiation: Thinking and Learning for the 21st Century* by Richard M. Cash, Ed.D., copyright © 2017. This page may be reproduced for use within an individual school or district. For all other uses, contact Free Spirit Publishing Inc. at www.freespirit.com/permissions.

Motivation Strategies Based on Assessment

The following activities acknowledge and respect what students already know and their need to know more.

- **Provide mini-lessons on facts and procedures** students will encounter in the unit of study. For advanced learners who require less time to learn facts and procedures this allows them to "buy" time for advanced levels of activities. For all other learners, this provides a warm-up or additional exposure to the material that will be covered.

- **Provide varied levels of reading materials,** from elementary to college-level texts and trade books and professional journals from the field of study. These materials will expose the learners to the professional language of the field of discipline, as well as provide a wider range of subject diversity. The students can then develop a professional vocabulary list.

- **Flexibly group students by ability or comprehension of content.** In these smaller groups, students can collaboratively work on authentic issues related to the content, develop questions they would like to explore, debate ethical ramifications, and investigate, interview, or contact experts from the field of study.

- **Have learning materials available other than text.** Not all learners enjoy or acquire knowledge from text, therefore use other materials such as audio recordings, videos/DVDs/CDs, websites, or computer simulations that will allow students to digest the required information.

- **Highlight key points in the text.** Some learners read text and believe all the material is highly relevant. Highlighting helps them focus on the most relevant and important notes.

- **Use creative activities** to assist learners in stretching beyond the basics in math and science. The experiences must require the practice of novelty, originality, and creating new ideas.

- **Use graphic organizers** to help learners organize their knowledge and connect prior learning to new ideas.

- **Adjust questioning practices** for the varied levels of learners in the classroom. Questions should encourage students to elaborate on points of discussion. All learners are able to think at higher levels, but advanced learners require a more sophisticated degree of analysis, synthesis, and justification.

- **Encourage reciprocal teaching.** Reciprocal teaching occurs when a student is secure in the knowledge and is willing to share or assist others in a greater sense of understanding. To teach requires a deep understanding of the material, therefore allowing students to become reciprocal teachers who can provide other students assistance in learning and guidance in understanding the material. Being a reciprocal teacher can build learners' confidence as well as their knowledge of the subject.

- **Develop discovery-based lessons and content** that use the Internet so students can access any piece of information at any time and in any sequence. This process must teach the learner how to discern and critically analyze information for bias, opinion, or irrelevance.

From *Advancing Differentiation: Thinking and Learning for the 21st Century* by Richard M. Cash, Ed.D., copyright © 2017. This page may be reproduced for use within an individual school or district. For all other uses, contact Free Spirit Publishing Inc. at www.freespirit.com/permissions.

Developing Student Self-Regulation

Acquiring higher mental functions allows children to make a critical transition from being "slaves to the environment" to becoming "masters of their own behavior."[1]

—Dr. Deborah J. Leong and Dr. Elena Bodrova, psychologists

The role of schooling in a child's life is to expose him or her to the common knowledge we hold true as a society. The teacher's role is to provide this information in compatible ways for the child's brain to retain and use for future success. The student's role in school is to become self-regulated and develop new knowledge for future generations. The theory of self-regulation is based on the interaction and balancing of affect, behavior, and cognition toward the formation of new knowledge, ideas, and products. Teachers provide those interactions when they offer students opportunities that encourage them to think and take authentic action.

Self-Regulation Theory

For over four decades, the idea of self-regulating has been an important area of educational and psychological research. The ideas behind how humans learn, both in academic and social settings, suggest that the competent, successful people believe that most things can be accomplished as long as one puts effort forward, has a goal in mind, knows how to deal with conflict, avoids distraction and impulsivity, stays focused on the task at hand, and acknowledges both success and failure. In addition, how a person manages his or her emotional responses and reflects on learning has a profound effect on his or her level of achievement. In the classroom, we call these abilities *self-regulation for learning*.

Self-regulation for learning is the process by which learners activate, sustain, manage, and reflect upon their affects (or feelings), behaviors, and cognition throughout learning. These interrelated dimensions of affect, behavior, and cognition (ABCs) must balance together for learners to experience success (see **Figure 5.1**). To achieve this balance, students must employ a repertoire of strategies to focus and improve on their learning.

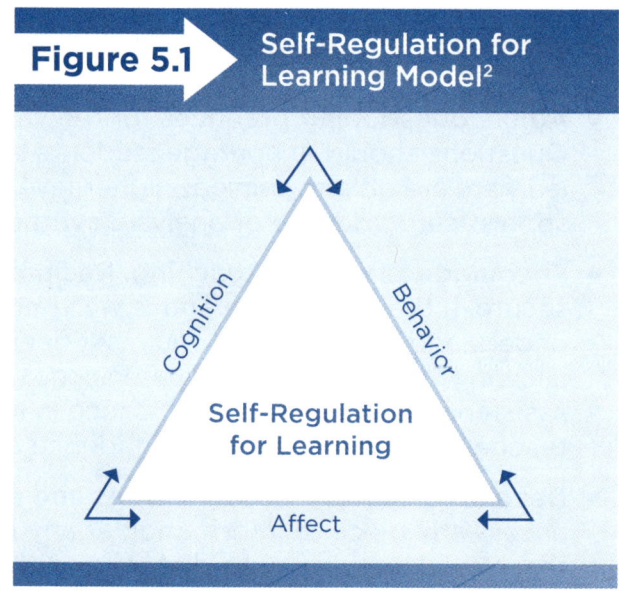

Figure 5.1 Self-Regulation for Learning Model[2]

---

1. Leong, D. J., and E. Bodrova. "Developing Self-Regulation: The Vygotskian View." *Academic Exchange Quarterly* (Winter 2006).
2. Cash, R. M. *Self-Regulation in the Classroom: Helping Students Learn How to Learn*. Minneapolis: Free Spirit Publishing, 2016. Used with permission.

ABCs Explained

Affect is the conscious awareness of our emotions and how we respond to them. These responses, often called feelings, are what can inhibit or promote learning. How learners feel about a situation determines the focus of their attention, therefore it is important for us to know how to help students attune their emotional responses appropriately for the situation.

Behavior is what we do to be successful or unsuccessful. In the academic setting, this includes everything from our body postures (such as how we sit at a desk, walk down the hall, and so forth) to our problem-solving skills (such as working backward or doing an experiment). Knowing how to be flexible in different settings and learning experiences is a component of effective learning behavior.

Cognition refers to our thinking processes. It moves from metacognition (reflective thinking) to infra-cognition (the advanced thinking processes used in school) to metaphysical cognition (thinking beyond the self). Having significant thinking tools is important for success in this ever-changing world.

Based on studies done by leading research scientists in the field of motivation and competence, Barry Zimmerman and Anastasia Kitsantas: "There is evidence that the attainment of peak levels of academic and athletic competence requires more than basic talent and high-quality instruction; it also involves self-belief, diligence, and self-discipline."[3] This development is completed in the four stages of self-regulation (see **Figure 5.2**).

Students have the capacity to learn how to self-regulate when the learning is effectively modeled for them. They can emulate or practice the modeled learning with others, they can use the learning during independent practice to employ it automatically, and they can transfer the learning to other learning activities.

The following skills guide learners in developing self-regulation:

- goal setting
- task strategies
- visual imagery
- self-instruction
- time management
- self-monitoring
- self-evaluation
- selecting and creating learning environments
- help-seeking

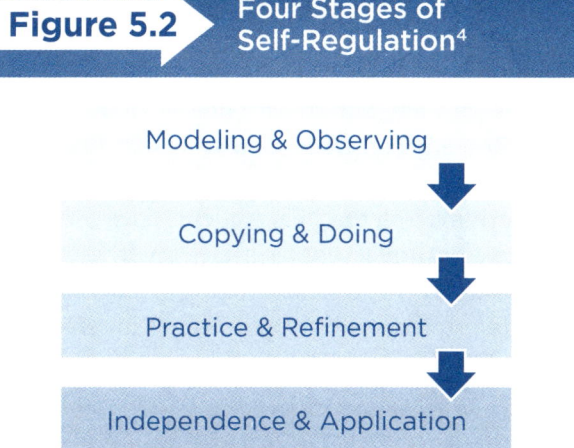

Figure 5.2 Four Stages of Self-Regulation[4]

Modeling & Observing

Copying & Doing

Practice & Refinement

Independence & Application

Zimmerman also proposed that the developmental process of how people acquire skills for success is cyclical in nature. As you can see in **Figure 5.3** on page 102, learning to develop self-regulation involves three cyclical phases.

In phase one, *pre-learning*, students set the stage for learning to occur. They examine the task to be completed and then establish a plan of action to complete the task. Students must also evaluate the meaningfulness of the task, as well as their own intrinsic beliefs about the task. At this point, students may want to use the Student Perception Questionnaire (Chapter 7, page 143) and also complete a Work Plan (Chapter 7, page 144).

In the *performance phase*, students monitor their attention and focus on completing the task. After reviewing their work plans, students may find that they need additional support and guidance or that they are on track to reach their goals. After the performance has been completed, the *self-reflection phase* begins, and students reflect upon the earlier phases of planning and performance. Students should review the work plan, looking back on the effectiveness of the goal setting, the availability of resources, whether they had the skills necessary to

---

3. Zimmerman, B. J., and A. Kitsantas. "The Hidden Dimension of Personal Competence: Self-Regulated Learning and Practice." In *Handbook of Competence and Motivation*. A. J. Elliot and C. S. Dweck (Eds.). New York: Guilford Press, 2005: 509.
4. Zimmerman, B. J., S. Bonner, and R. Kovach. *Developing Self-Regulated Learners: Beyond Achievement to Self-Efficacy*. Washington, DC: American Psychological Association, 1996; Zimmerman, B. J., and A. Kitsantas. "Developmental Phases in Self-Regulation: Shifting from Process Goals to Outcome Goals." *Journal of Educational Psychology*, 89 (1) (1997): 29–36.

complete the task, and to what extent they accomplished the goal. Key to the success at each phase of this model is the student's sense of self-efficacy. *Self-efficacy* is the personal understanding one has about his or her skills and abilities to perform tasks, as well as a sense of commitment to complete a given task. Students with high self-efficacy are more willing to take on challenges, put forth effort to complete tasks when faced with temptations or distractions, and can effectively self-evaluate. Students with low self-efficacy display more learning and test anxiety, are more distractible, possess less intrinsic motivation, and are often disengaged from learning. You can help students develop and maintain a healthy level of self-efficacy by setting up a classroom that fosters thinking, encourages risk taking, and provides opportunities for students to develop autonomy.

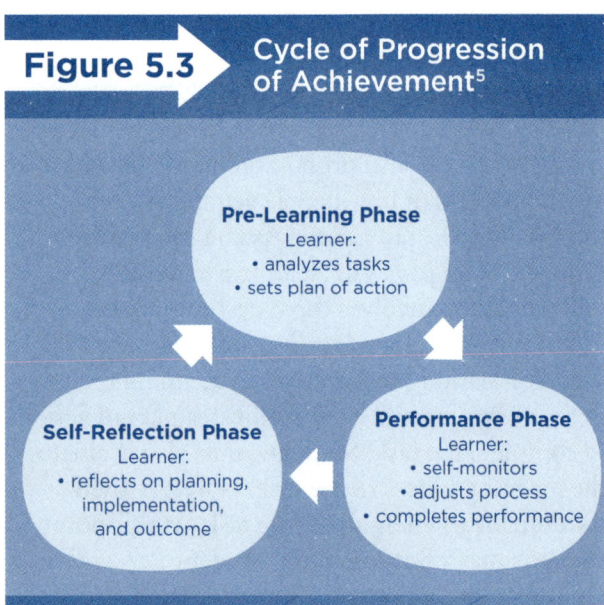

Figure 5.3 Cycle of Progression of Achievement[5]

Building Self-Regulation Through Goal Setting

An effective strategy for building self-regulation is through helping students set a goal, manage their progress toward the goal, and assess their attainment of the goal. Begin with short-term goal setting at the beginning of each day or lesson.

Steps in Short-Term Goal Setting

1. Model for students the writing of three goals at the beginning of class.
2. Have students write their own goals for the class session or the day.
3. Pause class midway through instruction to monitor and reflect on your goals, thinking aloud.
4. Have students do the same with their own goals, either with a partner or alone.
   Questions to ask:
   ▸ Have I met any of my goals?
   ▸ Why or why not?
   ▸ What should I do for the remainder of the class or day to make sure I meet my goals?
5. At the end of the class or day, repeat a verbalization of goal reflection, and have students do the same.
   Questions to ask:
   ▸ Did I meet my goals?
   ▸ Why or why not?
   ▸ How will I celebrate my success?
   ▸ What will I do differently next time to meet my goals?

To effectively help students build autonomy in goal setting, begin with very short-term goals, such as lesson-by-lesson, class-by-class, or day-by-day. Then move to a weekly goal that is reviewed midway through the week. Build up to long-term goals of monthly, quarterly, or yearly. Goal setting should be practiced every day, be made a part of instruction, and become an expectation of every student and teacher.

Building Self-Regulation Through Mindset

Another way to look at self-regulation is through the work of Dr. Carol Dweck. Dweck believes a person either has a fixed or a growth mindset. In a *fixed mindset*, a person believes his or her intelligence and talents are fixed traits that cannot be changed or enhanced. We maintain the fixed mindset through reliance on documentations, such as IQ tests and achievement tests, to tell us that a person can or cannot do something. When people have a fixed mindset, they measure success by the amount of intelligence or talent a person possesses. Failure is measured the same way.

---

5. Zimmerman, B. J. "Becoming a Self-Regulated Learner: An Overview." *Theory Into Practice*, 41 (2) (Spring 2002): 64–70.

Students with a fixed mindset have a difficult time admitting to or correcting mistakes. Advanced learners who spend many years in under-challenging courses don't develop an understanding of or a need for effort. But when they hit challenging courses, they believe they shouldn't need to put forth effort, so they think of themselves as not gifted. Failure threatens their sense of ability and therefore threatens their giftedness. Students who have not been challenged sufficiently do not develop important life skills such as patience, perseverance, or persistence (P^3).

A person with a *growth mindset* believes that most skills and abilities can be learned. We begin with what we have and build from there. It is through dedication, hard work, and effort that we gain success. "When people believe their basic qualities can be developed, failures may still hurt, but failures don't define them."[6] In other words, intensity as a learner is a far more useful trait than tested or perceived ability. Having a growth mindset encourages the development of self-regulation and valuable life skills. Students who develop a growth mindset learn useful tools for overcoming negative labels or stereotyping, learn how to mitigate difficult situations, and learn how to overcome perceived or real barriers to learning. These strategies can be most effective for students who are culturally or linguistically diverse. See Chapter 11, pages 203–204, for a suggested list of growth mindset questions, compliments, and strategies that are helpful to parents for developing self-confidence and a growth mindset in their children.

To help students shift from a fixed mindset to one of a growth mindset, we need to employ strategies that build their self-regulation. This can be done by creating classroom settings that are stimulating and that enable students to develop the ability to monitor their actions, thoughts, feelings, and behaviors in order to be academically and personally successful—in other words, by creating a *student-centered classroom*. The next section provides an overview of a student-centered classroom, along with numerous strategies and techniques for increasing student self-regulation.

The Student-Centered Classroom

A student-centered classroom is one where students are actively engaged in the discovery of information and are responsible for the learning. As you will see in Chapter 6, the roles of teaching and learning shift in a student-centered classroom from teacher-directed to learner-directed. Transitioning the roles of teacher and student build learner autonomy by developing an intrinsic desire to think and learn.

Students develop the following critical elements in a student-centered classroom (see the student checklist on page 111):

- responsibility for learning
- self-efficacy
- an intrinsic desire to succeed
- persistence, patience, and perseverance (P^3)
- metacognitive skills
- critical thinking skills
- problem-solving skills
- creative abilities and production
- a growth mindset

Teachers in a student-centered classroom have the following responsibilities (see the teacher checklist on page 112):

- facilitate learning
- guide students to success
- understand and encourage student differences
- employ a variety of instructional practices, interventions, and assessments
- know content essentials and curriculum standards
- set high expectations for all students

Five Keys for Creating a Student-Centered Classroom

1. Establish a Community of Scholars

Students learn best when they feel safe and are not threatened. Following this first rule of brain-compatible learning can also help students feel welcomed and connected to others through a

---

6. Dweck, C. S. *Mindset: The New Psychology of Success*. New York: Ballantine Books, 2006: 39.

sense of belonging. You can do this by making your classroom a "community of scholars." In a community of scholars, all participants are expected to act not only as learners, but as learners who develop a knowledge base in order to produce new knowledge. Being able to build upon prior knowledge and be innovative in developing new ideas are keys to students' success in the twenty-first century. In a community of scholars, students develop an understanding of why they are there, the shared responsibility of all class members, and the ways they can hold each other accountable.

IDEAS FOR ESTABLISHING A COMMUNITY OF SCHOLARS

Create a bill of rights. Have students construct a constitution or bill of rights in which the roles and responsibilities of each participant in the classroom are spelled out. An example of a classroom bill of rights might include:

All participants in the classroom have the right to:

- a safe and welcoming learning environment
- active and engaging learning experiences
- meaningful instruction and curriculum
- knowledge that is represented in a format most appropriate to the learning experience
- accurate, effective, and immediate feedback that can lead toward success

Develop classroom conventions. Have students collectively develop conventions for the classroom. Different from rules, conventions are agreements, compacts, or standards of practice. Examples of classroom conventions might include:

- All skills and processes are presented and approached as learnable.
- Patience, persistence, and perseverance are valued, modeled, and expected.
- All feedback will be constructive to inspire future success.

Form an oversight council. Have students elect members of the class to form a council that oversees the implementation of the bill of rights or classroom conventions.

Use restorative justice. Use the method of restorative justice to manage classroom conflicts and grievances. Restorative justice is a process that repairs the harm caused by infractions or offenses. It brings together the target, offender, and other members of the classroom community to meet and decide how to repair and transform the situation from one that is negative toward one that is positive. Through the use of sequential questioning justice is restored. Harms are repaired, wrongdoers are held accountable for their actions, targets feel empowered, agreements are negotiated, participants take ownership or responsibility for their actions, and closure is attained.

Sequential questioning:
What happened?
How did it happen?
What part did you play in it?
How were you affected?
Who else was affected?
What do you need to make it right?
How can we repair the harm?

2. Build Students' Empathy and Wisdom

Dr. Ben Dean states, "Wisdom is the product of knowledge and experience, but it is more than the accumulation of information. It is the coordination of this information and its deliberate use to improve well-being. In a social context, wisdom allows the individual to listen to others, evaluate what they say, and then offer them good (sage) advice."[7] Likewise, Robert Sternberg claims that people are wise when they use their intelligence to seek the common good and have an understanding of how their actions can affect others.[8] In essence, when a person is able to balance their personal needs with the needs of other individuals and of a greater community, they are more likely to be happy, healthy, and successful.

IDEAS FOR BUILDING EMPATHY AND WISDOM

Assign roles. To build cooperative learning skills, give each student a role within the group and have them report on how well they performed their duty. Also, ask other students in the group to give positive critique to each other on their performance within the group.

---

7. Dean, B. "Wisdom" (www.authentichappiness.sas.upenn.edu/newsletters/authentichappinesscoaching/wisdom).
8. Sternberg, R. "Schools Should Nurture Wisdom." In *Teaching for Intelligence*. B. Z. Presseisen (Ed.). Arlington Heights, IL: Skylight Training and Publishing, 1999: 55–82.

Use service learning projects in which students help others less fortunate than they are.

Use a buddy system. Help students develop a classroom, lunchtime, or playground buddy system. Older students buddy with younger students at least once per month. Activities could include a conversation; reading a book together; working on a project, game, or puzzle together; or helping with a homework assignment.

Hold a fundraiser. Have students investigate charities or other organizations that help people, and then hold a fundraising event.

Partner with an organization. Partner your class with a nursing home, a homeless shelter, or other social service organization. Students then develop plans to offer the partner assistance or volunteer work throughout the school year.

3. Develop a Supportive Classroom Environment

In a supportive environment, both you and your students understand people's fundamental needs to feel safe, welcome, and wanted. As the teacher, you ensure that the curriculum is rigorous and holds relevance for all students. Class members forge supportive relationships that can lead to individual student success.

IDEAS FOR DEVELOPING A SUPPORTIVE CLASSROOM

Mobilize resources. Help students develop an understanding of how to mobilize their resources. Post the following list in your classroom to encourage students to take on the responsibility for learning and to become more autonomous:

- Use what you have (believe in yourself).
- Draw on the expertise of those around you (teachers, classmates, parents, and other adults).
- Use the materials available.
- Ask questions, or ask for help.
- Request more support, information, or resources, if needed.

Express yourself. You and all of your students represent yourselves as individuals through an introductory display, poster, or performance.

Know names. You and all of your students know each other's names.

Know interests. You know quality information about your students that can inform instruction. Interest surveys are a wonderful way to gather this information.

Know abilities. You know the differing abilities of each student and respect those differences through tiered instruction and activities.

4. Develop Students' Metacognitive Skills

Metacognition is basically "thinking about your own thinking." In a student-centered classroom, you routinely focus students on how they are thinking, processing, and relating to the material being taught. Students also develop an awareness of their strengths and limitations. Gear activities and lessons toward helping students construct meaning, and use tools to help them solve problems, make decisions, and evaluate their productivity. Developing skills to think about how and what they are thinking can improve students' learning and increase intelligent behavior. (See Chapter 7 for more information about metacognition.)

IDEAS FOR DEVELOPING METACOGNITIVE SKILLS

Use KIQ charts. Start each lesson with a "What do you know?" and "What do you have questions about?" activity that focuses learners on what needs to be learned. Use a KIQ, KWL, or KWI chart (see page 87 for an example).

Use verbal repetition. Learning happens best when students can verbalize what they have learned. We store and process our memories through repeating information verbally. Think about the last time you tried to remember a phone number. You likely said the number over and over again. This type of rehearsal helps set the information into short-term memory. For the information to be stored into long-term memory, we must use the information repeatedly before it becomes automatic. For example, use this partner problem-solving strategy: one partner verbalizes the problem while the other partner listens and asks clarifying questions.

Keep thinking journals. Have students create a "thinking journal" to take notes on their ideas or thoughts throughout lessons. The journal can be used during study time, conferences, or end-of-unit reflection on what the student has learned. The "I Chart" can be incorporated into this journal (see page 85).

Encourage reflection. Allow students to reflect on their learning continually throughout the day. Provide time in each lesson for students to debrief, discuss, debate, and digest new ideas and information. Reflection should be done at least every 20 minutes. The reflection can be writing, oral, or graphic.

Require self-evaluations. Have students do self-evaluations at the end of every unit. Provide them with a checklist and rubric of the objectives and unit outcomes.

Use the 10:2/20:2 (or Richard's) Rule to help students remember information, stay focused, and remain active (see **Figure 5.4**).

Figure 5.4 — 10:2/20:2 Rule

10:2 (ten to two)
or
20:2 (twenty to two)

The brain learns information best when allowed time to process and connect new ideas. This rule takes into account the amount of time and information the brain can handle before it needs to download or use the information.

Elementary grades: For every 10 minutes of instruction, allow up to two minutes for discussion, application, movement, or restating what was just stated.

Secondary grades: For every 20 minutes of instruction, allow up to two minutes for discussion, application, movement, or restating what was just stated.

5. Develop Persistence, Patience, and Perseverance (P^3)

Life is a series of problem-solving actions. When faced with a problem, either major or minor, we are unlikely to successfully solve it without useful and effective strategies. In today's world, situations occur at an accelerated pace, so our students must be prepared with key skills to nimbly work through problems and find solutions. When developing persistence, patience, and perseverance (or P^3), students learn to reduce impulsivity and review their work to ensure accuracy.

IDEAS FOR DEVELOPING P^3

- Focus feedback and praise on the amount of effort students put forth rather than on their level of ability.
- Give students a pad of sticky notes so they can write down their thoughts rather than verbally interrupt a lesson.
- Establish and maintain a daily class routine so that students are aware of what is to come and when breaks or changes in activities will happen.
- To practice impulse control, provide students with games in the classroom that build patience and persistence.
- Model how students should take turns, ask questions, wait in line, and listen to others.
- For students who are impulsive, give them tactile fidgets or stress toys, such as squeeze balls, to use when they are most likely to interrupt or be impatient.
- Teach students proofreading and answer-checking skills, such as working backward in math to check answers, reviewing their writing for spelling errors, or asking a friend to review their work.
- Give students a list of commonly misspelled words, common punctuation errors, common grammatical errors, or common math computational errors.
- Before students hand in assignments, give them the grading criteria or scoring rubric so they can check over their work to ensure they have addressed all the objectives.
- Give students a list of questions to ask before they turn in work, such as:
  - Did I do what was asked?
  - How can I be sure I met the objective?
  - Have I reviewed my work?
  - Have I had someone else review my work?

- Give students logic problems (from easy to difficult) to solve over a period of time.
- Have students explain each step they take when solving a problem.
- Encourage students to try several different ways to solve a problem.
- Have multipiece puzzles in the room for students to work on over a period of time.
- Provide ample wait time. Counting to 10 in your head is a handy technique to help you offer students wait time.
- Expect students to redo assignments that do not show proficiency.

Using Centers and Stations to Develop Self-Regulation

In addition to the strategies discussed so far in this chapter, the use of learning centers and/or stations also can be helpful in the process of developing students' self-regulation. Based on work by Carol Ann Tomlinson, centers provide individualized instruction to students who may be struggling or need to be advanced within a lesson or unit.[9] One idea is to use centers after a lesson has been delivered. Post-assessments can reveal that some students are still not grasping the strategy or concept while others have met the goal. For students who struggle, the center can reinforce (or reteach in a different manner) the strategy or concept. Students who do grasp the lesson can work on either practicing, extending, or enhancing the strategy.

Learning Centers

Centers are typically a space within the classroom or a virtual location, as in a folder or website, where students can go to gather more information, have a lesson retaught, or work on an individual area of study. A successful learning center is engaging and interactive and allows for self-paced/self-directed learning. Teachers train students how to use centers, work independently, and complete tasks in a timely manner with limited teacher interaction.

For students who may be struggling or lacking the self-regulation skills to work independently, centers may not be the most efficient strategy. In this case, while you work closely with students needing reteaching, let students who have grasped the concept or skill use the center as a means for enrichment, extension, or enhancement (E^3) of the learning activities.

E^3 learning activities:
- Enrichment: focuses within the topic of study
- Extension: broadens the topic within the field or subject
- Enhancement: interrelates the topic outside the field or subject

Example: During a study of ratio and proportion, some students need reteaching of cross products; other students grasped the idea quickly. The latter students proceed to the math center in the classroom to work on topics such as:

- The use of ratio and proportion in daily life by finding examples in the local media (enrichment)
- The use of ratio and proportion in professions by researching disciplinarians who use the concept routinely, such as a grain buyer or demographer (extension)
- The misuse of ratio and proportion by finding ways the concept can be used to deceive or distract the public, for example, inaccuracies in political messages or materials (enhancement)[10]

Learning Stations

Stations, on the other hand, contain differentiated tasks that all students rotate through to learn content or develop strategies. Stations are used during lessons or portions of a unit, and they often are used to promote teamwork and collaboration among students. Not all students will visit each station, especially those students who gain understanding or proficiency quickly. In this case, you should design an "alternate" station for those students who don't need to visit every station. I call these "by-pass" stations. Ideas for by-pass stations can include:

- **Homework station:** Students can work on homework from any of their classes.
- **Reading station:** Students are allowed to read from a text of their choice—preferably materials from the class.

---

9. Tomlinson, C. A. *The Differentiated Classroom: Responding to the Needs of All Learners*. Alexandria, VA: ASCD, 2014.
10. For more on E^3 and numerous activity ideas, see Heacox, D., and R. M. Cash. *Differentiation for Gifted Learners: Going Beyond the Basics*. Minneapolis: Free Spirit Publishing, 2014.

- **Enrichment station:** Students are provided with a focused topic within the content (for example, in an astronomy class this station might offer an activity on black holes).
- **Extension station:** Students explore a broadening of the content (for example, when studying *Grapes of Wrath*, students might listen to John Steinbeck discuss his writing process).
- **Enhancement station:** Students connect the unit of study to other content areas (for example, biology class students might learn more about the economic costs associated with contagious diseases).
- **Exploration station:** Students are offered disassociated words to do an Internet search (for example, in a math class they might use the words *grief, economics,* and *division*. When I did a search, I came up with an article from *The Economist* (September 24, 2011) on the shake-up in the global labor market. This is a great way to get students to understand searching with keywords and/or to find information on new topics. The idea is to help students understand how one content area connects with others. In the math example, the word *grief* seems totally unrelated to math. But upon deeper investigation, students learn the breadth of language used within and across content areas. Try using one or two vocabulary terms directly connected to the content and one or two words from a different content area. You can also ask students to come up with their own disassociated terms to stump their classmates.

Ideas for stations during instruction, based on higher levels of learning:

- **"Meet with Me" station:** This is a rotation where the teacher has the opportunity to meet with small groups of students to either reteach or enhance learning.
- **Recall station:** At this station, students have access to varied levels of text or audio focused on a new idea or expanding on a topic already discussed. The activity at this station involves factual retrieval of the text or audio.
- **Comprehension station:** Considering the entirety of a lecture or reading/viewing material, the activity at this station reinforces or challenges the students' comprehension of the topic. Examples include debating a question or writing about the topic.
- **Application station:** Students work on various levels of computation, writing application, or experiments at this station. The idea is to have students practice a strategy they have learned and apply it to different situations.
- **Analysis/evaluation station:** At this station, students are given an issue related to the topic and asked to find ways to solve the problem or suggest solutions. For example, in a class on human interaction with the environment, students are asked to investigate new sources of energy and then debate which source is most valuable to their local community. Students then decide who had the best argument.
- **Creation/evaluation station:** Students come up with new ideas or unique ways to solve problems. Using the new sources of energy example, students are challenged to find ways to persuade legislators to enact rules for the use of renewable energies. The evaluation occurs when students defend their positions.
  - *Note:* In the analysis and creation stations, evaluation is a component of the activity.

For ideas on crafting learning center and station activities at each level of Bloom's Taxonomy, refer to Chapter 8, Figure 8.3 on page 149.

Tips for Successful Centers and Stations

Use this list when preparing learning centers and stations:

Determine clear outcomes. If your intent is to reteach, reinforce, or extend a skill or lesson, create learning centers where students visit only one center. If your intent is to directly teach skills or content, use stations. Be sure to articulate the outcomes to students so they know what is expected.

Have students practice moving around the room. Prior to using centers or stations, students must learn how to manage themselves while moving from space to space. When space is an issue, think creatively about what can be removed to provide more space (such as desks) or use file folders or boxes that move between individuals or groups of students.

Set up classroom norms or action protocols. When students are working collaboratively in centers or stations, they all need to participate and contribute. This is best accomplished by having no more than five and no less than three students in each group.

Ensure students can do the activities at each location. Practice sample activities with the whole class prior to developing a center or station.

Create clear directions for the students to follow. Use as few words as possible and try to include photos, illustrations, drawings, or videos of each step. Post directions at each location.

Ensure all activities take the same amount of time, are equally engaging, and require effort. Beware of the curse of "fluff and stuff" activities for advanced students!

Use formalized assessments after each center or at the end of a round of stations.

Provide students with choices whenever possible. Try to have two to three options at each center or station.

Keep the number of centers or stations manageable. I suggest that you have three to six stations total. To keep the number of students at each location practicable, you may need to have two to three of the same station. For example, if you have 30 students in your class and you want to have three stations, then you will need two of each station.

Critical to the success of centers and stations:

- **Preparation.** Think through each activity and be sure you have all the materials ready before the students arrive.
- **Organization.** Use file folders for papers, boxes or baskets for materials, bindings for utensils, and so forth. Especially when students are moving from station to station, be sure they know how to return items to the original organization.
- **Expectations.** Make sure students know how to move from place to place, what to do at each location, how to work with others, what to do when they have questions, and what to do when they finish early or don't finish in time.
- **Movement.** As a teacher, you must move between stations or centers to provide support, guidance, and encouragement. If you are co-teaching or have preservice teachers, classroom aids, or volunteers, adults can either be fixed at a center/station or follow a group of students from place to place.

Centers and stations are a great way to engage, enrich, and enhance your classroom and can help students achieve learning goals. I find that shifting the normal classroom routine from "teacher as knowledge provider" to "student as explorer" can have a profound effect on student motivation and achievement.

Five Understandings for Developing Self-Regulation for Learning

What do students need to be self-regulated in their learning? **Figure 5.5** (see page 110) presents five understandings necessary for developing self-regulated learners. These ideas can be used when working with students either on a group project or in individual study. As discussed throughout this chapter, the most successful learners know how to focus their attention and manage, adjust, and adapt their feelings, behavior, and cognition to achieve success. For more ideas, activities, and suggestions for developing self-regulation for learning, see other resources such as *Self-Regulation in the Classroom: Helping Students Learn How to Learn* (Cash, 2016).

Figure 5.5 Five Understandings for Developing Self-Regulation for Learning

Understanding 1: Intrinsic Motivation
Learners who are intrinsically driven by a love of learning achieve through:
- Working with others who are supportive and encouraging
- Understanding their hierarchical needs for:
  - Survival
  - Love and belonging
  - Power
  - Freedom
  - Fun

Understanding 2: Goal Orientation
Goal-oriented individuals have higher degrees of motivation, achieve greater success, and are generally more satisfied in life.
- Teachers can assist students in developing goals by using SMART goals:
  - **S**pecific
  - **M**easurable
  - **A**ssignable
  - **R**ealistic
  - **T**imely

Understanding 3: Self-Efficacy
Self-efficacy is the ability to recognize one's personal capacity and to organize and execute a course of action to gain skills necessary to achieve greater levels.
- Three forms of engagement involved in self-efficacy are:
  - *Behavioral:* the ability to complete a task
  - *Cognitive:* the ability to think at advanced levels
  - *Motivational:* the ability to take personal interest in and perceive the relevance of a task
- Self-efficacy is developed through relevant performance feedback.

Understanding 4: Metacognition
Metacognition is an awareness of one's learning process and involves:
- Monitoring progress
- Making changes and adapting when necessary
- Analyzing the effectiveness of learning strategies
- Recognizing the direct relationship between effort and learning (called *mindset*)

Understanding 5: Locus of Control
Levels of achievement are either internally or externally controlled.
- Individuals who believe achievement levels are due to the amount of effort put forth have an internal locus of control.
- Success without failure or effort is pure luck.

Student Checklist for a Student-Centered Classroom

AS A STUDENT:	NEVER	SOMETIMES	OFTEN	ALWAYS
I'm responsible for my own learning.				
I'm capable of doing most anything I put my mind to, as long as I work hard.				
I'm patient with myself and others when I/they don't get it.				
I persist and persevere until I do get it.				
I think about what I'm going to do before I do it.				
I think about what I'm doing while I'm doing it.				
I think about what I've done when I've done it.				
I know and use several different strategies to solve problems.				
I think "outside" the box to come up with new ideas, thoughts, and products.				

From *Advancing Differentiation: Thinking and Learning for the 21st Century* by Richard M. Cash, Ed.D., copyright © 2017. This page may be reproduced for use within an individual school or district. For all other uses, contact Free Spirit Publishing Inc. at www.freespirit.com/permissions.

Teacher Checklist for a Student-Centered Classroom

AS A TEACHER:	NEVER	SOMETIMES	OFTEN	ALWAYS
I facilitate learning rather than direct it.				
I guide students to success rather than lead them.				
I understand and encourage student differences rather than expect all students to learn the same way at the same time.				
I use a variety of instructional practices, interventions, and assessments to ensure my students are successful.				
I know the content essentials and curriculum standards so my students can achieve to their highest potential.				
I set high expectations for *all* students.				

Chapter 6

The Teaching and Learning Continuum: Building Success Through Autonomy

Success is about being your best self, not about being better than others; failure is an opportunity, not a condemnation; effort is the key to success.
—Carol Dweck, author and educator

The ultimate outcome of differentiated curriculum and instruction is to cultivate the passion for learning in your students. As you differentiate, you must be knowledgeable about what turns on a learner to new information and stimulates a desire to investigate a topic further. Learning becomes autonomous when students are driven to gain greater knowledge in any study without the prodding of a teacher. This is what we envision when we say "lifelong learners." You build learning autonomy by guiding your students to take responsibility for and control of their learning. Autonomous learners find more relevance in the material, are more intrinsically motivated, and show greater gains in achievement.

All people want to be competent at meaningful tasks; it is part of our nature. Our competencies define who we are, promote our self-esteem, and help make us valuable to others. When individuals feel competent and understand the relevance of information, they are more likely to be motivated toward autonomy in future pursuits. This autonomy is what propels us to success. Robert Sternberg states that people most efficiently achieve success when they engage in purposeful and meaningful tasks. Your students' attitudes toward learning are enhanced when you provide them with learner-centered situations that build student independence. Through these situations, students are taught skills for self-directed learning. Ultimately, the learner builds an attachment to the content and is able to initiate his or her own true learning.

Learner autonomy is sometimes misinterpreted as self-guided instruction, independent study, or self-initiated learning. While these are all strategies that can and should be used when building learner autonomy, autonomy goes beyond a set of strategies. To develop learner autonomy, students need to gradually build toward independence through stages in the teaching and learning process. Dr. Diane Heacox and I have created a teaching and learning continuum to assist you in guiding your students toward greater learning autonomy. This chapter presents the conceptual model of the Teaching and Learning Continuum (TLC) (pages 122–123), the frameworks supporting it, and the various teacher/student activities and assessments within each level.

What Is the TLC?

The TLC is intended to be a guiding framework to assist you and your students in developing learner autonomy. Students may progress through this model at different times and varied paces based on their need for challenge and complexity. Additionally, students may move up through the model and then back to lower levels as new skills and content are introduced.

For example, using the TLC model in a high school civics lesson on racial disparity in the court systems, you would begin instruction to the entire class by directly teaching the structure, systems, and vocabulary of the court network *(didactic instruction)*. You would then ask students to work in groups to research the number of court cases in a particular county, the outcomes of the cases, and the racial statistics of all the cases *(facilitated instruction)*. Next, you would ask the student groups to report on their findings and derive conclusions *(coached instruction)*. As an extension to this activity, some students may choose to pursue an independent study based on the findings of the class. They will look to you to be an advisor *(consultative instruction)*. Finally, these students will present their independent study results to an authentic audience suggesting actions for change. Authentic audiences consist of people who either are practicing professionals in the discipline, invested in the use of the information, or participants who can offer purpose or direction to the work. For each project, the audience will change based on the work and the level of feedback needed.

Examples of Presentations to Authentic Audiences

- presenting to professionals in the field
- presenting to professional organizations
- writing for publications (both electronic and print)
- participating in contests and competitions
- creating a public display outside the classroom or school

The TLC model shares ideas for how you and your students design learning goals, adjust instructional methods, and construct and enact assessments. Learning goals, modes of instruction, and assessments will vary through each of the levels of the model. Teachers and students are not restricted to any of the specific strategies or ideas presented. These ideas are intended to act as guides for moving students toward learning autonomy.

Why Build Autonomy?

Developing learner autonomy not only helps your students learn, it also helps you develop as a teacher.

Autonomy Is Essential for Student Learning

Learners in the twenty-first century will either be passive receptacles and storehouses of rote information or they will manipulate knowledge and ideas to create new ideas and products. Learning does not occur as a response to teaching, but rather *through* the authentic engagement in and application of this knowledge. Today's learners need to have the skills, attitudes, and confidence that come with learning autonomy to be successful in this century.

Self-confidence is an essential life skill. Students who lack self-confidence as learners rarely find success. In many cases, they have not developed the necessary skills, such as planning, organizing, and monitoring progress of learning, that could lead them to success. Many students lack self-confidence because they lack the opportunity to develop self-direction. As you guide students through the framework of the TLC model, they gain self-confidence by gradually taking control of and becoming responsible for their own learning.

As learners build self-confidence in learning, they also develop:

- a greater desire for academic challenges
- an awareness of their learning strengths
- abilities for planning and monitoring progress toward a goal
- increased usage of critical reasoning skills, problem-solving strategies, and creative idea generation
- a deeper curiosity for further investigations
- a significant motivation toward achievement

Autonomy Is Essential for Teacher Development

Leading motivation researchers Richard Ryan and Edward Deci suggest, "teachers who are autonomy supportive (in contrast to controlling) catalyze in their students greater intrinsic motivation, curiosity, and desire for challenge."[1] Teachers who facilitate and guide, who are supportive and caring, and who construct an environment that encourages learners to flourish, can develop autonomous learners. These learners continue to learn beyond the classroom, through alternative learning methods, and with a greater degree of creativity. Crafting this kind of

---

1. Ryan, R. M., and E. L. Deci. "Self-Determination Theory and the Facilitation of Intrinsic Motivation, Social Development, and Well-Being." *American Psychologist* (January 2000): 68–78.

environment requires you as a teacher to use more expansive skills beyond didactic/direct instruction.

A classroom that encourages learner autonomy requires you to hone pedagogical skills that advance differentiated instruction. The true goal of differentiated instruction is to guide students toward greater levels of success and competency. The Multi-Tiered System of Supports (MTSS) and Response to Intervention (RTI) models also utilize these strategies and interventions to move all students to greater levels of independence and autonomy. By focusing on the needs of the individual learner to become more autonomous in learning, you take on a new role as coach, guide, and consultant.

Framework Supporting the Teaching and Learning Continuum (TLC)

The TLC model builds upon decades of research on how teachers teach and students learn. It was developed to synthesize the most effective strategies of instruction, learning, and assessment. The following three theories provide the foundation for the TLC.

The Gradual Release of Responsibility Model

A model that has informed the TLC is the Gradual Release of Responsibility model (see **Figure 6.1**). This model is most often associated with the teaching of literacy and provides scaffolding for student learning using the following steps:

1. The teacher demonstrates or models a strategy.
2. The teacher offers guided practice in a large group setting.
3. Students practice independently in small groups.
4. Students apply the strategy independently.

The Gradual Release of Responsibility model has been used successfully for many years. Optimal learning is achieved when supports and scaffolds are gradually removed. Students also shape their responsibility to learn.

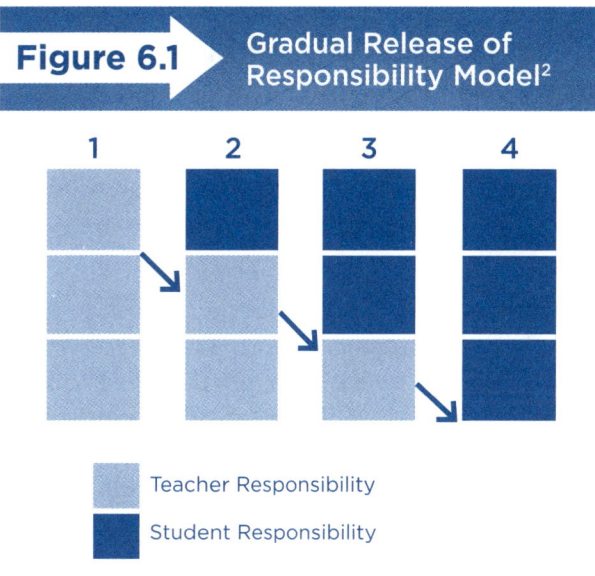

Figure 6.1 Gradual Release of Responsibility Model[2]

Self-Determination Theory

Self-determination is a theory of human motivation based on the psychological needs of survival, relatedness, and competence.[3] In a natural process of growth and development, individuals use life experiences to construct a sense of self. When people are more self-determined, they are more confident, perform better, develop greater persistence, display greater creativity, have stronger self-esteem, and maintain an overall healthier well-being.

Student Competence and Self-Regulation

Students feel empowered to learn when they have experiences and competence with skills that support new learning. When students recognize how new skills and knowledge can increase their quality of life, they build what is called *intrinsic achievement motivation*. Intrinsic achievement motivation is a personal desire or need for success or excellence. Additionally, students gain power when they can collaboratively work together with others to achieve success. (See Chapter 4 for an in-depth discussion of motivation.)

Each of the self-regulating skills listed in Chapter 5 are part of a cyclical progression of achieving academic competence (see Figure 5.3 on page 101). This design is naturally embedded within the TLC model and can act as a guide to developing learner autonomy.

---

2. Based on Pearson, P. D., and M. C. Gallagher. "The Instruction of Reading Comprehension." *Contemporary Educational Psychology*, 8 (1983): 317–345. Adapted by Richard Cash and Diane Heacox, 2008.
3. Ryan, R. M., and E. L. Deci. "Self-Determination Theory and the Facilitation of Intrinsic Motivation, Social Development, and Well-Being." *American Psychologist* (January 2000): 68–78.

As learners move upward in the TLC model, they acquire skill development, practice, reinforcement, and application of these self-regulating strategies and progress toward competency and autonomy.

Mindset Theory

As discussed in Chapter 5 on page 102, Carol Dweck has defined the mindset with which people view their own abilities as either *fixed* or *growth*. People who believe their abilities to be fixed often describe these traits as either "you have it or you don't." Those with a growth, or malleable, mindset believe that you can achieve almost anything you put your mind to with effort.

Using a Growth Mindset

Learners develop mastery of a skill through the awareness of their progress and success, which is communicated through descriptive, constructive feedback. When using a growth mindset with learners, you:

- develop a wholeness of learning
- spark innovative thinking
- strengthen a sense of belonging through partnership with others
- focus on a self-definition rather than an "others" definition
- put learners in charge of their own learning

The TLC model develops this growth mindset in both teachers and students by progressively building learner competence through relevant and meaningful tasks, descriptive and constructive feedback, and learning activities that gradually demand greater degrees of authenticity (real-world application).

The Four Levels of the TLC Model

The TLC model provides a framework for you to identify the progression of teaching, learning, and assessment systems from a teacher-controlled level to student autonomy. It is helpful to know that as a teacher you have control over your students' progress through the levels. The following are insights into how you might encourage this progression.

TLC Level 1: Didactic Instruction—Teacher Prescribed, Student Acted

At the didactic level, you (the teacher) are in charge of the learning process and control the content and the activities that build understanding. Student participation is limited based on the direction you offer. At this, the broadest level, students acquire information for recall, deliver and rehearse factual and procedural skills, and build a ground of conceptual knowledge.

Many would suggest that at this level you are enacting "direct instruction." The term "direct instruction," however, should not indicate that the learner is passively participating in the learning. On the contrary, the student is actively building an accurate understanding of the ideas and concepts at the heart of the content. You are also helping the student:

- learn a common language within the discipline
- know the vocabulary of the lessons
- gather the skills and processes

For instance, when you want to introduce a new skill, you would model the skill for the students showing them exactly the process to follow. Or, if you are introducing a unit on the Renaissance, for example, you might share artifacts and music to ground the students in the "sense" of the time period.

Through didactic instruction the student is able to build an understanding of the ideas and concepts to be covered in a unit of study. Students begin to make connections to prior learning experiences, build awareness of topics, and establish what is unique or common about the new information. At this level, you directly instruct, infuse, and prescribe specific self-regulating skills and development.

This is a very important phase of learning, especially for students from a language background other than English or for students who live in poverty. Students are developing the academic language and building the foundation for further learning. **Figure 6.2** shows how the learning is structured at this level from goal setting to instruction to assessment.

Figure 6.2 — TLC Level 1: Didactic Instruction

LEARNING GOALS	INSTRUCTION	ACTIVITIES	ASSESSMENT
Teacher: - Establishes learning goals based on state/provincial standards - Uses state/provincial standards to determine student needs - Plans for the group - Plans instruction so students cover same or similar goals - Defines and prescribes for class or groups of students	- Teacher presents lessons, provides exercises, arranges and supervises student applications (guided practice) - Teacher provides structure, direction, specificity, and clearly established purpose for learning - Teacher focuses on explicit, systematic, relevant teaching points - Teacher demonstrates explicit, deliberate, meaningful instruction - Teacher explains and models "what, how, why" prior to student independent work - Students may select activities from options provided by the teacher	- Whole-group direct instruction - Whole-group observations	- Teacher conducts evaluation and reports to students - Teacher uses established criteria - Teacher provides feedback on specified procedures as well as performance - Teacher provides students with information on their goal attainment - Students may self-evaluate based on teacher developed criteria

TLC Level 2: Facilitated Instruction—Teacher Differentiated, Student Acted

The facilitated level begins to see students more actively involved and teachers less dominating in the learning process (see **Figure 6.3** on page 118). As the teacher, you still maintain a range of control as the instructional manager of the curriculum and of the instructional and assessment processes.

You establish learning goals based on standards and allow students varied opportunities for addressing the standards through units that provide interdisciplinary connections. Learning at this level includes greater student participation through open-ended questioning and discussion. This interaction encourages students to share thoughts and ideas and to challenge beliefs and opinions. Additionally, students build listening, questioning, and thinking skills, which are essential for the more advanced levels of the TLC.

The importance of this level cannot be stressed enough. At the facilitated level, the student gains a greater degree of independence, but with your support and guidance. Learners engage in intellectual risk taking and practice self-regulation skills to stretch and grow toward autonomy. Students start to believe they have the means to learn and perform effectively on their own.

TLC Level 3: Coached Instruction—Teacher Differentiated with Student Input

The coached level of the TLC has teacher and student roles significantly changing (see **Figure 6.4** on page 118). Coaching is a learning technique. You observe the student at work and provide feedback to enhance performance or correct deficiencies. Effective feedback to enhance performance is the essential component at this level.

Figure 6.3 — TLC Level 2: Facilitated Instruction

LEARNING GOALS	INSTRUCTION	ACTIVITIES	ASSESSMENT
■ Teacher plans for specific goals based on state/provincial standards ■ Teacher uses diagnostic data to determine student specific goals	■ Student paced ■ Open-ended tasks ■ Flexible instructional groups ■ Simulations ■ Problem solving and decision making ■ Choice in content, process, or product ■ Problem-based learning ■ Critical thinking and reasoning ■ Socratic seminars	■ Small-group activities ■ Teacher-constructed learning groups ■ Stations ■ Cooperative learning groups	■ Teacher evaluates student performance based on shared criteria ■ Teacher provides feedback on content/process/product ■ Student and peer evaluation using shared criteria ■ Student and peer evaluation are reported to the teacher

Figure 6.4 — TLC Level 3: Coached Instruction

LEARNING GOALS	INSTRUCTION	ACTIVITIES	ASSESSMENT
■ State/provincial standards and teacher- and student-developed goals ■ Teacher provides students with information related to their strengths and needs and identifies individual learning goals ■ Students are given opportunity to pursue additional goals related to their learning preferences and/or interests ■ Student assumes primary responsibility for particular goals	■ Students assume primary responsibility for pursuit of particular learning goals ■ Teacher as "encourager" ■ Teacher provides resources, instruction in necessary skills and processes, feedback, and guidance ■ Student self-selection ■ Guided inquiry ■ Open choice and options ■ Compacting and acceleration ■ Active experiential learning	■ Independent learning activities ■ Flexible group options ■ Centers ■ Enrichment/extension/enhancement options ■ Service learning projects ■ Student-selected groups (special interest groups: SIGs) ■ Teacher-directed research and report ■ Project-based learning ■ Collaborative learning groups	■ Teacher and students confer regularly to monitor progress, evaluate work in progress, identify necessary improvements, and to make modifications ■ Teacher and student evaluation based upon agreed criteria

Your role as a teacher shifts from control of what and how students learn to mediation and support of student learning. During coached instruction, you engage in the students' learning by guiding their thinking, communication, data gathering and sharing, grouping configurations, and thinking techniques and strategies. You provide descriptive feedback to sustain your students' self-directed learning, and you monitor and reinforce students' self-regulating strategies for greater development of self-efficacy.

Your primary goals at the coached level are to build learners' sense of purpose, ownership, and meaning through activities and tasks that:

- anchor to larger authentic problems or issues
- involve emotional engagement
- challenge and test learners' beliefs and opinions
- reflect the complexity of the "real world"
- offer ambiguity
- require learners to cultivate and use advanced thinking tools
- encourage alternative methods of assessment
- provide opportunities for reflection on both the content and learning processes

TLC Level 4: Consultative Instruction—Teacher Managed, Student Designed and Guided

Once students guide their own learning process, they have entered the consultative level of the TLC model (see **Figure 6.5**). At this level the teacher and student roles change dramatically. Students now become the initiators and designers of their own learning, while you provide recommendations and advice. You no longer facilitate from the position of expert, but move to the position of skilled feedback provider and advisor.

Throughout this level, you act as a consultant to assist learners in applying the strategies

Figure 6.5 TLC Level 4: Consultative Instruction

LEARNING GOALS	INSTRUCTION	ACTIVITIES	ASSESSMENT
■ Students determine goals based on needs and interests with teacher advice and consultation ■ Teacher works with the student to plan the course of action but student assumes ownership, responsibility for the goal ■ Student-based goals	■ Student initiates the tasks, identifies and solves problems that arise, and faces challenges independently ■ Teacher as counselor and consultant ■ Resources/mentors beyond the classroom and school ■ Producers of knowledge ■ Innovation, transformation, ingenuity are exhibited ■ Self-awareness, self-advocacy, self-determination, and resilience are at the core for success ■ Task analysis ■ Hypothetical thinking ■ Personal critique ■ Need to defend thinking and work ■ Acceptance of personal responsibility for talent development and roles as learners	■ Self-directed learning ■ Passion projects ■ Authentic research and development ■ Problem-based learning	■ Student involvement in determining explicit criteria and evaluating performance ■ Teacher advises on criteria and provides feedback ■ Critical reflection

of self-regulation and autonomy developed in the lower levels. Learners are now in charge and responsible for constructing, implementing, and evaluating learning plans.

Assessment That Builds Autonomy

Teachers can build learning autonomy by offering appropriate intervention and assessment strategies. Students gain greater responsibility for learning when they:

- set, monitor, manage, and evaluate their own goals
- develop choice and voice (for example, What do I need? How can I get it?)
- negotiate the learning process
- utilize technology skills and competence

Inherent in the TLC is a model of assessment that can build learner autonomy (see **Figure 6.6**). As the learner moves upward toward the consultative level, the assessments naturally change from being based on a single discipline to being based on multidisciplinary projects and performances.

Assessment also shifts from imitational (regenerative tests of factual knowledge) to authentic performances (useful original products). Thinking expands from bilateral/convergent (yes/no questions) to multilateral/divergent (questions that have more than one correct answer). Learners also start to develop social interactions from collaborative production versus solo performances and move from passive recitation to social action.

By using the TLC model, you can ensure you are differentiating to build learning autonomy. Figure 6.6 gives you many examples and ideas at each stage of the model. The model can be used as a guide when reviewing your entire year's curriculum, as a pacing guide toward autonomy, or to plot units of study that can develop student autonomy. In some cases, you may find overlaps from stage to stage in the model. There is no clear delineation between stages; ascending to autonomy and self-regulation is a process along a spectrum of learning.

In addition, the TLC's design includes the three forms of assessment outlined in Chapter 4, from diagnostic (preassessments) to formative (assessment to guide the learner) to summative (assessment of completion).

Figure 6.6 — Assessment That Builds Autonomy

Axis labels: MULTIPLE DISCIPLINES ↔ SINGLE DISCIPLINE (left); AUTHENTIC ↔ IMITATION (right)

TLC LEVEL	KNOWLEDGE LEVEL	TYPE OF ASSESSMENT — DIAGNOSTIC	TYPE OF ASSESSMENT — FORMATIVE	TYPE OF ASSESSMENT — SUMMATIVE
Consultative — Student designs assessment to develop, monitor, and evaluate own learning process	**Self-Regulatory*** • Create • Produce • Hypothesize • Build • Compose • Critique • Extend • Invent • Originate • Transform	• Student-directed investigation to find problems • Personal goal setting • Proposal development	• Case study • Hypothesis development • Personal goal-setting update • Website • Progress report • Expert feedback	• Student-designed rubric • Student-designed product • Assessment by audience/expert
Coached — Teacher and student collaborate to design assessment	**Conceptual** • Evaluate • Design • Support • Adapt • Discriminate • Analyze • Connect • Deconstruct • Differentiate • Examine • Infer • Integrate • Test for	• Interest survey • Contract • Self-preassessment	• Lab/experiment • Thesis statement • Self-assessment/progress report • Discussion forum • Simulation • Wiki • Reciprocal teaching	• Student- and teacher-negotiated rubric • Teacher- and student-negotiated product • Self-assessment • Peer review • Portfolio • Research report • Contract completion
Facilitated — Teacher constructs assessment with options for individual learners or groups	**Procedural** • Construct • Perform • Solve • Reason • Understand • Analogize • Redesign • Predict • Map • Relate • Show • Examine • Inspect • Categorize • Classify • Clarify • Compare • Conclude • Contrast • Demonstrate • Distinguish • Explain • Illustrate • Interpret • Paraphrase • Predict • Represent • Reorganize • Summarize • Translate • Apply • Develop • Display • Execute • Implement • Model • Solve • Use	• KWL • Guided questioning • Group discussion • Mind map • Inventory of learning styles/modes/preferences	• Discussions • Reflections • Demonstration • Homework • Research • Exit cards • Oral presentation • Games • Check-ins • E-bulletin boards/e-chats	• Subjective assessment (open-ended essay) • Poster • Research paper • Teacher-designed rubric • Debate • Group project • Assessment stations
Didactic — Teacher constructs assessment based on whole-group learning	**Factual** • Recall • Remember • Verify • Respond • Match • Choose • Define • Describe • Identify • Label • List • Locate/Find • Name • Recite • Say • Tell	• Teacher-constructed pretest	• Quizzes • Homework • Practice exams • Class participation • Performance assessments	• Objective assessment (multiple choice, true/false) • Standardized tests

*Note: Self-regulatory replaces metacognitive as the fourth knowledge dimension in this chart.

Teaching and Learning Continuum (TLC)

CONSULTATIVE

TEACHER ROLE	STUDENT ROLE	LEVEL OF INDEPENDENCE	LEARNING FOCUS
Advisement on learning plan	Conduct self-guided learning	Autonomous	Metacognition Self-awareness
<ul><li>Provide consultation and feedback as needed</li></ul>	<ul><li>Develop, implement, and complete a learning plan</li><li>Seek advisement as necessary and appropriate</li><li>Produce, present, and evaluate</li><li>Develop self-efficacy</li></ul>	Student independently: <ul><li>Develops a learning plan</li><li>Monitors progress</li><li>Documents process and progress</li><li>Seeks advisement as necessary and appropriate</li><li>Concludes learning</li><li>Presents results authentically</li><li>Evaluates process and results</li></ul>	Students: <ul><li>Evaluate</li><li>Critique</li><li>Create</li></ul> By: Innovating, designing, and creating new authentic plans, ideas, and products

COACHED

TEACHER ROLE	STUDENT ROLE	LEVEL OF INDEPENDENCE	LEARNING FOCUS
Monitor and support learning progress	Refine skills and deepen understanding	Collaborative	Conceptual
<ul><li>Feedback/ conferencing</li><li>Guided practice</li><li>Resource channel</li></ul>	<ul><li>Listen, consider, practice, retry</li><li>Rethink, revise, reflect, refine, recycle</li><li>Develop self-regulation</li></ul>	Student poses and teacher refines: <ul><li>Problem</li><li>Design</li><li>Timelines</li><li>Process</li><li>Evaluation criteria</li></ul>	Students: <ul><li>Apply</li><li>Analyze</li><li>Create</li></ul> By: Applying analyzed information to formulate or compile to make new ideas

Based on work by Richard Cash and Diane Heacox, 2008.

continued ➡

Teaching and Learning Continuum (TLC) (continued)

FACILITATED

TEACHER ROLE	STUDENT ROLE	LEVEL OF INDEPENDENCE	LEARNING FOCUS
Provide structure for and facilitation of learning	Actively participate in constructing, examining, and extending meaning	Guided	Procedural
Examples include: - Discussion - Problem-based learning - Questions (open-ended) - Socratic seminar	Examples include: - Listen, question, consider, explain - Pose/define problems, solve, evaluate - Answer and explain, reflect, rethink - Consider, explain, challenge, justify	Teacher provides options and student: - Selects from among topics - Completes open-ended assignments - Poses and answers questions - Follows preset timelines - Performs self-evaluation according to prepared criteria - Develops skills of problem solving - Documents stages in the process	Students: - Understand - Apply By: Translating, interpreting, reorganizing, and applying information

DIDACTIC

TEACHER ROLE	STUDENT ROLE	LEVEL OF INDEPENDENCE	LEARNING FOCUS
Provide direct instruction	Passive participant who receives, takes in, and responds	Directed	Factual
Examples include: - Demonstration/modeling - Lecture - Questions (focused on convergent thinking)	Examples include: - Observe, attempt, practice, refine - Listen, watch, take notes, question - Answer, give responses	Teacher constructs and student: - Makes choices - Finds answers - Uses resources - Plans time - Uses basic elements of critical and creative thinking - Sets goals - Follows through - Discusses goal attainment	Students: - Remember - Recall By: Verifying factual knowledge

Based on work by Richard Cash and Diane Heacox, 2008.

From *Advancing Differentiation: Thinking and Learning for the 21st Century* by Richard M. Cash, Ed.D., copyright © 2017. This page may be reproduced for use within an individual school or district. For all other uses, contact Free Spirit Publishing Inc. at www.freespirit.com/permissions.

PART TWO

Putting Thinking Skills to Use in the Classroom

When you differentiate instruction, you provide students with avenues to own their learning. Students accomplish this by thinking critically and creatively about the content and by solving problems that are meaningful and relevant to their lives. The following five chapters supply an understanding of the essential thinking skills and offer tools to help your students develop these skills.

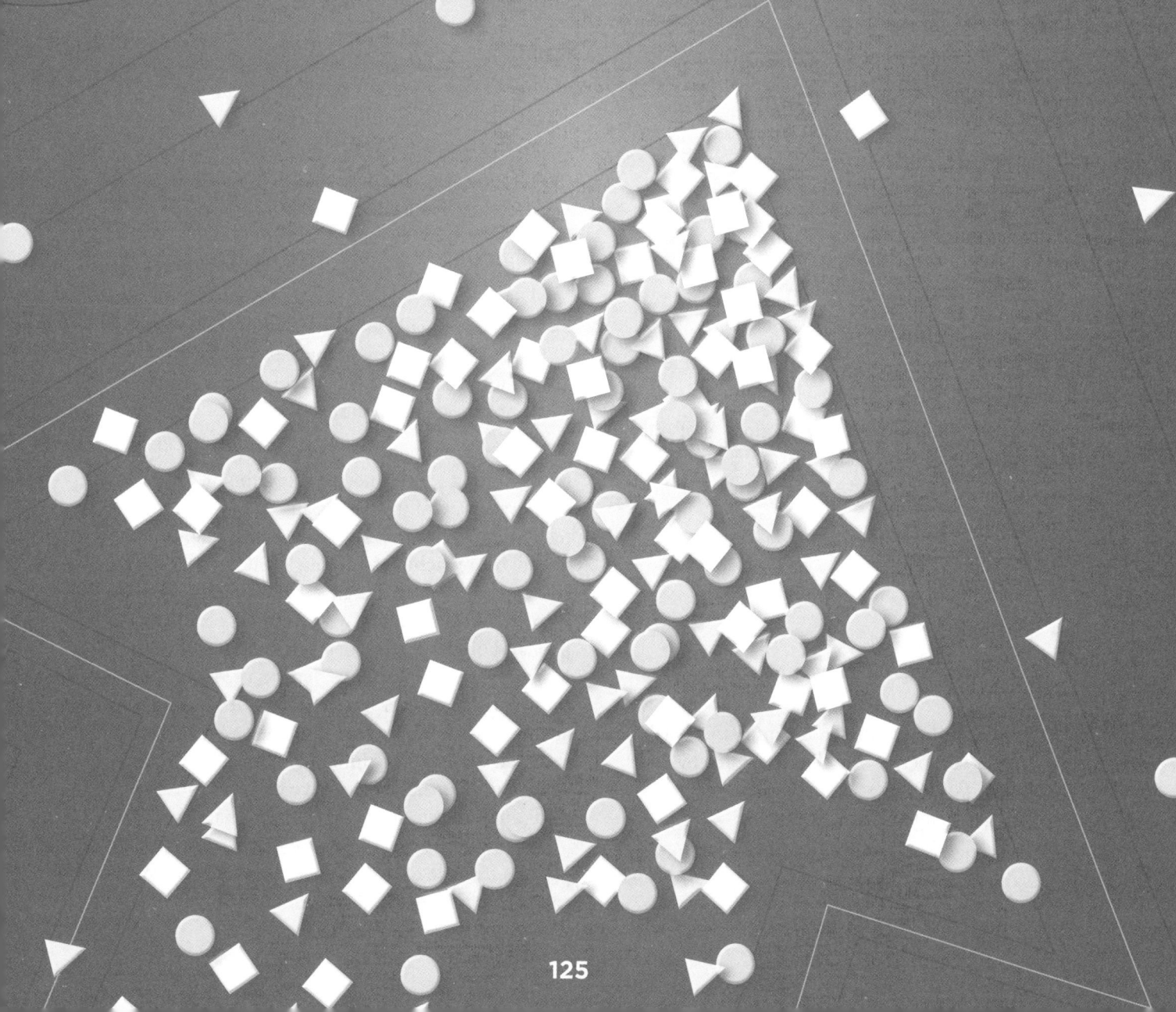

Chapter 7

The Thinking Classroom

I like a teacher who gives you something to take home to think about besides homework.

—Edith Ann (played by Lily Tomlin)

As we continue into the twenty-first century and our world grows increasingly more complex, the need for our students to be active thinkers becomes more apparent. Every day new problems arise that require more sophisticated solutions. Huge developments in communication and technology have occurred in a relatively short span of time. Just think:

- the first iPad was released in the United States in 2010
- social media sites with widespread use, such as Facebook and Twitter, didn't exist prior to 2004
- E-readers, such as the Kindle, were not in popular use until 2007
- YouTube was a "revolutionary" concept as recently as 2005

Jobs that didn't exist at the beginning of this century are now in big demand:

- search engine optimization (SEO) strategist
- social media manager
- blogger
- app designer
- content developer

According to the Institute for the Future (IFTF):

- People are living longer, meaning there will be greater competition in the workforce by 2020.
- Technologies will be able to increase our capacities and extend our abilities, meaning that which *can* be automated *will* be automated, extinguishing repetitive labor.
- Computation and mathematics will be more in demand, meaning that data will be used to make our world both more efficient and more complex.
- New communication tools will replace our current modes, meaning students will need to be savvy with multiple forms of communication, especially visual.
- Organizations will expand to "superstructures," meaning the workers of the future will be interacting with greater numbers of people and forms of production and creativity will be essential.
- The world will continue to be more connected, meaning the United States and Europe will no longer hold the key to future job growth, innovation, and political power.

The flattening and shrinking of the world necessitates a greater need for collaboration and cooperation. Unfortunately, automation and new technologies have made it more convenient for us to rely on a machine to do our thinking, which creates a concern I call "intellectual laziness." Students who rely on technology to solve their problems, plan and organize their days, or simply tell them what to eat, are, in essence, letting the technology think for them. Over time, the practice of thinking atrophies to a point where students are reluctant to think on their feet or think for themselves. To guard against intellectual laziness, we teachers must infuse thinking into our everyday instructional practices.

In addition to all these exponential changes happening, the role of a teacher is also changing. We can no longer be considered fonts of all knowledge preparing students for the expected. Just the opposite, we now need to be facilitators of learning that prepares our children for the *unexpected*.

10 Skills for the Future Workforce

The IFTF states that expanding globalization, smart machines, and advances in new medias are reshaping the skills necessary for success in the future workforce. Based on the work of IFTF and other organizations, I crafted a list of 10 skills every teacher should be teaching and infusing into today's classroom.[1]

1. **Flexibility.** Teaching students how to be flexible in their thinking and behavior will be essential for the rapid changes ahead.

2. **Social awareness.** Students who can "read" the social landscape, adapt as necessary, and connect in meaningful ways will be best able to make an impact in their chosen careers.

3. **Cross-cultural competencies.** The workforce of the future will be more globally connected, requiring workers to operate in various cultural settings.

4. **Conceptual thinking.** Rather than thinking factually, workers will be going beyond specific content and connecting diverse content areas, which requires thinking conceptually.

5. **Technology adaptability.** As technology expands and becomes more sophisticated, workers will be creating new forms of media and using them to grow the economy.

6. **Creativity.** The ability to go beyond the consumption of knowledge and create new ideas is critical for success.

7. **Self-regulation.** With the expansion of technology and the ever present load of information, students must learn how to balance their affect, behaviors, and cognition to avoid distractions, remain persistent, and follow through on tasks.

8. **Critical reasoning to solve complex problems.** Both divergent and convergent thinking will be necessary to solve yet unknown problems.

9. **Communication.** Beyond the face-to-face, our students will need to learn how to work productively and efficiently through various forms of media and technology.

10. **Resiliency.** Students must learn how to bounce back from mistakes or failures, learn from them, and move on to create new ideas.

How many times have we said to our students, *"Now think about this..."*? Sometimes we may have been amazed by what they came up with, while other times we were frustrated because they did not think deep enough or generate any new information. What may be lacking in our teaching and instructional process is the art of constructing a framework, or context, for students to do their thinking. This chapter will define what thinking is, share some characteristics of a thinking student, and suggest how you might frame your curriculum to encourage students to do a better job of thinking.

What Is Thinking?

Thinking is the mental process of using information to reach a conclusion. For students to do a good job at thinking, they must be presented with frameworks that can assist them in being more proficient at the act of thinking. Students can be at least four different types of thinkers at any given time.

Four Types of Thinkers

Receivers are those who ingest information at face value. They don't seek to analyze or validate the information. They simply take it "as is."

Intuitive thinkers use their gut feelings to validate thoughts. Based on past experiences, they evaluate what they are receiving and then make a decision based on that information. This type of thinker will often be critical of authority.

Sequential thinkers hold information to a set of criteria to interpret, such as rules or procedures. Sequential thinkers take time to think things through in a step-by-step manner. Then they form opinions based on the information. This type of thinker may overthink information or spend too much time thinking about solutions and find it difficult to reach a conclusion.

---

1. Institute for the Future. "Future Work Skills 2020." Palo Alto, CA: Institute for the Future for the University of Phoenix Research Institute, 2011 (iftf.org/uploads/media/SR-1382A_UPRI_future_work_skills_sm.pdf); Oxford Economics. "Workforce 2020: Building a Strategic Workforce for the Future." (2015) (oxfordeconomics.com/workforce2020); PwC. "The Future of Work: Reshaping the Workplace." (2014) (pwc.com/gx/en/issues/talent/future-of-work.html); Ettling, M. "Workforce 2020: How Ready Are You?" *Forbes.com* (Sept. 11, 2014) (forbes.com/sites/sap/2014/09/11/workforce-2020-how-ready-are-you).

Finally, **connected thinkers** are able to connect what is learned in one discipline to another. These thinkers take into account the views of others and are open and fair-minded. They stretch to look beyond the facts to find new perspectives that may explain the implications of actions. Connected thinkers are the thinkers we should be developing in our classrooms.

Divergent Thinking vs. Convergent Thinking

In addition to different types of thinkers, there are different types of thinking. The two main types are divergent thinking and convergent thinking. Both are useful and necessary, depending on the situation.

Divergent thinking is the process of generating and creating new and imaginative ideas. When you "diverge" from the usual pathways of thinking and attempt to find more than one right answer, you are using divergent thinking.

Guiding principles to keep in mind for divergent thinking are:

- **Keep an open mind.** Don't critique or judge ideas until all ideas have been considered.
- **Come up with many ideas.** The more ideas you have to choose from the better the outcome.
- **Be accepting of all ideas.** You never know when and if something will work.
- **Use all of your senses.** Think with your eyes, ears, nose, mouth, and skin. The brain acquires information through your senses; using all of them opens up multiple avenues of thought.
- **Sleep on it!** Sometimes the best solutions come after a good night's sleep.
- **Take risks.** Break out of your comfort zone and boldly go where you've never gone before.
- **Hitchhike on others' ideas.** Listen to other people's ideas and add to them, elaborate on them, or attach your own ideas to them.

Convergent thinking is thinking through a set of logical steps to come up with one right answer. Convergent thinking is not necessarily in opposition to divergent thinking. Whereas divergent thinking seeks multiple answers, you will eventually need to settle on the one answer that will solve the problem (convergent thinking).

Principles to keep in mind for convergent thinking are:

- **Clarify the problem.** Find out exactly what needs to be solved or resolved.
- **Evaluate the solution.** Just finding a solution is not enough. You must know if the solution is working or not.
- **Look at all options.** Problems may require different solutions than those that were tried in the past.
- **Be reflective.** Keep asking yourself, "Is this working? Am I getting to resolution?"
- **Sleep on it!** Again, sometimes the best solutions come after a good night's sleep.
- **Be positive.** Don't be critical of your ideas or others' ideas. Look for the strengths and positive aspects of all ideas.

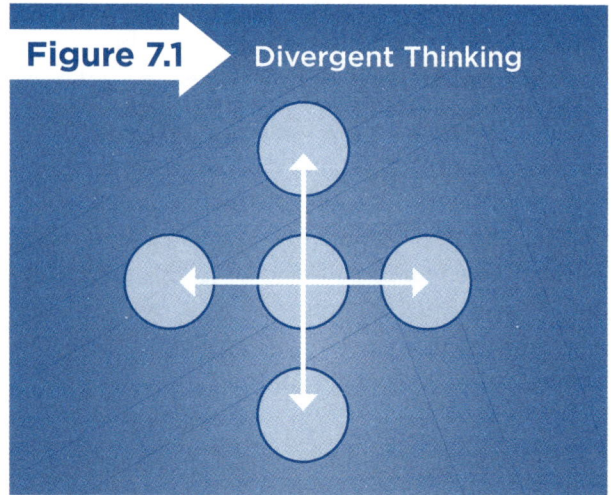

Figure 7.1 Divergent Thinking

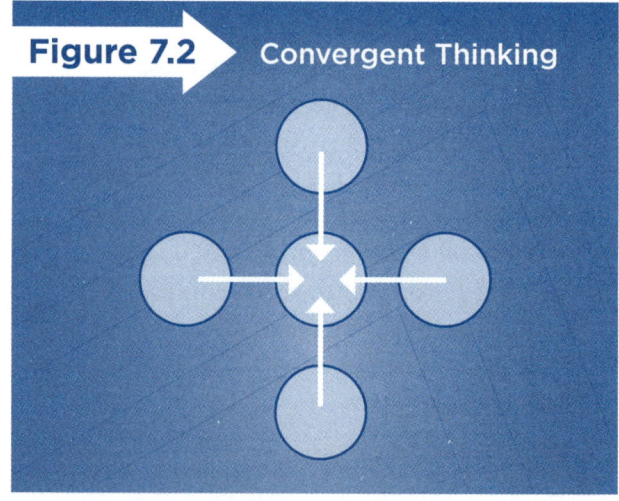

Figure 7.2 Convergent Thinking

Characteristics of a Thinking Student

For students to do well in the act of thinking, they must possess several characteristics (see checklist on page 137).

Thinking students have the following capacities:

- **Openness.** They have an active imagination, are alert to their own and others' feelings, are curious, and enjoy variety.
- **Ego-control.** They are able to look both inside and outside themselves for solutions and understand that ideas are limitless.
- **Spontaneity.** They are free from the constraints of their feelings and are willing to trust their own instincts.

Thinking students have a willingness to be:

- **Flexible.** Like athletes, thinkers are able to bend and think of things in new and different ways.
- **Adaptable.** They can take what was learned in one setting and apply it to a new setting or problem.
- **Intellectual risk takers.** They are open to trying new lines of thinking or doing.

Thinking students have a tolerance for:

- **Ambiguity.** They can appreciate the uncertainty of problems and situations.
- **Complexity.** They realize any given situation or problem has many different layers, perspectives, and points of view.
- **Disorder.** They understand, respect, and anticipate the unpredictable nature of life.

Finally, thinking students are:

- task and learning motivated
- persevering
- not expecting immediate gratification or closure

Characteristics of a Thinking Classroom

For a classroom to be conducive to effective thinking, it must have the following traits (see checklist on page 138).

- **Encourages intellectual independence.** Students are encouraged and expected to think beyond what is delivered in the curriculum.
- **Recognizes and nurtures brain development.** All aspects of the classroom support and care for the basic needs of the students as well as provide for greater cognitive growth.
- **Allows and encourages intellectual risk taking.** Students are encouraged to stretch intellectually and explore new fields of study.
- **Eliminates stereotyping, bias, oppression, and bullying.** Students feel safe being themselves.
- **Delays gratification.** The emphasis in a thinking classroom is on hard work and effort, not on immediate reward.
- **Nurtures social relationships and community.** All students feel part of the classroom and school community. Each person has something to offer the group.
- **Fosters a supportive environment where all learners have choices and a sense of control.** Choices are meaningful to learners, and learners must feel as though they have control over making those choices.
- **Builds learners' responsibility for the learning.** Your job is to teach; the learner's job is to learn.
- **Is enjoyable and fun!** Students must want to be in the classroom. That can be accomplished with an environment that includes humor as well as pleasurable activities.

Characteristics of a Thinking Curriculum

For a curriculum to promote thinking skills, it must include the following characteristics (see checklist on page 139).

- **Focuses on learning goals.** Students are clear about where they are going and what they will learn in each lesson.
- **Presents essential questions.** The unit is designed around essential questions worth investigating (see Chapter 2).
- **Is concept-based.** The unit has a focus on the "big picture" concepts.

- **Scaffolds intellectual readiness toward independence.** Students are provided with sufficient modeling, practice, and independence to become autonomous in their learning (see Chapter 6).
- **Provides interrelated learning.** Units are interdisciplinary or provide cross-curricular connections.
- **Inspires emotional engagement.** Students find emotional reasons (joy, trust, surprise, anticipation, and excitement) to engage in learning tasks or discussions.
- **Offers ambiguity.** At times, not all the answers are available, and students will be expected to do further investigation to unravel the mysteries.
- **Introduces provocative issues that challenge students' beliefs, understanding, or prior knowledge.** The content stimulates conversations that arouse feelings and move students to action.
- **Contains room for further questioning and investigation.** Some students may be interested in seeking out additional information within a unit of study. Resources and materials should be made available for such studies.
- **Is relevant to the learner and encourages personal connections.** Students find the content personally meaningful and relevant to their current lives.
- **Provides authentic learning opportunities that require authentic products.** The best learning and outcomes occur when the products are useful and are reviewed by the audience who will use them or by a professional in that field of study.
- **Challenges all students and builds competence.** Building competence is building confidence. All learners want to be competent at meaningful tasks.
- **Includes assessment and evaluation that are focused on student learning development.** For quality student growth, students must be informed about what they don't know, where they are in the learning, and how close they are to meeting the goal.
- **Builds reflective practices into every learning experience.** All students need time to reflect on what they are learning. You must provide time within the lessons for students to stop, make notes, discuss with others, and document what they have learned.

The checklists on pages 137–139 of the characteristics of a thinking student, classroom, and curriculum can be used as guides before, during, and after instruction. They can also be used and posted as general guidelines of what is expected in a thinking classroom. Students can use the student checklist to monitor their own thinking. You can use the curriculum checklist as a reminder when developing units, lessons, and activities. The thinking classroom checklist can also be shared with parents to show them the expectations in the classroom.

Methods for Developing Intellectually Disciplined Thinkers

Just like the skill of walking, thinking is a natural process that begins with small baby steps (everyday thinking, such as which shirt to wear, what to eat for lunch, and when to go to bed) and develops to running (advanced levels of thinking, such as which route to take when a road is closed or what to do about oil spills in the Gulf of Mexico).

Though our brains are designed to think, advanced levels of thinking occur in a relatively newer area of our brain. Our brains have evolved in such a way that we have progressed from simply solving problems of daily survival to more advanced levels of thinking and problem solving. The advanced levels of thought take place in the neocortex or "new brain" (frontal lobe and prefrontal cortex).

All students are capable of advanced levels of thinking, not only the gifted students. Just as learning to walk takes practice, so too does the art of thinking. And just as learning to be a good runner requires stamina and endurance to continually run faster and farther, so too does developing techniques for advanced thinking. As a teacher, your job is to coach students in achieving these advanced levels of thinking.

Method #1: Explicitly Teach Thinking Skills

Students cannot learn to think critically or creatively on their own or by simply being asked to think. Direct, systematic instruction of thinking skills and creativity-building activities—through introduction and development of the skills and repeated practice in application—are required. Each skill should be labeled as it is being taught so students understand the skill is a specific tool that they own and can use whenever appropriate—at school, at home, at work—throughout life.

Students need to be made aware of when each skill is best employed. Students also need practice and guidance with the skill and shown how it can be used in a variety of settings and ways.

The Teaching Thinking Skills: Lesson Format Template on pages 140–141 can help you directly teach a thinking skill or strategy. See **Figure 7.3** for an example.

Method #2: Use Guided Thinking

Guided thinking is the practice of helping students improve their thinking by engaging them in

---

Figure 7.3   Teaching Thinking Skills: Lesson Format Example

Thinking Skill: SCAMPER

Focus Activity
Display a smartphone, a telephone, and two tin cans connected with a piece of string. Ask students:
- "What do all these items have in common?"
- "How did we get from the tin cans to the telephone to the smartphone?"
- "What do you think will be the next great invention in communication?"

Objective
Students will be able to use the technique of SCAMPER to come up with innovative ideas.

Modeling
Definition of the skill: SCAMPER is a thinking technique to help you come up with new ideas by using seven different strategies: substitute, combine, adapt, modify, put to other uses, eliminate, and revise.
Explain how and when to use: SCAMPER can be used when you are asked to create a novel idea or project, or you are trying to solve a common everyday problem. Come up with a new idea for each of the seven strategies.
Ways to remember the skill: The word SCAMPER is an acronym that stands for each of the seven strategies: **S**ubstitute, **C**ombine, **A**dapt, **M**odify, **P**ut to other uses, **E**liminate, **R**evise.

Practice Activity
Ask students: "How could you improve upon a pen?"
- "What could you **substitute** on a pen to make it better?"
- "What could you **combine** with a pen to improve upon it?"
- "How could you **adapt** a pen for use in various situations?"
- "In what ways could you **modify** a pen to meet your needs?"
- "How might you **put it to uses other** than writing?"
- "What characteristics of a pen could you **eliminate** to make it better?"
- "What characteristics of a pen could you **revise**, reorder, or rearrange to make it better?"

Reflection/Metacognition
Ask students:
- "When might you use SCAMPER in your school or personal lives?"
- "Can you think of products that may have been designed using the SCAMPER method?"
- "How could you use the SCAMPER method to help you be more successful?"

knowing what they are thinking at the beginning of a study, monitoring their thinking throughout the study, and understanding what they have accomplished at the end of a study. Using formative assessment (see Chapter 4, page 78) is an excellent way of keeping students in tune with where they are in the thinking process from the beginning to the end of the unit. Activities within the unit should also be designed to engage students in actively thinking about and processing important ideas, topics, and issues. See page 142 for a blank Guided Thinking Template, and **Figures 7.4** and **7.5** for partially completed subject-specific examples.

Method #3: Teach Students to Think *About* Thinking: Metacognition

All great thinkers spend time thinking about the process of thinking. We should also be teaching our students this process as well. When René Descartes, the renowned French philosopher said, "I think, therefore I am," he was not only speaking about existing as a human, but about what makes us human: the profound ability to think about our actions, thoughts, and ideas. Thinking is a process that helps us develop our "self," the person who we are or want to become.

Students must learn the process of metacognition in order to achieve greater success in learning. Metacognition assists in the development of self-regulation (described more completely in Chapter 5). When students are able to think through all steps of the learning process, from beginning to end, they can better judge what their outcome will be. During the learning process it is very important that students monitor their efficacy—their capacity to produce the required effect. This capacity to produce comes from the effort the learner is willing to put forward. Students achieve because of working hard and using effort, not from innate ability.

Students sometimes fail or do not achieve success due to low self-esteem. Self-esteem is a primary key to well-being and happiness. Building self-esteem is about recognizing what you are good at and what strengths you possess. Knowing these abilities, putting them to use, and then identifying how those abilities and strengths propelled you toward success is a major factor in developing self-esteem. Learners must also understand that mistakes or failures may be signals to put forth more effort next time. Remember, success without failure or effort is pure luck!

Student Perception Questionnaire

Page 143 provides a questionnaire that teachers can administer to their students to help them guide their own metacognition and self-regulation. First, students need to identify their level of motivation or attention for the upcoming activity, because how they feel about a learning situation will determine how much focus they give to the learning. Students should find ways to monitor, control, or adjust their attitude throughout the activity (**efficacy**). Secondly, students should be openly aware of all the tasks involved in the activity and the skills required (**regulation**). If they don't understand any component of the activity they should know who to ask questions and how to ask, or they should have the resources available to them to find the answers. Students also need to have an understanding of how they will use previously learned skills and processes within the new learning, and how to apply those skills and processes. Thirdly, students should build their support network and strengths as a learner by building their own confidence (**self-esteem**). They should know who to ask for emotional or moral support throughout the learning, recognize their strengths, and celebrate their accomplishments. Finally, students must be able to reflect on what they learned, how they felt about the learning process, and what changes they might make in the next round of learning (**metacognition**).

Method #4: Create Work Plans

Another strategy for assisting students in building self-regulation and metacognition is to have them create a work plan before a project begins. Page 144 includes a work plan template that students can use to set their direction, maintain and monitor their progress, and evaluate how effective they were in completing a project.

Set a SMART Goal

The work plan begins with students setting a SMART goal. SMART is an acronym used as a planning device to help students focus their efforts

Figure 7.4 — Guided Thinking: Math Example

GUIDED QUESTION	PRIOR TO INSTRUCTION	DURING INSTRUCTION	AFTER INSTRUCTION
What is an unknown?	I'm not sure what an "unknown" is.	I learned that the "unknown" is a number we are looking for and it is represented by the letter X.	When I see a problem with a bunch of letters in it rather than numbers, I know that I can use math to figure out all the unknowns.
Describe the process of finding an unknown.	In most of my math, I have either added or subtracted to find the answer.		
How does working backward help identify missing numbers?	I'm not sure.	When I work backward I can use the opposite operation to make sure I have the right answer.	

Figure 7.5 — Guided Thinking: History Example

GUIDED QUESTION	PRIOR TO INSTRUCTION	DURING INSTRUCTION	AFTER INSTRUCTION
Describe independence.	It's when I do things on my own.	In this unit, independence is about a city, state, or country being self-governed.	
In what ways did the colonists work toward building their own government?	I learned in my elementary classes that the colonists tried several different types of governments that failed before they decided upon the democracy structure we now have.		
List the colonies in order.	I only remember: Connecticut, Delaware, Massachusetts, Pennsylvania, Rhode Island, Virginia		

on what they want to accomplish. The goal is formatted to define *what* the student will do, *how* they will do it, and *why* it's important. The more precise the goal, the better the goal can be measured and students can realize their learning.

SMART Goals

S = Specific: In plain language, students spell out exactly what it is they must accomplish. Tell them to avoid general statements such as "Get an A on this assignment." A more specific goal would be "Achieve at least 90% of the total points on this project."

M = Measurable: Students set a time line and criteria for measuring their progress toward the goal. This will help them stay on track, see their progress, make adjustments when needed, and feel the satisfaction of their efforts. Measurable goals answer the questions of "Where?" "When?" "For how long?" and "By how much?"

A = Achievable: Have students set goals they can truly achieve. Setting unattainable goals will only hinder their growth. Instruct them to set the goal high enough to be challenging, but still within reach.

R = Realistic: Similar to achievable, students should make the goal something they want, are willing to work toward, and have the skills and support to achieve. Tell students to avoid being overly aggressive or under achieving. They must believe in themselves and be willing to stretch to reach the goal.

T = Timely: Related to measurable, students must set an end point for the goal. They should keep the time line reasonable and short-term, and plan to meet the goal within six weeks.

Once students set a SMART goal, they must decide what work habits they need to employ to achieve their goal. For example, if the goal is: "Achieve at least 90% of the total points by the end of this project," work habits might include:

- Attendance and punctuality: be in school and on time every day
- Productivity: get motivated to work hard
- Initiative: get started doing the work without being reminded or prodded
- Cooperation: get along with, listen to, and support my class members
- Accuracy: pay attention to details and ensure I am working through mistakes
- Diligence: put forth effort and work until the work gets done
- Open-mindedness: be willing to try new ideas, graciously accept constructive criticism, and embrace creativity
- Honesty, fairness, and trustworthiness: be a good person, do unto others as I would have them do to me

Everyone needs support from time to time. Ask students: Who or what will be your supports? Support can be people who can assist them when they make mistakes, have questions, or need a shoulder to cry on. Or support may be a place they can go for quiet, reflection, time alone, or to rejuvenate their thinking. Support can even be an item such as a lucky hat that brings them ideas, joy, or strength. Ask students: Do you believe yourself to be "someone who can do it" or do you believe yourself to be "someone who can't"? Tell them to decide which frame of mind they are in and make sure that it is one that supports them in achieving their goal.

Use Check-Ins

While students are working toward their goal, they can use check-ins to help them stay on task. When they check in with you, encourage them to ask guiding questions such as:

- How can I make my project better?
- Am I getting close to what is required?
- Are there things I could be doing that can help me go above and beyond what is required?

When checking in with a peer, students can ask questions such as:

- What suggestions do you have that could improve my project?
- How might I enhance the components I've included so far?
- What part of my project stands out to you?

Students can also check in with parents or other adults as a way to inform them of what is occurring in the classroom. In this case, students may want to start a discussion in the following ways:

- The part of my project that I am most proud of is . . .
- The most difficult aspect of this project has been . . .
- I have worked the hardest on . . .

Finally, encourage students to check in with themselves and reflect on the effort they put forth. They can ask themselves questions such as:

- If I were to do a project like this again, I might . . .
- The most time-consuming part of this project was . . . Therefore, I will need to . . .
- Because of this project, I have come to understand that I am good at . . .

Method #5: Reflection Logs

When the work is complete, have students reflect on how they did. They should truthfully evaluate their initial estimation of what they wanted to accomplish, how they felt working on the project, how much effort they put forth throughout the process, how close they came to meeting the goal, and how they feel about their accomplishment. As with every accomplishment, students should take time to celebrate the good work they did and reflect on what they might do better next time.

The Student Reflection Log (page 145) can be used to assist learners in building reflection and metacognitive skills. At the beginning of the lesson or unit of study, students fill in the top part of the form that seeks information about what the student already knows about the topic and what they wonder about the topic. At the end of the unit of study, students document what they have learned about the topic and what they would like to know more about related to the topic. There is also space for students to let you know what they liked about the unit, what they didn't like, what they didn't understand, and what suggestions they have for improvements for future teaching of the unit.

General Strategies to Improve Student Thinking

Use thinking skills every day and all the time—both you and your students.

- Use broad, open-ended questions.
- Use wait-time #1. Before asking students to respond to a question, allow at least 10 seconds for students to process their ideas and answers.
- Use wait-time #2. After students have answered questions, ask them to pause and think for at least 10 seconds about which answers seemed most reasonable, which answers they would add to, which answers were less grounded in evidence, and so on.
- Use follow-up statements or questions for deeper thinking, such as:
  - "Tell me more."
  - "Can you clarify your answer?"
  - "Provide me with evidence to support your answer."
  - "Tell me how you got to that answer."
- Use focused, directed thinking strategies in every lesson.
- Plan instruction that incorporates and uses Higher Order Thinking Skills (HOTS) and expect students to use HOTS in questioning, product work, and group work every day.
- Make students aware of their thinking process.
- Model thinking and share your own metacognition on thinking with students.
- Always encourage students to ask questions.

Teach Students How to Ask Questions

Students must move beyond simply answering questions to having the ability to ask good questions. Based on the work by the Right Question Institute (rightquestion.org) and their Question Formulation Technique (QFT), here are steps to teach your students how to ask good questions and more effectively participate in class. Use the following strategy to encourage your students to produce, improve, and align questions that contribute to robust classroom discussions (see **Figure 7.6** on page 136).

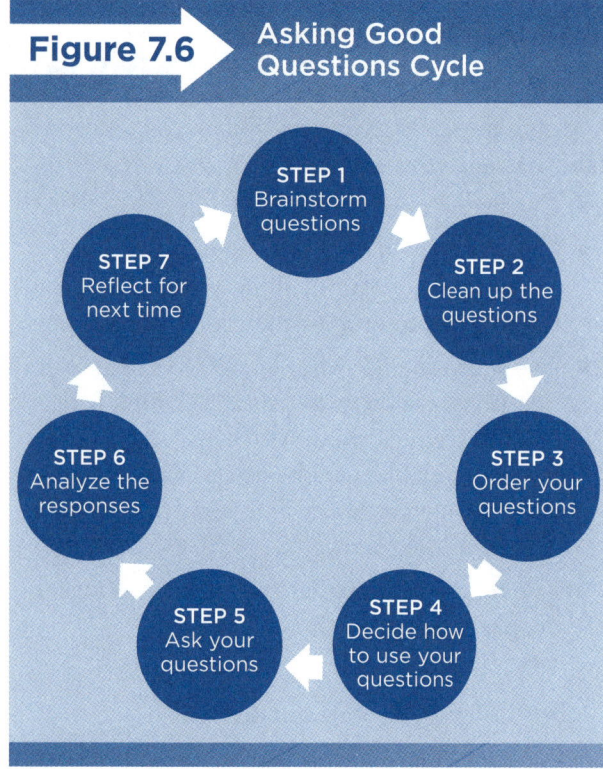

Figure 7.6 — Asking Good Questions Cycle

- STEP 1 Brainstorm questions
- STEP 2 Clean up the questions
- STEP 3 Order your questions
- STEP 4 Decide how to use your questions
- STEP 5 Ask your questions
- STEP 6 Analyze the responses
- STEP 7 Reflect for next time

Seven Steps to Asking Good Questions

Step 1. Brainstorm questions. Keep in mind the rules of brainstorming (see page 185):

- Write down as many questions as you can think of.
- Don't evaluate the questions at this point.
- Listen to others' questions and try to piggyback on them.
- Make sure you are asking a question and not making a statement.

Step 2. Clean up the questions. After you have generated a good number of questions:

- Put the questions into categories, such as fact-finding questions, hypothetical questions, or creative questions.
- Review the pros and cons of each question, looking for strong questions that are open-ended, divergent, and will require intellectual energy to answer.
- Rewrite questions if necessary to make them more complex or sophisticated.

Step 3. Order your questions.

- Put your questions into an order that makes sense, with the most important, "need to know" questions first and the more complex, deep questions last.
- Be able to articulate why you ordered the questions the way you did.

Step 4. Decide how to use your questions. Will the questions be used to deepen understanding, uncover information, or further the discussion? Know how you intend to use the questions and why.

Step 5. Ask your questions.

- Be sure to listen to the questions others are asking; you don't want to ask the same or similar questions.
- Listen to the responses to others' questions and to your questions.
- Record the responses; don't try to write the entire response, just a summary.

Step 6. Analyze the responses. Analyze the responses by answering some of the following questions:

- What kinds of answers did you receive?
- What kinds of answers did others receive?
- Why did you or others receive better responses?
- How well did others understand your questions?
- Did you need to clarify or restate the questions?
- How well did your questions add to the discussion?
- Did your questions produce a new line of thought?
- Were your questions ones that kept people thinking?

Step 7. Reflect for next time. Now that you have asked some questions and analyzed the responses, consider what you will do again and what you will change next time.

Checklist of Characteristics of a Thinking Student

CHARACTERISTIC	NOT YET	JUST BEGINNING	I'M TRYING	ALMOST THERE	THIS IS ME!
Open to new ideas					
Able to see from others' points of view					
Spontaneous					
Flexible					
Adaptable					
Intellectual risk taker					
Enjoys ambiguity					
Likes complexity					
Understands disorder					
Motivated to complete a task					
Will persevere until an answer is found					

From *Advancing Differentiation: Thinking and Learning for the 21st Century* by Richard M. Cash, Ed.D., copyright © 2017. This page may be reproduced for use within an individual school or district. For all other uses, contact Free Spirit Publishing Inc. at www.freespirit.com/permissions.

Checklist of Characteristics of a Thinking Classroom

CHARACTERISTIC	NOT YET	JUST BEGINNING	WE'RE TRYING	ALMOST THERE	THIS IS US!
Encourages intellectual independence					
Recognizes and nurtures brain development					
Allows and encourages intellectual risk taking					
Eliminates stereotyping, bias, oppression, and bullying					
Focuses on hard work, not instant gratification					
Fosters relationships and community					
Provides all students with choices and empowerment					
Builds students' responsibility for learning					
Understands disorder					
Creates a fun and enjoyable environment					

From *Advancing Differentiation: Thinking and Learning for the 21st Century* by Richard M. Cash, Ed.D., copyright © 2017. This page may be reproduced for use within an individual school or district. For all other uses, contact Free Spirit Publishing Inc. at www.freespirit.com/permissions.

Checklist of Characteristics of a Thinking Curriculum

CHARACTERISTIC	NOT YET	JUST BEGINNING	WE'RE TRYING	ALMOST THERE	THIS IS US!
Learning goals are well articulated					
Essential questions are worth investigating					
Concepts are clearly defined					
Activities are designed to move the learner toward independence					
Activities build student confidence					
Content is interdisciplinary					
Activities are emotionally engaging					
Situations involve ambiguity					
Provocative issues are raised					
There is room for additional questions and deeper investigations					
The content is relevant to the learners					
Activities and projects are authentic					
Assessments and evaluations are designed to provide learners with quality feedback					
All lessons involve some form of student reflection					

From *Advancing Differentiation: Thinking and Learning for the 21st Century* by Richard M. Cash, Ed.D., copyright © 2017. This page may be reproduced for use within an individual school or district. For all other uses, contact Free Spirit Publishing Inc. at www.freespirit.com/permissions.

Teaching Thinking Skills: Lesson Format Template

Instructions

Thinking Skill: Identify the thinking skill that will be introduced to the students. Clearly articulate what the skill is and when it may be most efficient to use that skill.

Focus Activity: This is your "anticipatory set." Do something that will grab the students' attention in regards to the skill and will help them concentrate on what will come next.

Objective: Inform students what they will learn in this lesson and why it's relevant. Give examples of when the skill can be used. Communicate the objective of the skill before, during, and after the lesson.

Modeling: Demonstrate the skill with the students. Provide information regarding this thinking skill including:

- A clear definition (add synonyms where relevant)
- An explanation of how and when the thinking skill is used
- An easy way to remember the mental operations used in the thinking process (mnemonics)

Students who have a working knowledge of the thinking skill may benefit more from an inductive approach. Instead of giving a definition and description of operations, try posing a problem to solve. Use questions to help the class generalize a definition and list the operations they used. Are any rules to be followed?

Practice Activity: Allow students time to practice the skill in context. You will act as a guide or facilitator while the student builds independence with the skill.

Reflection/Metacognition: Give students time to debrief, discuss, or reflect on the use of the skill and how it can help them achieve learning goals. You might use journal writing, PMI, Think-Pair-Share, or other activities.

continued

From *Advancing Differentiation: Thinking and Learning for the 21st Century* by Richard M. Cash, Ed.D., copyright © 2017. This page may be reproduced for use within an individual school or district. For all other uses, contact Free Spirit Publishing Inc. at www.freespirit.com/permissions.

Teaching Thinking Skills: Lesson Format Template (continued)

Thinking Skill: _____

Focus Activity: _____
_____
_____
_____
_____

Objective: _____
_____
_____
_____
_____

Modeling
Definition of the skill: _____
_____
_____
_____

Explain how and when to use: _____
_____
_____
_____

Ways to remember the skill: _____
_____
_____
_____

Practice Activity: _____
_____
_____
_____

Reflection/Metacognition: _____
_____
_____
_____

From *Advancing Differentiation: Thinking and Learning for the 21st Century* by Richard M. Cash, Ed.D., copyright © 2017. This page may be reproduced for use within an individual school or district. For all other uses, contact Free Spirit Publishing Inc. at www.freespirit.com/permissions.

Guided Thinking Template

GUIDED QUESTION	PRIOR TO INSTRUCTION	DURING INSTRUCTION	AFTER INSTRUCTION
Question related to the CONCEPT			
Question related to the PROCESS			
Question related to the FACTS			

Student Perception Questionnaire

ATTITUDE/Efficacy

How do I feel about this learning activity? _____
_____

What issues am I dealing with that may be distracting my attention? _____
_____

What can I do to adjust my attitude toward this learning activity?_____
_____

What do I need in order to make this a more successful experience?_____
_____

SKILL/Regulation

Do I completely understand the tasks involved in this activity? _____

Do I have the skills required to complete the tasks? _____

Do I have all the resources I need? _____

Do I have the time to complete the tasks?_____

Do I have the support to complete the tasks?_____

CONFIDENCE/Self-Esteem

Who can I ask for help if I need it? _____

Who can I ask for support if I need it?_____

What skills do I possess that will help me do well on these tasks?_____
_____

What will I do to celebrate my accomplishment?_____
_____

REFLECTION/Metacognition

This was my best work because:_____
_____

I could have worked harder on:_____
_____

Next time I will:_____
_____

From *Advancing Differentiation: Thinking and Learning for the 21st Century* by Richard M. Cash, Ed.D., copyright © 2017. This page may be reproduced for use within an individual school or district. For all other uses, contact Free Spirit Publishing Inc. at www.freespirit.com/permissions.

Work Plan

Before You Begin Work
Set a SMART goal

SPECIFIC   **M**EASURABLE   **A**CHIEVABLE   **R**EALISTIC   **T**IMELY

At the end of this unit I will: _____

_____

_____

How do you plan on achieving the goal?

Work habits I need: _____

Support I will need: _____

Mindset for achievement: _____

While You Are Working
How is the work progressing?   DATE   NOTES

Check in with a teacher   _____   _____

Check in with a peer   _____   _____

Check in with a parent or other adult   _____   _____

Check in with self   _____   _____

After the Work Is Complete
How close to your goal did you come?

- ☐ I did better than I thought I would do.
- ☐ I accomplished my goal.
- ☐ I didn't accomplish everything I wanted to, but I learned some new things.
- ☐ I tried but didn't really learn much.
- ☐ I didn't really try to accomplish my goal.

What specifically can you work on next time to improve your performance? _____

_____

_____

_____

From *Advancing Differentiation: Thinking and Learning for the 21st Century* by Richard M. Cash, Ed.D., copyright © 2017. This page may be reproduced for use within an individual school or district. For all other uses, contact Free Spirit Publishing Inc. at www.freespirit.com/permissions.

Student Reflection Log

Name: _____

Date: _____

Topic: _____

What I **know** about this topic: _____
_____
_____

What I **wonder** about this topic: _____
_____
_____

What I **learned** about this topic: _____
_____
_____

What I **want to learn more** about related to this topic: _____
_____
_____

I liked: _____
_____
_____

I did not like: _____
_____
_____

I did not understand: _____
_____
_____

I'd like the lesson more if: _____
_____
_____

From *Advancing Differentiation: Thinking and Learning for the 21st Century* by Richard M. Cash, Ed.D., copyright © 2017. This page may be reproduced for use within an individual school or district. For all other uses, contact Free Spirit Publishing Inc. at www.freespirit.com/permissions.

Chapter 8

A Framework for Thinking: Digging Deeper into Bloom's Taxonomy

I cannot teach anybody anything, I can only make them think.
—Socrates, philosopher

All students have the right to think at high levels. Some need more scaffolding to reach those high levels, while others require greater degrees of sophistication when working in the highest levels. When differentiating the thinking process for students, you need to pay attention to the variances in students' abilities to work at high levels of thinking.

Teaching our students to think more deeply and with more complexity means we need to provide them with a thinking framework. The process of structuring deep levels of thinking must be connected to classroom curriculum and standards. Most prepared curriculum and textbooks do not offer activities that can systematically guide students into the deep thoughtful process of learning. This chapter will explain a sequential method, built on Bloom's Taxonomy, for moving students into greater depths of learning.

A Brief Introduction to Bloom's Taxonomy

In 1956, Benjamin Bloom and his colleagues published the *Taxonomy of Educational Objectives, The Classification of Educational Goals, Handbook I: Cognitive Domain*.[1] The main purpose of this text was to define a taxonomy (a classification system) to help educators design hierarchic learning objectives and deal with curricular and evaluation issues. The taxonomy became known simply as Bloom's Taxonomy (see **Figure 8.1**). It provided teachers and curriculum designers with a framework for advancing student thinking through a hierarchy of learning objectives. Beginning with the recall of information—the knowledge base of all disciplines—the taxonomy provided a common language that educators could use in the development of more precise objectives that would lead students through increasingly complex learning activities that required them to apply, dissect, and appraise learned content.

Bloom's Taxonomy was one of the most influential educational tools of the twentieth century. It continues to be a standard reference in defining quality curriculum, instruction, and assessments. Virtually every administrator and teacher at all levels of education is familiar with this tool and has applied it in one form or another. Bloom's Taxonomy has had a significant influence on helping teachers translate educational theory into effective practice. The enduring power of the taxonomy may be linked to its sequential intellectual scaffolding to higher levels of thought. Cognitive science suggests that the brain learns best when information is connected, richly practiced, and then reflected upon.

The taxonomy provides a logical structure for students to build both learning and thinking. To most effectively use the taxonomy, you should be aware of how each level interacts with and supports the succeeding levels. This chapter discusses the levels of the taxonomy, offers a broad framework for each level, and then makes suggestions for how you can apply the taxonomy in a

---

1. Bloom, B. S. *Taxonomy of Educational Objectives, The Classification of Educational Goals, Handbook I: Cognitive Domain*. White Plains, NY: Longman, 1956.

meaningful way for students. Finally, the chapter provides a structure for constructing advancing levels of tiered assignments by delving more deeply into Bloom's Taxonomy.

Performing Automatically to Performing Consciously

The base levels of Bloom's Taxonomy are intended to assist learners in constructing a solid foundation of content knowledge in order to support more advanced cognitive processes. As stated in Chapter 4, the function of automatic performance is situated in the lower levels of the brain (cerebellum). This automaticity is very important in allowing energy to be concentrated in the higher levels of the brain (the cerebral cortex). This higher level of brain activity is called *conscious performance*; because we don't have to think about the basic processes, we can instead focus our attention on more mindful, sophisticated thoughts. For example, when students have achieved automaticity of multiplication facts, they can more rapidly and fluently complete advanced algorithms without pausing to think about the basics. Having proficiency at the basic skill level is an important step toward internalizing the content (metacognition) and then realizing the benefit of learning (self-regulation).

Building on Bloom's

With each generation of educators, Bloom's Taxonomy has been refined to adhere to the needs of the marketplace students will be entering, which speaks to the valuable contribution this taxonomy has sustained. In 2001, researchers Lorin Anderson and David Krathwohl revised the taxonomy to realign the upper two levels and include a second dimension. Anderson and Krathwohl, students of Dr. Bloom's, suggest that the mental activity of creativity (synthesis) is more complex than that of evaluation, thus moving synthesis to the highest level. The original taxonomy was developed within a single dimension of cognitive processes. The second interrelated dimension added by Anderson and Krathwohl is the knowledge dimension, which includes the three main types of knowledge: factual, procedural, and conceptual, as well as metacognitive knowledge.

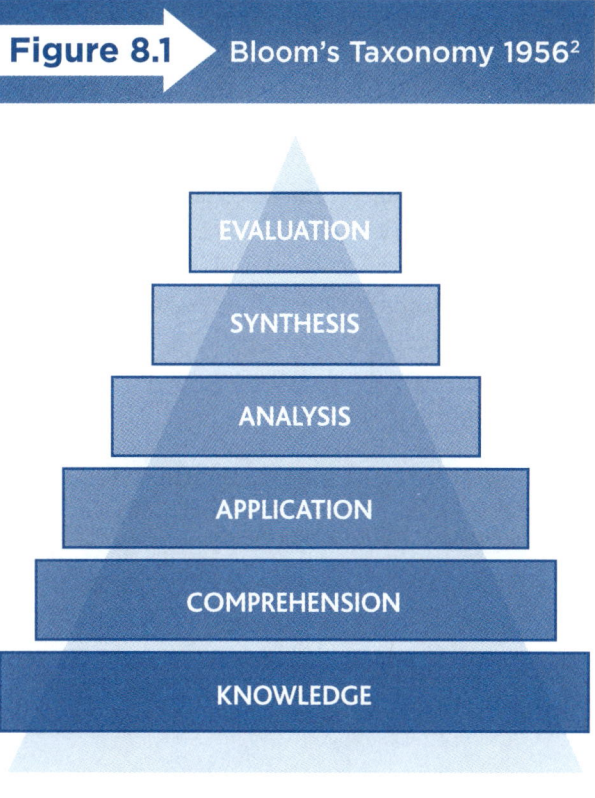

Figure 8.1 Bloom's Taxonomy 1956[2]

The addition of the knowledge dimension to the taxonomy provides for more flexibility in constructing more complex tasks and for moving students to greater degrees of autonomy. The knowledge levels progress students from basic tasks to more sophisticated undertakings. As previously discussed in Chapter 2, curriculum is framed in factual, procedural, and conceptual knowledge. Cognitively, learners are also storing memories in the same three ways: factually, procedurally, and conceptually. Therefore, including this second dimension to the taxonomy is supported both within a quality curriculum and by effective brain learning strategies.

As we continue into the twenty-first century, I have built on the work of Anderson and Krathwohl by including suggestions for tiering to deeper and more complex activities at every level of Bloom's Taxonomy to respect the varying needs for academic difficulty in a mixed-ability classroom. I have also added a frame for assessment options to consider at each of the stages in the learning process. In this new era of standards, classroom assessment takes on a much more prominent role. Many highly regarded assessment experts suggest

2. Ibid.

that formative assessment/assessment for learning be used to identify the comprehensive understanding of student learning throughout the process and the effectiveness of instructional strategies.[3] This is why I suggest that assessment should be implemented at *each* stage of the taxonomy, not just at the end of the process (see **Figure 8.2**). Assessment in this context is more about understanding where students are in the learning process, how close they are to reaching the academic goals, and to what degree the instructional activities and procedures are affecting their learning.

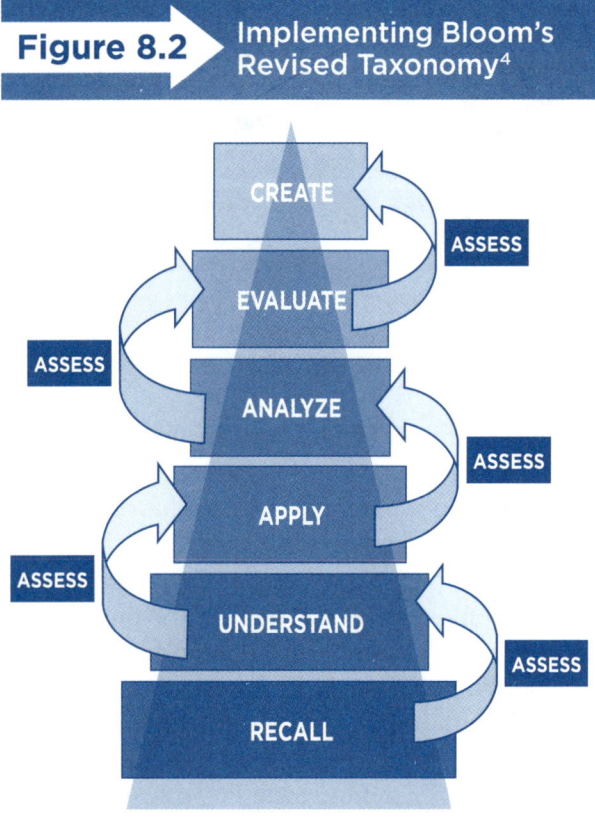

Figure 8.2 Implementing Bloom's Revised Taxonomy[4]

Every student can think at higher levels, and some students need more sophisticated activities that stretch them into more advanced levels of thinking. All students can work at Level 1 *(factual knowledge)*, some students may work to Level 2 *(procedural knowledge)*, and the advanced learner possibly will move deeper into Level 3 *(conceptual knowledge)* (see **Figure 8.3**). In this template, the number and letter in parentheses in each box are code for the cognitive process *(recall, understand,*

apply, analyze, evaluate, and *create)* and level of knowledge acquisition *(factual, procedural,* and *conceptual)*. The darkest shaded boxes are activities appropriate for all students or whole-group instruction. The medium shaded boxes are activities appropriate for most students or small groups. The lightest shaded boxes are activities intended for individual students or advanced learners. Notice that the assessment techniques become more sophisticated and performance-oriented as students progress through the taxonomy.

Another modification I have made to Anderson and Krathwohl's work is to consider the metacognitive domain *within* both the assessment level and throughout the learning process as a self-regulation strategy for autonomy (see Chapters 5 and 6). This does not require the teacher to prepare separate activities to help students build self-regulation. As stated in Chapter 5, self-regulation and metacognition develop when students are provided with supportive descriptive feedback and encouraged to take intellectual risks to stretch through their zone of proximal development.

The next section will describe each of the six cognitive process dimensions of the revised Bloom's Taxonomy (with my new suggestions for implementation) and share ideas of how to dig deeper into those dimensions. Three example units of study are used to demonstrate how to apply the revised taxonomy (see **Figures 8.4, 8.5,** and **8.6** on pages 150, 151, and 152–153) and a planning tool, the Digging Deeper Matrix (DDM), is provided on page 158, preceded by ideas and instructions for use.

Recall: Retrieving Information and Developing a Knowledge Base

At the lowest level of the learning continuum is Recall, or sometimes denoted as Remember. Simply, the learner is to recall or recite previously learned material. At the first level (factual knowledge) of Recall, the student may recite vocabulary, facts, names, dates, or terms within the discipline or unit of study. Having this basic level of knowledge is important for students to support higher levels of cognition. As they move into Level 2 of Recall (procedural knowledge), students define the

---

3. Fisher, D., and N. Frey. *Checking for Understanding: Formative Assessment Techniques for Your Classroom*. Alexandria, VA: ASCD, 2014; Guskey, T. R., ed. *The Teacher as Assessment Leader*. Bloomington, IN: Solution Tree Press, 2009; Marzano, R. J. *Transforming Classroom Grading*. Alexandria, VA: ASCD, 2000; O'Connor, K. *How to Grade for Learning: K–12*. Thousand Oaks, CA: Corwin Press, 2009; Reeves, D. B. *Making Standards Work: How to Implement Standards-Based Assessments in the Classroom, School, and District*. Denver, CO: Advanced Learning Press, 2002.
4. Based on Anderson, L. W., and D. R. Krathwohl, eds. *A Taxonomy for Learning, Teaching, and Assessing: A Revision of Bloom's Taxonomy of Educational Objectives*. New York: Longman, 2001.

Figure 8.3 Bloom's Revised Taxonomy with Additional Assessment Layer[5]

COGNITIVE PROCESS DIMENSION →

	RECALL (R)	UNDERSTAND (U)	APPLY (A)	ANALYZE (Z)	EVALUATE (E)	CREATE (C)
LEVEL 1 FACTUAL	*FOR ALL STUDENTS* **Specific/Concrete (1R)** Recall specific concrete information **Key words:** *vocabulary, names, symbols, facts, dates, sources of information, basic elements*	**Translate (1U) WHAT?** Translate the facts into one's own words **Key words:** *retell, recap, repeat*	**Original Way (1A)** Apply the information in the original context **Key words:** *apply, use, utilize*	**Individual Elements (1Z)** Analyze the individual elements **Key words:** *observe, examine, survey, organize, find*	**Check Clarity (1E)** Check information for clarity **Key words:** *check, test, assess, question, evaluate, monitor*	**Reorganize (1C)** Reorganize elements of the original information **Key words:** *reorder, rearrange, restructure, change, alter, fashion, form, craft, generate*
LEVEL 2 PROCEDURAL	**Tools/Skills (2R)** Remember procedural definitions, tools, and skills **Key words:** *problem solving, process, algorithm, structure, method, steps, model, parts, organization, action, criteria, technique*	**Interpret (2U) SO WHAT?** Interpret the meaning of the information **Key words:** *paraphrase, restate, summarize, reword, explain, construe, clarify, give details, describe, represent*	*FOR SOME STUDENTS* **Practical Way (2A)** Apply the information in a practical, authentic way **Key words:** *implement, employ*	**Relationship Among Elements (2Z)** Analyze the relationship among elements **Key words:** *determine, establish, ascertain, differentiate, distinguish*	**Judge Accuracy (2E)** Judge information for accuracy **Key words:** *judge, ensure, confirm, review, authorize, decide*	**Formulate (2C)** Formulate designs for new uses for the information **Key words:** *design, devise, plan, express, articulate*
LEVEL 3 CONCEPTUAL	**Abstract Information (3R)** Retrieve abstract knowledge **Key words:** *theory, theorem, classification, taxonomy, periods, laws, principles, generalization, relationships, understandings*	**Extrapolate (3U) NOW WHAT?** Extrapolate the information into another context **Key words:** *illustrate, model, exemplar, paradigm*	*FOR ADVANCED STUDENTS* **Creative Way (3A)** Apply in a creative way **Key words:** *execute, relate, perform, stage*	**Principles Governing Elements (3Z)** Analyze the principles that govern the elements **Key words:** *appraise, connect, dissect, probe*	**Critique Validity (3E)** Critique information for validity **Key words:** *critique, validate, verify, scrutinize*	**Innovate (3C)** Create innovative and original ideas or products **Key words:** *create new, produce, build, invent, deconstruct, originate, initiate*
ASSESSMENT: EXAMPLES	Objective tests True/false Matching Fill in the blank Multiple choice Short answer One right answer Standardized tests Checklists Vocabulary recitations Q&A periods	Subject tests Open-ended questions Essays Constructed responses Selected responses Journals/reflections Short answer Q&A periods Discussions Oral reports Posters/displays/dioramas	Performances Re-creation of product Demonstrations/ presentations Games/simulations Open-ended essays Experiments Projects Research reports	Compare/contrast charts Hierarchical diagrams Research reports/papers Essays Open-ended/subjective tests	Criterion-referenced assessments Surveys Research reports Experiments	Speeches/debates Research proposals Graphic representations Designs Research proposals Performance-based productions

← KNOWLEDGE DIMENSION

5. Ibid.

Figure 8.4 — Digging Deeper into Bloom's: Science Example (Lower Grades)[6]

Unit: Health/Nutrition
Standard: Students will understand how healthy behaviors lead to a healthy life.[7]
Students will know: vocabulary related to healthy eating and the Food Guide Pyramid
Students will be able to: explain how the body uses nutrients and design a healthy eating and living plan
Students will understand: healthy eating leads to a healthy life

	RECALL (R)	UNDERSTAND (U)	APPLY (A)	ANALYZE (Z)	EVALUATE (E)	CREATE (C)
LEVEL 1 FACTUAL	*FOR ALL STUDENTS* **Specific/Concrete (1R)** List vocabulary words related to healthy eating and living.	**Translate (1U) WHAT?** Describe the Food Guide Pyramid.	**Original Way (1A)** Keep a journal of the foods you eat for one week.	**Individual Elements (1Z)** Review your journal to calculate the average amount of nutrients you receive each day.	**Check Clarity (1E)** Graph how well you did at meeting the daily average nutrients needed by a child like you.	**Reorganize (1C)** Create a weeklong menu that would provide a healthy diet for you.
LEVEL 2 PROCEDURAL	**Tools/Skills (2R)** Describe how nutrients supply our body with energy.	**Interpret (2U) SO WHAT?** Define why the Food Guide Pyramid is important for a healthy life.	*FOR SOME STUDENTS* **Practical Way (2A)** Using the school lunch menu for one week, place all items on the Food Guide Pyramid.	**Relationship Among Elements (2Z)** Analyze the school's lunch menu and calculate the average amount of nutrients students receive each day.	**Judge Accuracy (2E)** Graph how well the school does in meeting the daily average needs of nutrients for a child like you.	**Formulate (2C)** Using the average amount of nutrients needed for a student your age, create a weeklong healthy school lunch menu.
LEVEL 3 CONCEPTUAL	**Abstract Information (3R)** Describe how healthy eating and living can lead to a healthy life.	**Extrapolate (3U) NOW WHAT?** How might we use the Food Guide Pyramid as a school/class?	*FOR ADVANCED STUDENTS* **Creative Way (3A)** Build a healthy school lunch menu for one week.	**Principles Governing Elements (3Z)** Evaluate the school's lunch, defining strengths and weaknesses in the menu, and devise suggestions for change.	**Critique Validity (3E)** Why do you think the school has strengths or weaknesses in its school lunch menu related to nutrients needed by a child like you?	**Innovate (3C)** Create a healthy school lunch menu using only local or organic products.
ASSESSMENT	Vocabulary quiz Poster Short essay	Poster/report Short essay Newspaper article Position statement	Journal/log Poster/report	Report	Graph Editorial	Lunch menu Report

6. Ibid.
7. Adapted from the Joint Committee on National Health Education Standards. *National Health Education Standards: Achieving Excellence*. Atlanta: American Cancer Society, 2007.

Figure 8.5 Digging Deeper into Bloom's: History Example (Upper Grades)[8]

Unit: Revolution and the New Nation 1763-1820

Standard: The student will demonstrate knowledge of how the principles of the American Revolution became the foundation of a new nation.[9]

Students will know:

1. Important vocabulary, dates, and events (such as treaties, battles, political uprisings, and relations with foreign nations and Native Americans) related to the American Revolution
2. Important political, economic, military, and cultural figures related to the American Revolution (such as George Washington, Samuel Adams, John Adams, Paul Revere, Thomas Jefferson, Charles Cornwallis, Marquis de Lafayette, Thomas Paine, Patrick Henry, John Locke, and Baron de Montesquieu)
3. Important debates and facts over slavery; statues of free blacks, women, and Native Americans; migration to Canada; and the westward movement of white settlers

Students will be able to:

1. Analyze major economic, political, and philosophical conflicts leading to the American Revolution
2. Explain how and why the American colonists won the war against the more superior British resources
3. Interpret the impact the Revolutionary War had on groups within American society
4. Infer the impact of revolution on nations and groups of citizens within those nations

Students will understand: the causes, effects, and consequences of revolution

	RECALL (R)	UNDERSTAND (U)	APPLY (A)	ANALYZE (Z)	EVALUATE (E)	CREATE (C)
LEVEL 1 FACTUAL	*FOR ALL STUDENTS* Specific/Concrete (1R) List important dates of the Revolutionary War.	Translate (1U) WHAT? What led to the colonists' revolt against Britain?	Original Way (1A) How did the Treaty of Paris change the mapping of territories of North America?	Individual Elements (1Z) What were the basic disagreements among the Native Americans, colonists, British, and French?	Check Clarity (1E) Why did the Native Americans, colonists, British, and French have their disagreements?	Reorganize (1C) Put yourself in the role of a colonial ambassador. What message would you send to Britain or France?
LEVEL 2 PROCEDURAL	Tools/Skills (2R) Describe how the Red Coats attacked Boston.	Interpret (2U) SO WHAT? Why was this revolt important?	*FOR SOME STUDENTS* Practical Way (2A) How did the change of territories after the Treaty of Paris affect the colonists?	Relationship Among Elements (2Z) How did these disagreements relate to each other?	Judge Accuracy (2E) In what ways might any or all of the disagreements have been avoided?	Formulate (2C) Put yourself in the role of a British ambassador. What plans would you make to settle disputes in the colonies?
LEVEL 3 CONCEPTUAL	Abstract Information (3R) Define a revolution.	Extrapolate (3U) NOW WHAT? What effect has the American Revolution had on our nation and Britain?	*FOR ADVANCED STUDENTS* Creative Way (3A) Describe a modern day conflict where map boundaries were redrawn.	Principles Governing Elements (3Z) Why did each group seek control?	Critique Validity (3E) What made one group's claim more valid than the other group's claims?	Innovate (3C) Create a position statement that would either support or oppose colonization.
ASSESSMENT	Paper/pencil test	Essay	Performance	Graphic representation	Essay Persuasion speech Role play	Speech/debate Research proposal Graphic representation

8. Based on Anderson, L. W., and D. R. Krathwohl, eds. *A Taxonomy for Learning, Teaching, and Assessing: A Revision of Bloom's Taxonomy of Educational Objectives.* New York: Longman, 2001.
9. Adapted from Minnesota Academic Standards in History and Social Studies, United States History Grades 4-8, Minnesota Department of Education, May 15, 2004.

Figure 8.6 Digging Deeper into Bloom's: Math Example (Intermediate Grades)[10, 11]

Unit: Area and Perimeter of Rectangles
Standard: CCSS 4.MD.A.3

Students will know:
1. How to find area and perimeter of rectangles
2. How to identify rectangles and their attributes
3. Basic multiplication/division facts

Students will be able to:
1. Apply area and perimeter formulas for rectangles to real-world and mathematical problems
2. Write and solve equations involving area and perimeter of rectangles

Students will understand:
1. Multiplication and division model
2. Real-life situations involving measurement
3. How multiplication and addition are related to area and perimeter
4. How using the mathematical practices creates the mindset of a mathematician

	RECALL (R)	UNDERSTAND (U)	APPLY (A)	ANALYZE (Z)	EVALUATE (E)	CREATE (C)
LEVEL 1 FACTUAL	*FOR ALL STUDENTS* Specific/Concrete (1R) Create a vocabulary map/brainstorm for all the mathematical words you need when solving problems involving the area and perimeter of rectangles	Translate (1U) WHAT? Write a "how to" poem about finding either the area or perimeter of a rectangle. Share with a partner that chose the measurement you didn't.	Original Way (1A) Find at least 5 examples of how area and perimeter are used in the real world.	Individual Elements (1Z) Describe a way to find the area of a rectangle without using multiplication.	Check Clarity (1E) Write a problem and solution using area and perimeter that has an error. Have a partner read the solution, locate the error, and write a corrected solution.	Reorganize (1C) Draw a diagram of your future backyard created entirely of rectangles
LEVEL 2 PROCEDURAL	Tools/Skills (2R) Create a visual model (poster, brochure, etc.) for finding the area and perimeter of a rectangle.	Interpret (2U) SO WHAT? Summarize how addition and multiplication are necessary in solving problems involving area and perimeter of rectangles.	*FOR SOME STUDENTS* Practical Way (2A) Write an area and perimeter problem and solution from a real-world setting.	Relationship Among Elements (2Z) Compare/contrast the process for finding area and perimeter of rectangles using a poem in two voices.	Judge Accuracy (2E) Research and record any formulas that exist for area and perimeter of rectangles. How does each formula work? Why does the formula work?	Formulate (2C) Draw two rectangles and show their areas and perimeters. In a second picture, increase or decrease one side length. Calculate the new area and perimeter. How did the area and perimeter change? What patterns do you notice in the relation of side lengths to the area perimeter?

LEVEL 3 CONCEPTUAL	Abstract Information (3R) Why are multiplication and division critical to finding the area of rectangles?	Extrapolate (3U) NOW WHAT? Illustrate with a visual model why multiplication is used for finding the area of rectangles and addition is used for finding the perimeter.	FOR ADVANCED STUDENTS Creative Way (3A) Write an area or perimeter problem and solution that could exist in a real-world setting that uses different unknown values within the area and perimeter formulas.	Principles Governing Elements (3Z) How do multiplication and division and addition and subtraction model mathematical situations involving the area and perimeter of rectangles?	Critique Validity (3E) Research how perimeter and area formulas are used in science. How are the formulas similar or different from the math formulas? What types of precision are scientists concerned about when working with area and perimeter?	Innovate (3C) Create your own strategy for how to find the area and perimeter of a triangle using what you know about rectangles. Create detailed directions including pictures.
ASSESSMENT	Vocabulary map/list Visual (poster, brochure) Essay	How-to poem Summary Visual model	Examples of real-world use Real-world problem and solution Predictive real-world problem and solution with unknowns	Description Compare/contrast poem Essay	Problem and solution with error Research on formulas	Backyard diagram Drawings with calculations Self-created strategy

10. Based on Anderson, L. W., and D. R. Krathwohl, eds. *A Taxonomy for Learning, Teaching, and Assessing: A Revision of Bloom's Taxonomy of Educational Objectives*. New York: Longman, 2001.
11. Reprinted with permission from Holly Young, Making Mathematicians LLC.

---

steps in a process; learn problem-solving and thinking skills; are trained in algorithms, models, and structures; and learn the steps in experiments, how to write reports, or how to list events in a sequence or on a timeline. At Level 3 of Recall (conceptual knowledge), students are able to outline or define theories, taxonomies, periods of time, laws, and principles or generalizations.

In the American Revolution example (see Figure 8.5), students reinforce their knowledge base by listing important dates sequentially, giving the students a broad understanding of when the Revolutionary War took place and how long the events unfolded. Moving into Level 2, students describe methods of warfare that were used by the different armies. This helps them recognize the organizational structures of the two governments and how they each approached conflict. Finally, students define the concept of a revolution either from their personal experience or through the context of the introductory material.

Assessment at the Recall Level

Assessment at the Recall level is intended to validate that the students have acquired the fundamental factual information and are able to recite or recall it correctly.

Types of assessment at the Recall level include:
- objective exams/tests/quizzes
- true/false questions
- matching
- fill in the blank
- multiple choice
- short answer
- one right answer
- standardized tests
- checklists
- vocabulary recitation
- question and answer period

Understand: Grasping the Meaning of the Information

The Understand (or Comprehension) level involves students restating information in their own words to show they understand the information. This level can be thought of as the "What?

So What? Now What?" level (see **Figure 8.7**). At stage one, the "What?" stage, the student would restate the words used at the Recall level into their own words or summarize the meaning behind all the words: what was just said, done, or learned. In the example (see Figure 8.5), students identify what led up to the revolution, framing the context for the revolt.

Next is the "So What?" stage, defining what makes this information important. The learners must interpret what the information means to them personally or put it into the context of the study. Students paraphrase, restate, or summarize the information in personally meaningful ways. The example asks students to define why they believed the revolution has importance. This kind of open-endedness forces the students to inductively reason through the content.

Finally, at the "Now What?" stage, students extrapolate the information to hypothesize or theorize how things will change or what will happen next. Students generate examples and illustrations. Notice in the example (see Figure 8.5), students connect a past event to current situations. For an additional example of What? So What? Now What?, see Figure 11.5 on page 200.

Assessment at the Understand Level

Assessment at the Understand level is designed to display student comprehension of the content and concepts. Assessing understanding is more complex here than at the Recall level. Students must be able to summarize the information and put it into their own words.

Types of assessment at the Understand level include:

- subject tests/open-ended questions/essays
- constructed responses where students supply the answers
- selected response where students choose the answers
- journals/reflections
- short-answer tests/quizzes/exams
- question and answer periods
- discussions
- oral reports
- posters/displays/dioramas

Apply: Putting It to Use

Once information has been gathered and given meaning, students then put it to use. Students must correctly apply and demonstrate the information learned. Initially, at Level 1 of Apply, the student puts the information to use in the original context (inauthentic practices, such as worksheets or teacher-guided work). In the example (see Figure 8.5), students demonstrate their knowledge of the effect of the Treaty of Paris on changes to the mapping of territories in North America. This is an authentic activity, one directly related to the content.

Moving into the next level, students use the information in a more practical way (more authentic practices within the domain of the content, still with the support and coaching of the teacher). In the example, the students must think about the greater effects the Treaty of Paris had on people years later. The students are required to use the content information more broadly.

Finally, at the deepest level of application, the student applies the information or process in a variety of new contexts. This may include applying laws, theories, or principles learned in one content area

Figure 8.7 — The Three Stages of the *Understand* Level

WHAT?	SO WHAT?	NOW WHAT?
What led to the colonists' revolt against Britain?	Why was this revolt important?	What effect has the American Revolution had on the United States and Britain?
The development of semi-autonomous states that longed for independence from British finances	It led to the foundation and formation of the United States.	Losing the American colonies forced Britain to reevaluate its fiscal and military might and to seek a more collaborative connection to the newly formed United States.
Increasing numbers of immigrants from other nations		The United States and Britain have since been very strong allies.

to another content area. The example has students applying learned information to a new context, such as a modern day conflict that resulted in a similar boundary change to that of the Treaty of Paris.

Assessment at the Apply Level

At the Apply level, students must be able to perform the skills being learned. These types of assessments require a greater degree of authenticity and practicality.

Types of assessment at the Apply level include:

- performances
- re-creation of product
- demonstrations/presentations
- games/simulations or other interactive exercises
- open-ended essays
- experiments
- projects
- research reports

Analyze: Recognizing Relationships of the Parts

The analysis level of Bloom's Taxonomy is one that overlaps with the levels before and after, so it should not be considered a stand-alone level in the process. In fact, it is hard to do analysis without some level of understanding and application. As in all levels of Bloom's Taxonomy, a degree of evaluation is involved. Analysis is the beginning of what can be defined as higher levels of thought or learning and is essential to critical reasoning and decision making. The cognitive activity at this level requires a more sophisticated amount of attention paid to both individual parts of the content as well as to the content as a whole.

To dig deeper into the Analyze level, students begin by identifying and classifying the characteristics of the individual elements of the content. The American Revolution example (see Figure 8.5) has students defining the various disagreements each group held prior to the war. Through this activity, students come to understand the complexity of the issues. Next, the students compare and contrast the relationships between the individual characteristics or elements. Once the students have defined the multiple disagreements, they analyze how the issues interrelate. Finally, based on the information gleaned from the previous steps, students make an inference to articulate principles or generalizations that govern the content. At this stage, students are making conjecture as to why each of the groups would want to seek control. Use the compare and contrast organizers found in Chapter 9 (pages 174–175) to assist students in making deeper levels of analysis.

Assessment at the Analyze Level

At the analytical level, students reason through information to form purpose, solve complex problems, and draw conclusions about the importance of the data. Authenticity of assessment is much more significant at this level.

Types of assessment at the Analyze level include:

- compare/contrast charts with reports
- hierarchical diagrams
- research reports/papers
- essays
- open-ended/subjective tests

Evaluate: Determining Clarity, Accuracy, and Validity

At the evaluation level, students are using critical thinking skills to ensure information is clear, accurate, and valid. Evaluation, in this sense, is not summative as in a final exam. At this stage in the learning, students must be able to look back on how well information has been applied and analyzed. This can be done by using criteria created by the students, by the teacher, or by an expert in the domain. The three tiers of Evaluate begin with students being able to clarify how the facts come together to support or oppose building new ideas. At Level 2 of Evaluate, students determine how accurately a skill has been implemented and in what ways this procedure can be refined to reach the Create level. In the most advanced stage of evaluation, students critique the merits of ideas that have been presented and justify the positive or negative outcomes that have occurred because of these ideas.

Assessment at the Evaluate Level

The evaluation level involves students reflecting back on previously learned information, skills, and ideas and looking forward to how they can construct new thoughts and knowledge.

Types of assessment at the Evaluate level include:

- criterion-referenced assessments
- surveys
- research reports
- experiments

Create: Generating New Ideas

Building on the previous levels of Understand, Apply, Analyze, and Evaluate, students can then move up to the level of Create (also called Synthesis). Synthesized thoughts and ideas are created from an understanding of the information, knowing how it is put to use in varied and new settings, and being able to take parts and recombine or reconstruct them into entirely new forms. Synthesis is the use of creative thinking skills (see Chapter 10) where students are "putting elements together to form a coherent or functional whole."[12] Thinking and acting creatively is more than a freewheeling practice of making things up. Creating requires constructing ideas or products that address learning objectives or outcomes, offer feasibility of implementation, and can produce the required effects. Creative ideas and products must have practical applications.

Students begin the creative process by reorganizing, restructuring, or rearranging information learned in previous experiences to generate ideas to solve problems or develop new products. Most students can manipulate information in some way to generate new ideas or outcomes. This may be done by describing a situation in context that needs resolution and suggesting several alternative solutions. In the American Revolution example (see Figure 8.5), the students put themselves in the role of colonial ambassadors to develop a message for Britain or France. This activity uses information that is in the content, but it must be shaped by the student's creativity.

Going deeper into Level 2 of Create, students draw on elements from various sources to articulate and design a viable plan for a unique solution or product. Students use hypothetical predictive and deductive thinking to devise resolutions. Notice in the example, the students are taking on the role of the opposing side, which requires a greater degree of creative thinking, since not all information may be readily available.

In the most advanced stage of Create, the student develops innovative products that are original. In the final activity of the example in Figure 8.5, the students must move beyond the information provided and create their own position statement on the colonization by the British. This requires the student to use all the resources and knowledge built from prior activities. When considering objectives or activities that seek unique or innovative outcomes, originality takes different forms based on the individual or group. Younger children may be taking newly learned information and rearranging it in a way that is new to them, such as designing a new ending to a story or writing it from a different perspective. Older students may develop a new hypothesis as to why certain chemicals interact or react to one another after several experiments and studies. Both outcomes are original, based on the level of the student.

Many of the ideas shared in Chapter 10 can help your students move to deeper levels of creativity. Consider using the SCAMPER method (pages 131 and 187) as a way to ignite your students' creative ideas.

Assessment at the Create Level

Types of assessments at the Create level include:

- speeches/debates
- research proposals
- graphic representations
- designs
- performance-based productions

Assessment: Making Judgments About the Knowledge Throughout the Process

As I suggest in Figure 8.2, assessment is not a final step in the learning process. It is an ongoing integrated practice of using critical reasoning at each stage of Bloom's Taxonomy. At every level of the learning process, students continually contemplate how they are doing, their correctness, and their proficiency or mastery toward a set goal. Forms of assessment move from concrete, inauthentic

---

12. Based on Anderson, L. W., and D. R. Krathwohl, eds. *A Taxonomy for Learning, Teaching, and Assessing: A Revision of Bloom's Taxonomy of Educational Objectives.* New York: Longman, 2001: 84.

regeneration of knowledge, to more abstract, authentic representations of acquired knowledge or new thoughts or ideas. As seen in Figures 8.4, 8.5, and 8.6, the flow of assessment goes from internal reflection up to external reviews by others, progressing from tests or checklists to essays, performances, or representations, and, finally, to speeches or debates. This is accomplished through applying both internally defined criteria and externally imposed norms.

Internally defined criteria include self-evaluative questions such as:

- Does this make sense to me?
- How can I more specifically define this topic?
- Does this feel right?

Externally imposed norms offer guidelines that include:

- teacher-designed objectives
- teacher-constructed tests, quizzes, or checklists
- state standards and benchmarks

Putting It All Together: The Digging Deeper Matrix (DDM)

The Digging Deeper Matrix (page 158) can assist you in developing unit plans that can move all students into advanced levels of thinking.

The DDM can be used:

- as a guide for instruction
- to assign activities during lessons or for homework for all students
- as selected activities used during lessons or homework provided to all students in small flexible groupings
- as sequential movement from recalling to creating
- to offer students choices to work at greater degrees of difficulty (*Note:* Do not allow students to work at levels below their abilities)
- to suggest topics of greater research, investigation, or exploration
- as an assessment tool for curriculum and instructional practices

Steps to using the DDM:

Use the following six steps as a guide to adding rigor for all students and deeper degrees of complexity for students who require more sophisticated activities.

1. At the top of the model, record the topic and unit title.

2. Using your district, state, or provincial standards, create objectives of what you want students to know (facts), what you want them to be able to do (procedures and processes), and what you want them to understand (concepts).

3. Using a previously prepared unit or a newly developing unit, place activities in the appropriate level of thinking on the matrix. Check the keywords in Figure 8.3 to ensure you have placed the activity at the right level.

4. Design activities or assignments that address open boxes. In most cases you will be developing activities and assignments that are more complex and/or difficult. Again, use the keywords in each column and level to guide you. Be careful not to create new activities and assignments that are just more work. All activities within the model should be equally engaging and interesting and have a degree of fun.

5. According to the shaded tiers, activities can be constructed for individual students, small groups, or whole-group instruction. If students are doing the more advanced level activities, they may not need to do the activities in the other boxes.

6. Assess the activities for each of the learning objectives using the appropriate assessment strategies. Assessment for the learning objectives of *Recall*, *Understand*, *Apply*, *Analyze*, and *Evaluate* should be used formatively to guide the learner to the final learning objective *Create*.

Moving students to higher levels of thinking requires a comprehensive knowledge of Bloom's Taxonomy, an awareness of the varying degrees of sophistication to which students can perform at each of those levels, and the ability to differentiate activities to greater depth and complexity. The DDM provides you with a structured format for ensuring all students are maximizing thinking and learning to their greatest degree.

Digging Deeper Matrix (DDM)

Unit:

Standard:

Students will know:

Students will be able to:

Students will understand:

	RECALL (R)	UNDERSTAND (U)	APPLY (A)	ANALYZE (Z)	EVALUATE (E)	CREATE (C)
LEVEL 1 FACTUAL	*FOR ALL STUDENTS* Specific/Concrete (1R)	Translate (1U) WHAT?	Original Way (1A)	Individual Elements (1Z)	Check Clarity (1E)	Reorganize (1C)
LEVEL 2 PROCEDURAL	Tools/Skills (2R)	Interpret (2U) SO WHAT?	*FOR SOME STUDENTS* Practical Way (2A)	Relationship Among Elements (2Z)	Judge Accuracy (2E)	Formulate (2C)
LEVEL 3 CONCEPTUAL	Abstract Information (3R)	Extrapolate (3U) NOW WHAT?	*FOR ADVANCED STUDENTS* Creative Way (3A)	Principles Governing Elements (3Z)	Critique Validity (3E)	Innovate (3C)
ASSESSMENT						

From *Advancing Differentiation: Thinking and Learning for the 21st Century* by Richard M. Cash, Ed.D., copyright © 2017. This page may be reproduced for use within an individual school or district. For all other uses, contact Free Spirit Publishing Inc. at www.freespirit.com/permissions.

Chapter 9

Critical Thinking: Developing Reasoned Thought

Learning without thought is labor lost; thought without learning is perilous.
—Confucius, philosopher

The essence of differentiated instruction and the backbone of a quality education is for students to be proficient in understanding concepts, knowing facts, and being able to perform procedures successfully. However, recalling facts and executing procedures does not directly lead students to the understanding of concepts. It is through the critical thinking process that students come to grasp the concepts that link all knowledge together into a coherent and cohesive education.

The nature of human thought is self-serving. It's about getting what we want and need, and supporting what we believe. We don't naturally see the world the way it really is; we filter our thoughts and perceptions of the world through our various lenses of emotion, past experience, culture, ethnic background, gender, social status, history, and so on. Unconsciously we see the world that fits us. We all rely on the unconscious form of thinking to get us through the day. This kind of thinking is innate to us; it's our survival thinking. However, it's the more evolved, conscious form of thinking that will lead us to a productive and successful life. And this kind of conscious thinking is not "natural"; it must be taught.

Unconscious thinking is ill-formed thinking; it is disorganized, biased, narrow, and without clear direction. Effective conscious thinking is organized, open- and fair-minded, well-reasoned, and able to be clearly communicated to others. This conscious thinking is also known as *critical thinking*, or reasoning. This chapter will provide an overview of critical thinking and offer an array of strategies and tools for developing critical thinking.

Students are bombarded by all kinds of information from television to the Internet to social media. This overload of information may not always be accurate, precise, factual, or correct. Therefore, we must teach our students how to use the skills of critical thinking and reasoning to be able to take command of their own thinking and use their minds for the better of our world.

What Is Critical Thinking?

Critical thinking contrasts with creative thinking in some unique ways. Whereas creative thinking is more intuitive, is shaped somewhat randomly, and seeks multiple answers, critical thinking is more ordered, directed, and controlled. Both types of thinking require advanced levels of brain energy and seek to generate reasoned solutions. They each approach the solution in a different and valuable fashion.

Students are often exposed to curriculum that is grounded in facts and issues devoid of a wider context. Progressing from learned facts to concept development may feel disjointed to students because of this lack of context. Facts outside of context are just that: facts. Additionally, students may disengage from the material since they are not encouraged to question or critique the validity of the curriculum materials. The student is passive in the curriculum.

"Social relations in the classroom that glorify the teacher as the expert, the dispenser of knowledge, end up crippling student imagination and creativity; in addition, such approaches teach students more about the legitimacy of passivity than about the need to examine critically the lives they lead."[1] Students who actively engage in the questioning and critiquing of content validity are developing critical thinking skills. When students review information from different points of view and legitimize arguments and claims, they are constructing a foundation of thinking skills that doesn't presuppose the validity of any facts out of context or promote concepts disjointed from the facts.

Critical thinking is not about raising skeptics. It is about developing autonomous thinkers who can identify, evaluate, and reason through information in a broader context outside themselves. Critical thinking is about "awaking the student's awareness that the world contains unrealized possibilities for thoughts and action."[2]

Critical Thinking Is Sound Decision Making

Critical thinking is *making good decisions based on evidence and facts*. The thinker has to take on an impersonal or objective stance, limiting their emotions, bias, opinions, assumptions, and perceptions from the process. This does not mean that the decision maker lacks empathy. It means that the decision maker is guarded against information that can lead to a faulty outcome. Gathering and using evidence and factual information will help in making a better decision. Factual information needs to be corroborated through credible sources.

Critical Thinking Is Analysis and Criticism

Discerning the credibility of information is vital in the critical thinking process, therefore, critical thinkers must have the ability to analyze and criticize. They must be able to scrutinize the source of the information and what views the source holds. To criticize is not to belittle or disparage; it is to critique. When the thinker can assess the validity of an argument, appraise a situation from different angles, and even question as the "devil's advocate," he or she is more likely to form solutions that are well reasoned.

Critical Thinking Is Inductive and Deductive Reasoning

Critical thinking, like creative thinking, requires the use of both inductive and deductive reasoning. Basically, inductive reasoning is going with your gut feelings about the information you have received. Deductive reasoning takes into account all the facts presented with the information. To critically think through information, we cannot deny our internal feelings about the information, but we must temper it with the facts. We must come to conclusions based both on what we infer and what we have as factually tested knowledge.

Essential for skillful critical thinking is the ability to guard against bias, fallacies, persuasion, and rumor. Political campaigns, advertisements, newspapers, magazines, websites, music, art, film, and theater all have an agenda: to get a message to the viewer. The message intends to persuade you to agree or disagree with a candidate, buy a product, espouse a line of thinking, and so on. Good critical thinkers listen to the message, analyze the information presented, seek out hidden messages, acknowledge the propaganda, and make decisions about the information using all of these resources.

General Critical Thinking Strategies

To help your students do a better job of critical thinking, you need to provide them with graphic organizers, templates, and designs to frame their thinking. Following are several examples of general critical thinking strategies.

Validate Information

The broadest strategy of critical thinking is validating information. This strategy requires the student to appraise the source of the information, the credibility of the source, and the validity of the information. When validating information, the student must look at such things as the credentials of the author, date, and source of the information. In addition, knowing the intended audience of the original work can help identify:

- point of view
- stereotyping and bias

---

1. Giroux, H. A. "Toward a Pedagogy of Critical Thinking." In *Re-Thinking Reason: New Perspectives in Critical Thinking*. K. S. Walters (Ed.). Albany, NY: State University of New York Press, 1994: 202.
2. Maxine Greene quoted in *Re-Thinking Reason: New Perspectives in Critical Thinking*. K. S. Walters (Ed.). Albany, NY: State University of New York Press, 1994: 207.

- propaganda
- assumptions and generalizations

On page 173 is an excellent spider-design graphic organizer to help students substantiate and validate information. When validating information, the student is also discovering both relevant and irrelevant information, sorting out fact from opinion, and uncovering reliable and unreliable sources. (**Figure 9.1** shows a partially completed example.)

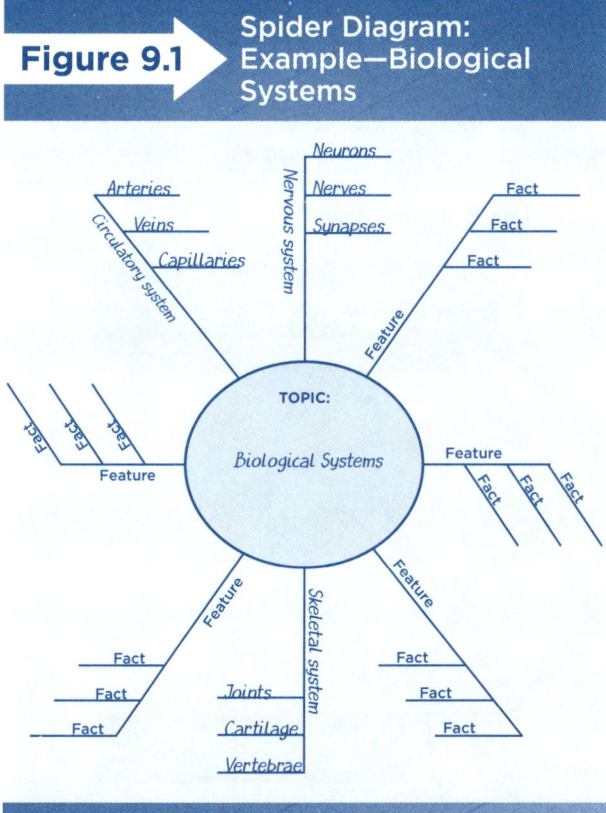

Figure 9.1 Spider Diagram: Example—Biological Systems

Compare and Contrast

Comparing and contrasting is an excellent way for students to categorize attributes of similar and dissimilar things and to analyze the individual parts. Page 174 shows a compare and contrast graphic organizer that can help students discern individual characteristics, plot out significant similarities and differences, and then interpret what those similarities and differences mean.

Figure 9.2 on page 162 shows two different types of compare and contrast graphics. The T-Chart is designed to provide parameters for the line of thinking required for an assignment or lesson. In the example, the student is asked to list how U.S. President Abraham Lincoln's administration compared to President John F. Kennedy's administration on key issues. The second design takes the basic two-ring Venn diagram to a higher level by providing three rings within which to compare and contrast. The example seeks out broad characteristics of three U.S. presidents (Washington, Lincoln, and Kennedy) to compare and contrast.

A more advanced level graphic organizer for comparing and contrasting is the Cross-Impact Matrix (CIM) (page 175). The CIM analyzes more than three variables or items and the relationships between them. This form of convergent thinking considers multiple interacting situations or issues. Depending on how you would like to use the CIM, columns and rows can be adjusted (see the two different examples in **Figure 9.3** on page 163). Notice in the Three Little Pigs example that Row 1 and Column A are the same, whereas in the American Civil War example, Row 1 and Column A use different variables. The CIM can be used in various ways depending on the line of thinking you are trying to achieve.

Sequence and Prioritize

Sequencing and prioritizing is used when a student must list characteristics or information, which will then be prioritized in order of importance. This skill can be helpful when solving problems, thinking through large amounts of information, setting work plans, understanding cause and effect, or organizing one's life. **Figure 9.4** on pages 164–165 offers several examples of sequencing and prioritizing graphics.

Critical Thinking Strategies in Reading

Reading critically is different from reading for pleasure. Students read critically to discover information. Using critical thinking strategies supports the students' efforts in validating the information. Critical thinking while reading helps students monitor their understanding of the information, recognize the author's point of view, and take into account assumptions and generalizations, all by utilizing their own prior experience with the information. Critical reading requires readers to be active, careful, and reflective about what they are reading. The reader must stand back from the text, distance themselves from the emotions or beliefs

Figure 9.2 — Advanced Compare and Contrast Graphic Organizer: Examples

T-CHART EXAMPLE

Characteristic	Abraham Lincoln	John F. Kennedy
Leadership Qualities	Had the interest of protecting the union over self	Surrounded himself with advisors that were liberals and conservatives
Major Accomplishments	Liberated the slaves Saved the union of the United States	Civil Rights bill passed after his death Sent the United States to the moon
Political Skills	Patient, calculated, shrewd	Skillful statesman
Character/Integrity	Self-made man, humorous, sullen	Intelligent, well-spoken

ADVANCED VENN DIAGRAM EXAMPLE

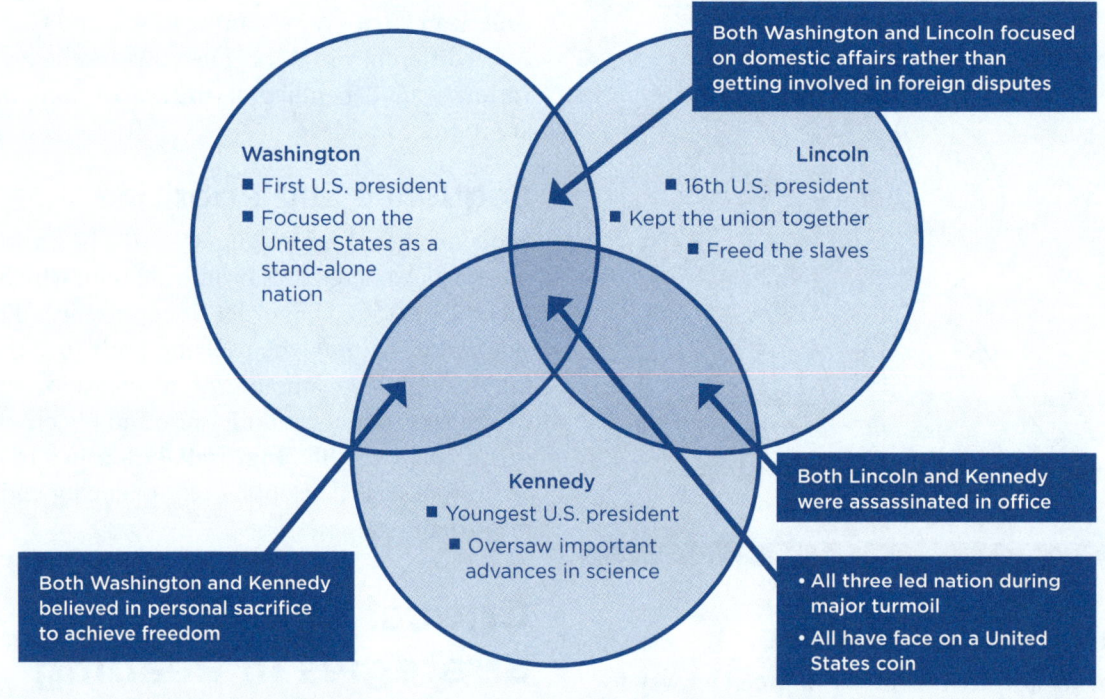

- **Washington**
  - First U.S. president
  - Focused on the United States as a stand-alone nation
- **Lincoln**
  - 16th U.S. president
  - Kept the union together
  - Freed the slaves
- **Kennedy**
  - Youngest U.S. president
  - Oversaw important advances in science

Both Washington and Lincoln focused on domestic affairs rather than getting involved in foreign disputes

Both Washington and Kennedy believed in personal sacrifice to achieve freedom

Both Lincoln and Kennedy were assassinated in office

- All three led nation during major turmoil
- All have face on a United States coin

---

it contains, and validate the evidence that supports the author's line of thinking. Critical thinking in reading requires the readers to:

- read for the central idea or purpose of the text
- identify the audience for which the text was written or intended
- understand the historical, political, social, and economic context of the writing
- recognize the discipline within which the text was positioned

Specific critical thinking strategies for reading:

- **Scanning or previewing:** Students look for specific words or repeated words in the table of contents, section or chapter headings, and introduction or conclusion paragraphs. This is also an effective strategy to pique interest in the topic.
- **Skimming:** Students read the text quickly the first time through and focus attention on the main points and ideas for further investigating.

Figure 9.3 — CIM: Examples

LOWER GRADES: THREE LITTLE PIGS

What impact does this → have on this? ↓	A Pig 1	B Pig 2	C Pig 3	D Big Bad Wolf (BBW)
1 Pig 1	■			
2 Pig 2		■		
3 Pig 3			■	
4 Big Bad Wolf				■

Pig 1 to Pig 1: **N/A**
Pig 1 to Pig 2:
Pig 1 to Pig 3:
Pig 1 to BBW:

Pig 2 to Pig 1:
Pig 2 to Pig 2: **N/A**
Pig 2 to Pig 3:
Pig 2 to BBW:

Pig 3 to Pig 1:
Pig 3 to Pig 2:
Pig 3 to Pig 3: **N/A**
Pig 3 to BBW:

BBW to Pig 1:
BBW to Pig 2:
BBW to Pig 3:
BBW to BBW: **N/A**

UPPER GRADES: THE U.S. CIVIL WAR

What impact does this → have on this? ↓	A The 1860 election of Abraham Lincoln	B The attack on Fort Sumter	C The Emancipation Proclamation	D Lee's Surrender to Grant in 1865
1 Economy				
2 Politics				
3 Race Issues				
4 Social Structure				

- **Annotating or note taking:** As readers begin a more in-depth or intensive read of the text, they should take notes that succinctly summarize the main ideas in each section. They should also write questions or comments that will suggest further investigation.

- **Highlighting:** Using a highlighter, readers may want to draw attention to specific words or phrases. Be careful students don't overuse this strategy; not everything is important and they shouldn't end up citing entire sections rather than statements. Keywords or sentences that

Figure 9.4 — Sequencing and Prioritizing Graphics

RANK ORDER of facts from most important to least important.

1 _____ 2 _____ 3 _____ 4 _____ 5 _____

CONTINUUM: Place each fact on the continuum from most important to least important.

Most ←——————————————————————————→ Least

CYCLE: Place the facts in a sequence to show how it represents a cycle.

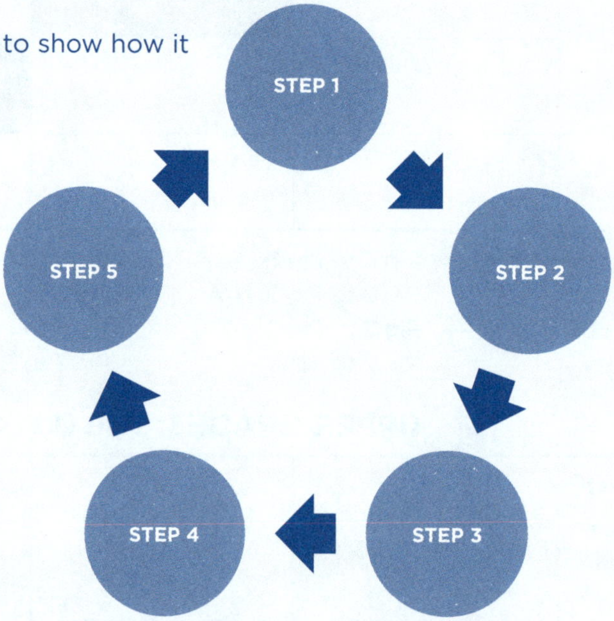

- STEP 1
- STEP 2
- STEP 3
- STEP 4
- STEP 5

SEQUENCE CHAIN: This tool can be used when trying to solve a problem that may have many types of solutions. It helps students understand that "if at first you don't succeed, try, try again" until you resolve the problem.

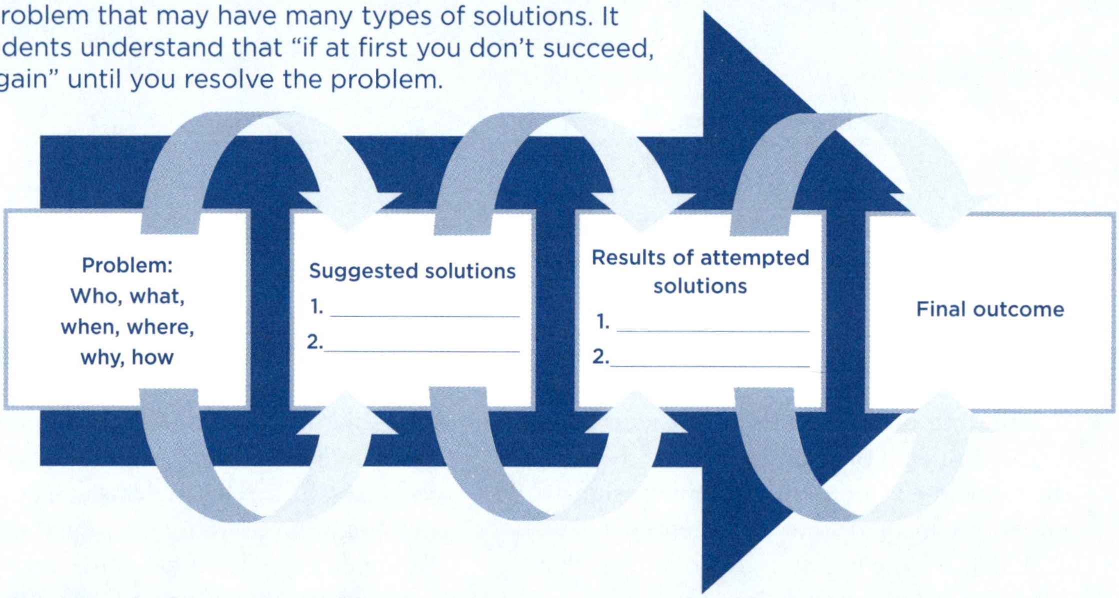

Problem: Who, what, when, where, why, how

Suggested solutions
1. _____
2. _____

Results of attempted solutions
1. _____
2. _____

Final outcome

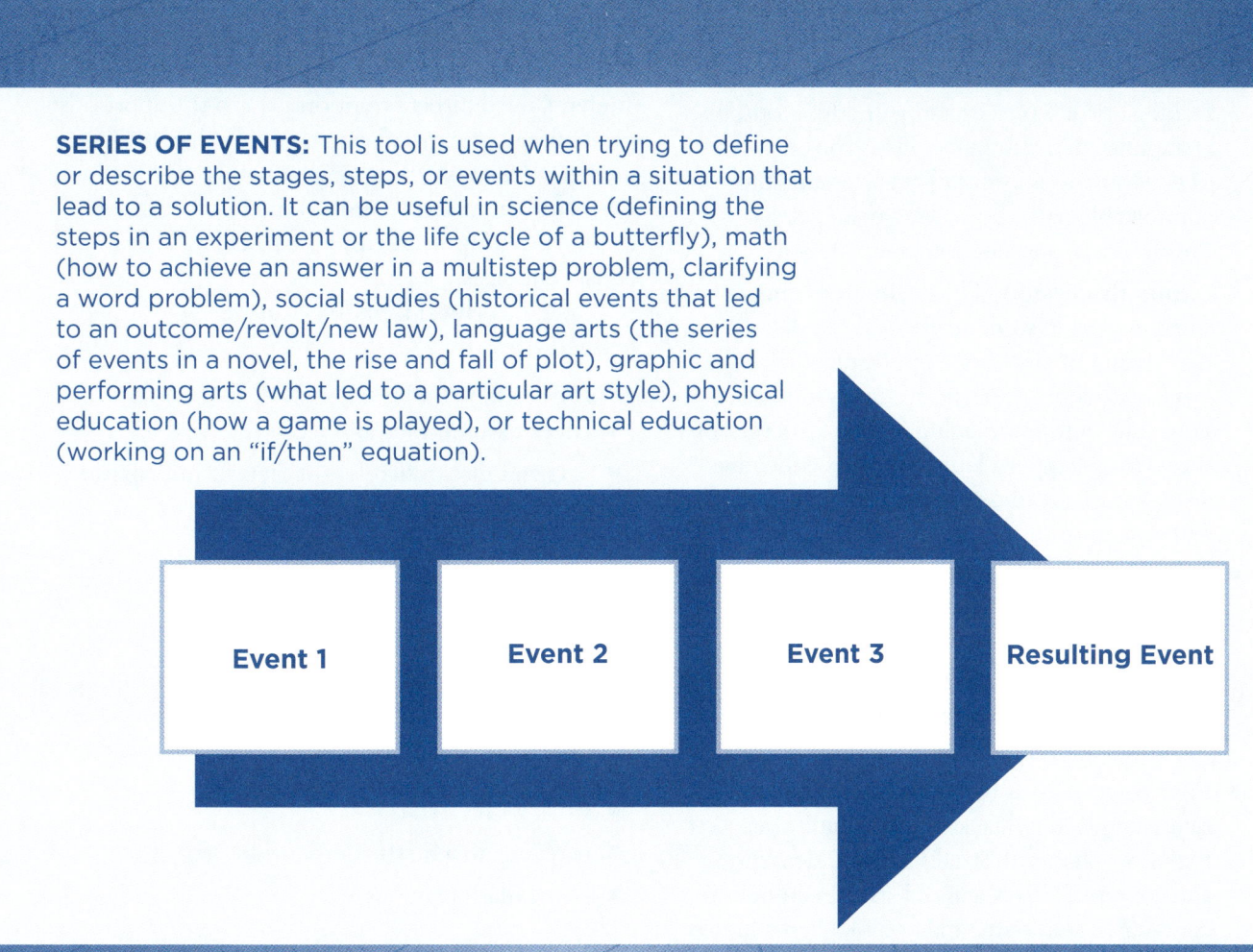

SERIES OF EVENTS: This tool is used when trying to define or describe the stages, steps, or events within a situation that lead to a solution. It can be useful in science (defining the steps in an experiment or the life cycle of a butterfly), math (how to achieve an answer in a multistep problem, clarifying a word problem), social studies (historical events that led to an outcome/revolt/new law), language arts (the series of events in a novel, the rise and fall of plot), graphic and performing arts (what led to a particular art style), physical education (how a game is played), or technical education (working on an "if/then" equation).

may support or provide evidence for validation should be selected.

- **Contextualizing:** Readers should investigate the historical, political, economic, and social context of the writing for greater understanding of the author's lens.
- **Inferring:** Most new standards have a specific focus on the readers' ability to make inferences based on increasingly complex text. Inferring is the ability to derive logical conclusions from the text or through observation, whether the information is implied or directly stated. See Infer: Justify Your Thinking (page 176) for a graphic organizer to help students make inferences while reading.
- **Reflecting:** Students should take notes of their thoughts and reflections on their own beliefs and values and compare and contrast them with the author's.
- **Evaluating arguments:** After substantial reading of the text, students should begin to evaluate the author's arguments or ideas. At this point, readers may find other sources that support or oppose the author's point of view.

Critical Thinking Strategies in Writing

The act of critical thinking in writing cannot be isolated from that of critical thinking in reading. As students write they should be aware that the reader will be reading their text with a critical eye. In order to communicate effectively through writing, students must keep in mind that judgments, interpretations, arguments, or opinions will need to be supported not only through quality writing structures but also through effective thinking.

Specific critical thinking strategies for writing:

- **Free writing:** Students write nonstop for a period of time (10 to 15 minutes) without making corrections, crossing anything out, or critiquing their thoughts. This type of "stream of consciousness" writing gets students more comfortable with the act of writing, allows for a flow of ideas, and uncovers new ideas.
- **Group discussion:** This technique brings small groups of students together to discuss the writing of either one or all students in the group. Students act as peer editors of ideas only. The editing of techniques or structure of the writing happens later. Students collectively discuss how the ideas are formed, supported, and argued.
- **Editing:** After students have formulated their ideas and structured and supported their arguments, they are ready to have their writing edited. This can be done by a peer or teacher. The editing process is one of collaboration with the editor and the writer.
- **Peer review:** This technique is also known as refereeing. Individual students submit their text to peers to be scrutinized for form, structure, and content. This is a useful strategy in building confidence as a writer and helps students understand how powerful their writing can become.
- **Publication:** Students should have the experience of making their text public. When they subject their writing to publication, they are putting their ideas in view of others for critique and discussion. Publication can take many forms: classroom displays; writing contests; submissions to newspapers, magazines, websites, or professional journals; and submissions to classroom or school publications.

Critical Thinking Strategies in Mathematics

The curricular area of mathematics naturally lends itself to the use and development of critical thinking. During the mathematics process, a student has a need to concisely articulate mathematical meaning, make decisions, solve problems, draw conclusions, use logical/deductive reasoning, and recognize known and unknown facts, among other needs. Some students may use a commonsense approach to solving math problems, while other students need direct attention paid to the appropriate usage of particular critical thinking strategies that are most effective in solving problems. Therefore, you should embed the instruction of critical thinking strategies in mathematics on a consistent basis.

Specific critical thinking strategies for mathematics:

- justify answers or conclusions
- check assumptions and facts
- sort and discard irrelevant facts or information
- estimate realistic solutions
- reflect, rethink, and rework
- comprehend and analyze information
- do logic and math puzzles
- decode messages or cryptograms
- play Sudoku
- design magic squares
- work with fractals
- take part in a math competition
- join a math team

Critical Thinking Strategies in Science

Like mathematics, science naturally lends itself to critical thinking. Every day, we try to understand the world around us. Scientific thinking *is* critical thinking. The methods used in science—observing, describing, hypothesizing, predicting, testing, experimenting, evaluating, and reporting—all require the use of critical thinking. We also use critical thinking when evaluating scientific claims, such as those in advertisements, opinions, or media.

Specific critical thinking for science:

- identify problems worth solving
- use evidence to support claims
- access relevant data and information
- be able to control data
- be able to validate evidence by repetition
- avoid subjective thinking
- view unreliable information with skepticism

- be aware of specious arguments
- use logical reasoning
- avoid fallacies
- judge the ethical and moral decisions made with science
- anticipate the consequences of scientific claims
- complete science fair projects
- undertake independent investigations
- debate controversial issues (for example, evolution, abortion, stem-cell research, etc.)
- read science mysteries/play crime scene investigations games
- take part in science competitions

Seven Critical Questioning Strategies to Use Daily

A wonderful strategy to use with students is to offer them critical thinking questions to ponder. This can be done as a sponge activity, before class begins (to get their brains in gear), or during class for those students who finish first, or it can be infused within the content or assessments. Critical thinking questions can even be used on bulletin boards or posters. Students can keep a journal of their responses to the questions and share these responses at conference time or include them in a portfolio assessment of their thinking. It is important to remember when students are answering critical reasoning questions, they should always support their answers with evidence (textual, graphic, or other media forms). Following are a list of the types of critical thinking questions and several examples of each type.

1. Analogy

Analogy is the cognitive process of transforming information from one context to another. Developing analogous thinking is an important step in creative production and innovation as well as critical thinking. Try using a concept (abstract) and a person/place/thing (concrete), as follows.

▶ **Sample questions and activities:**

How is a car (concrete) like an idea (abstract)?

How is a house like a storm?

How is an airplane like a thought?

How is a playground like democracy?

How is a turtle like an education?

How is a bus like awareness?

How is a classroom like indoctrination?

How is a rug like insight?

How is a sidewalk like a paradox?

How is a desk like a perception?

▶ **Or, turn it around:**

How is change like school?

How are systems like a computer?

How is tragedy like a book?

How is joy like a candy bar?

How is conflict like a clock?

How is conversation like a strawberry?

How is migration like a tomato?

How are rituals like a movie?

How is wisdom like a state capital?

How is courage like a cup?

▶ **Or, have students create an analogy** that would explain a novel, a concept, a mathematical problem, or their state capitol, city, or school.

2. Analysis of Point of View

In the study of historical documents or nonfiction materials, such as reports, research studies, newspaper or magazine articles, or websites, knowing the point of view of the author or creator is critical to the interpretation of the validity or foundation of the information. Knowing the factors that surround the document—how, where, when, why, and for what purpose it was produced—as well as whether the document was meant for public or private consumption, provides the reader multiple lenses through which to view the information.

▶ **Sample questions:**

What biases does the author represent in this article?

How does the author portray his or her point of view?

In what ways can you identify the assumptions of the author?

Why might this author see things the way she or he does?

How might this author's point of view change if he or she were . . . ?

How might someone else see this issue?

What are the various perspectives one could have on this writing?

What economic/cultural/historical/personal context contributed to the author's point of view?

What makes this author's point of view important?

What insights can you gain from this author's point of view?

After reviewing the data from the graphs/charts, what point of view/biases might the researcher have?

3. Complete an Incomplete

When not all the facts are in place, the learner must use prior knowledge and other resources to complete the problem-solving process. Questioning an incompletion is a sophisticated level of questioning, since the learner must have a solid foundation of both experiential and factual information

▶ **Sample questions and activities:**

Find the missing numbers in this sequence: 20, __, 16, __, 12, __.

Fill in the missing word in this sentence: George Read, Benjamin Rush, and John Adams were all____.

The Scientific Method:

1. Ask a question
2. _____
3. Construct a hypothesis
4. _____
5. Analyze your data
6. Communicate your results

Name the two missing steps and tell why they are important.

Fill in the blank and support your answer with reasoned evidence: Mars is NASA's next frontier. _____ will likely be selected to make the first journey.

4. Webbing

Webbing is an excellent tool that can help students see the "ripple effect" of an issue or conflict. Students can also use webbing as an analysis tool to uncover and mine into the complex interrelated causes and effects that develop from one source.

This questioning strategy is useful for visual/spatial learners and for those students needing assistance with "unpacking" their thinking.

▶ **Sample questions and activities:**

Graphically represent the effects of Hurricane Katrina, the recession, the gun laws in your state, El Niño/La Niña, etc.

Map out the relationships of all the characters in a particular novel.

Create a graphic organizer or thinking map to show where your lunch comes from.

Create a social web to represent your connections to all students in the classroom. (Social webs are similar to webbing in that students place themselves at the center of the web and connect themselves to others in the classroom.)

Create a drawing to show the impact of global warming on your school.

Diagram the effects of the war in Iraq.

Diagram how technology has changed your life.

Graphically represent the effects of alternative energy sources on the economies of the United States and other nations.

5. Hypothetical Thinking

This is a sophisticated level of thinking that requires the learner to use logical questioning and abstract thinking. When thinking hypothetically, the student learns to investigate problems in a careful and systematic fashion.

▶ **Sample questions and activities:**

What if there is no rain this summer?

What would happen if the schools ran out of money?

What would be the outcome if school ran all year long?

How might this experiment come out?

What if all modes of transportation were limited to bicycles?

How would life change if you had three legs?

What if a gallon of milk cost $10?

In what ways would society change if immigration were not allowed?

What would your life be like if you had a choice whether or not to attend school?

What effect would an overland trucking ban have on the United States economy? Support your answer with evidence.

6. Reversal of Thinking

This is an effective strategy to stimulate new thinking or when a student is "stuck in a rut." The process reframes the information and allows the student to look at the problem from a different point of view.

▶ **Sample questions and activities:**

Suppose the loser of the political race actually won. In what ways would legislation change?

From the perspective of a parent, what are the important factors to consider when sending your child to school?

How is life different in countries where an education is not a legal right?

How has life changed in Afghanistan since 2001?

What is your opinion on climate change? Support the opposing position on the issue.

7. Application of Different Symbol Systems

This strategy is effective when working with learners who think in a more visual manner, especially boys. It also forces learners to step outside their comfort zones to transform information in more than just a written symbol system. Students may transform an arithmetic problem into musical notes, the theme of a poem into chemical elements, a historical event into a mathematical equation, or a scientific theory into an editorial cartoon.

▶ **Sample questions and activities:**

Act out a math problem.

Draw a picture without words that represents the Gettysburg Address.

Draw a picture without words or numbers that represents linear equations.

Sketch the ideas in your essay.

Use movement to show your understanding of gravity.

Use vectors (line segments with directional arrows) to represent all forces acting on a car traveling at constant velocity.

Make sounds or music to depict a character, situation, or theme in a novel.

Critical Thinking Tools

Following are several specific tools that help build critical thinking skills. The idea behind these tools is that critical thinking is a fluid activity and requires students to think beyond themselves and consider multiple factors when forming responses. After using any of these tools, students should debrief the process they followed and reflect on the thinking that occurred.

PNI: Positive, Negative, Interesting

The PNI (page 177) helps students frame their thinking by asking them to think of positive, negative, and interesting or intriguing ideas about a statement or item. Using the PNI (sometimes called the PMI: plus, minus, interesting) can ferret out students' points of view on a subject, reveal their own assumptions and generalizations, incorporate cause and effect logic, and separate fact from opinion. The PNI also requires students to use both deductive and inductive reasoning.

Figure 9.5 on page 170 shows how the tool can be introduced to lower grade students. For very young students, have them use simple shapes to develop an understanding of positive/negative and interesting characteristics of each shape. Start with a circle. Using a large sheet of paper, have students divide the paper into three columns and three rows, creating nine boxes. Next, have the students label the far left column with a plus sign (+), the middle column with a minus sign (−), and the far right column with a question mark (?).

- Focusing the students' attention on the left-hand column, ask them: "What are some examples of positive (good) circles?" The students should then draw in examples of those things that make a circle positive, such as a smiley face, lollipop, or the planet Earth.

- Turning to the middle column, ask students: "What are some examples of negative (bad) circles?" Students can then draw in examples such as a sad face, pothole, or an ink stain.

- Moving to the far right column, ask students: "What are some examples of what makes a circle interesting?" Students may come up with ideas such as, "A circle has no corners to hide in," "It's hard to draw an exact circle," or "Circles are used to represent life."

Expand from simple shapes in the first chart (with circles) to ideas generated by the curriculum in the second chart (with statements generated from a Frog and Toad book).

Figure 9.5 — PNI: Examples (Lower Grades)

What Makes a Circle Positive, Negative, or Interesting?

+	−	?
○	○	○
○	○	○
○	○	○

Toad wants to wait until tomorrow to clean his messy house.

POSITIVE	NEGATIVE	INTERESTING
He will not have to clean today.	His house will be messy.	What will happen if he puts off cleaning his house again tomorrow?
He won't have to spend all day inside the house.	He won't have clean dishes to eat from or a clean sofa to sit on.	What if Toad has company?
He can do other things that he wants to do.	His house will be even dirtier tomorrow, so it will take him longer to clean it.	Why does Toad procrastinate?

Figure 9.6 shows an example of how this tool can be used for upper grades as a note-taking device regarding a statement from the curriculum (*December 18, 1865: Slavery was abolished in the United States*). You may also consider using this tool to discuss current events.

The PNI can be used as an individual thinking tool, sponge activity, brain warmup, or whole-class activity. You may also think about using this design as a bulletin board in your classroom. I suggest placing the bulletin board near your classroom door, so students can write on it while waiting in line to leave class. Write a statement on the board that gets students actively engaged in serious discussions. You can leave the statement up for several days or weeks to see how students' thinking, opinions, and ideas on one statement can change over time.

Figure 9.6 — PNI: Example (Upper Grades)

December 18, 1865: Slavery was abolished in the United States.

POSITIVE	NEGATIVE	INTERESTING
Involuntary servitude was outlawed.	It resulted in a loss of income for those who made a living trafficking humans.	The 13th Amendment was the first constitutional amendment in 60 years.
The 13th Amendment led to the 14th and 15th Amendments (civil rights in the states and ban on racial restrictions of voting).	Social structures were not put in place to support freed slaves. Not much changed in the South for them and the Union Army could not offer much protection.	The abolishment of slavery was mainly associated with the Republican party.
This began the Era of Reconstruction.	Andrew Johnson, Lincoln's successor, had little interest in helping freed slaves.	Laws were passed after the 13th Amendment that actually kept slaves in poverty.

CAI: Consider All the Issues

A more advanced level of the PNI is the Consider All the Issues (CAI) tool (see page 178). With this tool, students not only are using the PNI method, they are adding in specific facts to consider in relation to a particular issue. CAI can be a useful tool to help students consider all the relevant factors that can inform their decision making. It can be used when the students need to decide an action, plan an event, or predict an outcome. To develop students' abilities to use the CAI effectively, begin by offering them a practice scenario.

Sample CAI Scenario

After much financial planning, the school district has to cut $1 million from its budget. To balance the budget for the coming school year, the school board has decided to close one elementary school. This would mean that students from the closed school would be sent to at least three different school buildings in the next year. Many families are opposed to this option. A senior organization has agreed to buy the school building once it has closed to use as a senior center. What factors should be taken into consideration when deciding which school to close?

Another possible scenario:

A major pharmaceutical company has developed a pill that can increase intelligence. Your school is considering testing the pill. What should be considered?

Students can work on this issue either individually or in groups. Or, students can work individually on the CAI, then meet with a partner to compare ideas, and continue to meet with up to four new partners to share ideas. After the students have shared their CAI with at least five partners, reunite the class to create a class CAI on the scenario.

PL: Priority Ladder

We are often confronted with issues that are complex and have multiple causes. The Priority Ladder is a useful tool in helping students align their thinking about complex issues and put the multiple causes into a sequence of least to most relevant. This tool may be useful when using the CAI, in that the students must justify the order of factors and the amount of attention or weight each factor should receive. As with the CAI, students can use this tool individually, with partners, in small groups, or as a class.

Sample PL Activities

Students examine the contents of their desks and rank the contents from least to most valuable in solving:

- a math problem
- a homework problem
- an issue with a classmate
- being stranded on a desert island
- being called to the principal's office

Another way to practice using the PL is to put students in small groups and have them use the following list of items to accomplish one of the following activities:

Items:

- battery
- paper clips
- pens/pencils
- notepaper
- rubber band
- ruler
- permanent markers
- string
- pushpins
- scissors

Activities:

- solve a math problem
- find your way home
- help you do your homework
- survive on a deserted island

Each team will share how they organized their list and why they put items in the list the way they did. Students will see many creative ways to use everyday items.

To develop your own activity like the previous one, open your junk drawer at home and list 10 items in the drawer. Create four to five distinctly different scenarios for which the students can prioritize the list.

Figure 9.7 on page 172 shows an example of a Priority Ladder. A blank template is included on page 179.

Figure 9.7 — Priority Ladder: Example

Issue: The school board has decided to close one elementary school in the community.

MOST IMPORTANT
- Savings of up to $1,000,000 each year
- No teacher lay-offs
- Goodwill in the community
- Students may have to be bused to new school site
- School community is disrupted
- Parents upset with board's decision and won't vote for board members
- The building to be closed needs many repairs
- The building may be needed in the future if community grows
- Negative impact on neighborhood home values
- What to do with all of the fixtures in the building?
- Neighbors of the school like having the children present
- Local residents would have to go to another site to vote

LEAST IMPORTANT

Synthesis 3+1

This tool takes the common 3-2-1 Exit/Entrance Ticket to the next level (see page 180). Students complete the 3-2-1 portion of the graphic and add their creative thinking by coming up with one analogy, metaphor, or simile to summarize what they learned in the unit or lesson.

Structured Thinking Organizer (STO)

This tool will help students organize information in multiple formats for easier memorizing (see page 181). You can use the STO as an exit ticket or an additional component in a formative or summative assessment. Students should use this tool as a note-taking device throughout a unit or lesson. The follow-up questions can be used as homework, test preparation, or questions on the final exam.

No Easy Answers

Students often assume that there are answers for everything, which obviously is not true. One way to show students that we (and they) don't have all the answers, that knowing everything is impossible, and that finding solutions can be difficult, is to provide a wall space in your classroom for a bulletin board titled, "Things We Don't Know" or "No Easy Answers."

Students can place sticky notes on the board containing their ideas, thoughts, and questions, or they can write directly on a large sheet of paper. This bulletin board can be directly related to a subject matter or to general daily life. Subject matter questions may be framed around controversial issues (such as stem-cell research, abortion, medical use of marijuana, or assisted suicide) or information the students have an interest in knowing. For daily life issues, students may ask questions such as "When will the global recession end?" "How much will college cost by the time I graduate?" or "What is the best field of study for the future?" The bulletin board can be changed weekly, monthly, or kept up all year to see what kinds of questions and ideas students generate. If a question is answered, it is removed from the board.

Your students will vary in their degrees of sophistication when using any of the thinking tools and strategies listed in this chapter. Hence, it is essential for you to know where students are in the learning process, develop differentiated activities to scaffold students to higher levels of thinking, and provide students with differing avenues to show what they know. When students are skilled in critical thinking, they form meaningful questions, develop self-regulation, and can think for themselves.

Spider Diagram

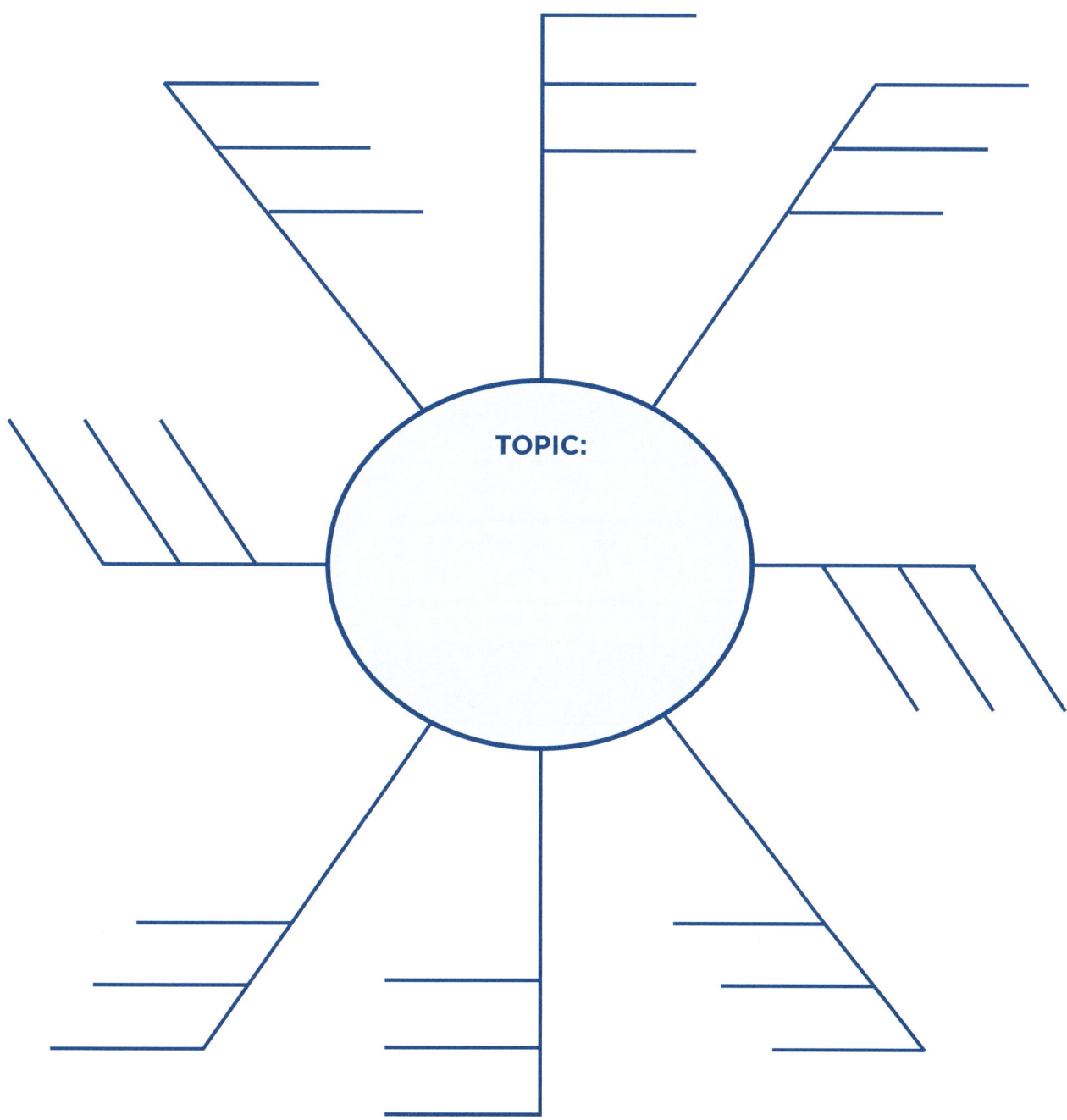

Compare and Contrast Graphic Organizer

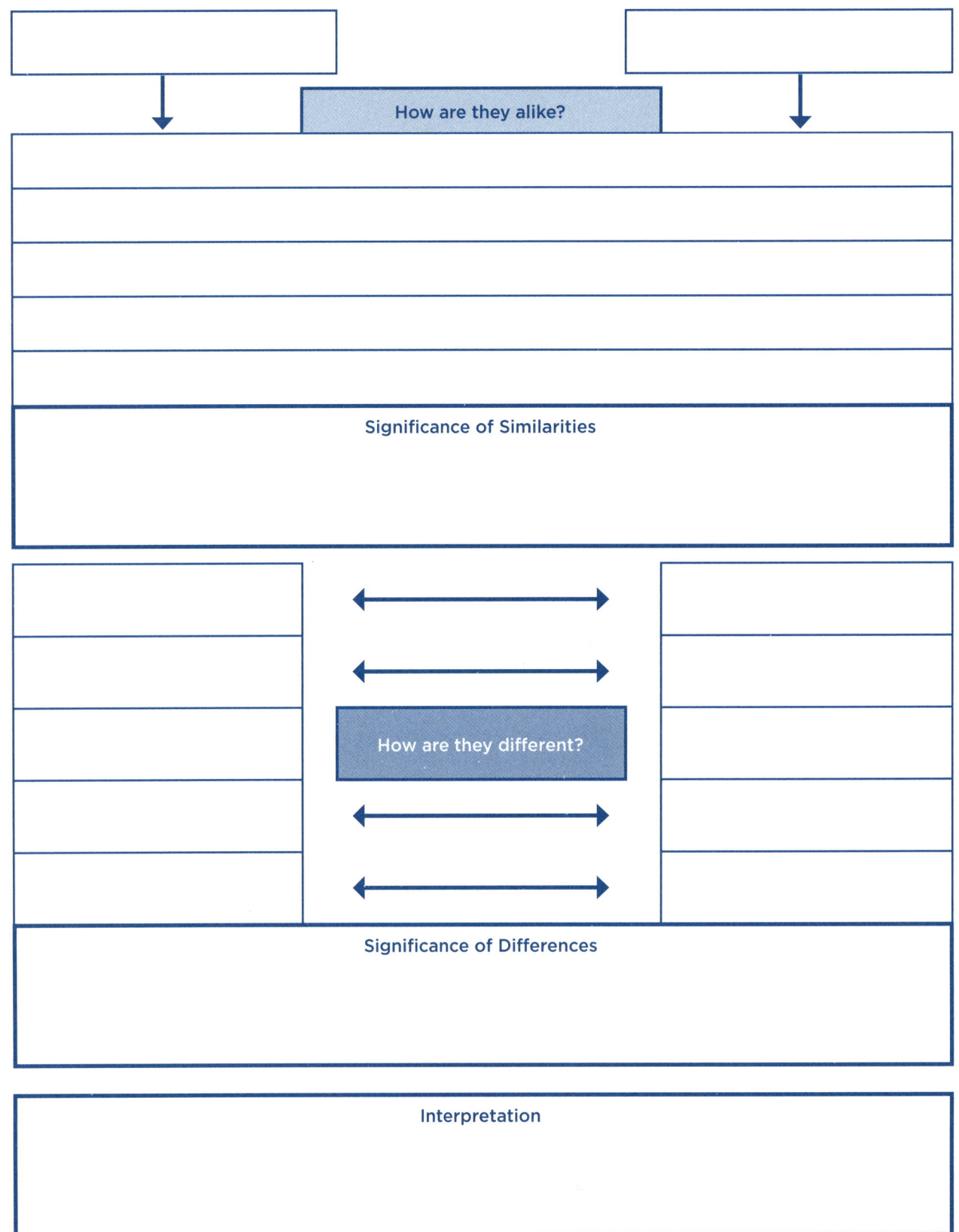

How are they alike?

Significance of Similarities

How are they different?

Significance of Differences

Interpretation

Cross-Impact Matrix (CIM)

What impact does this → have on this? ↓	A	B	C	D	E
1					
2					
3					
4					
5					

From *Advancing Differentiation: Thinking and Learning for the 21st Century* by Richard M. Cash, Ed.D., copyright © 2017. This page may be reproduced for use within an individual school or district. For all other uses, contact Free Spirit Publishing Inc. at www.freespirit.com/permissions.

Infer: Justify Your Thinking

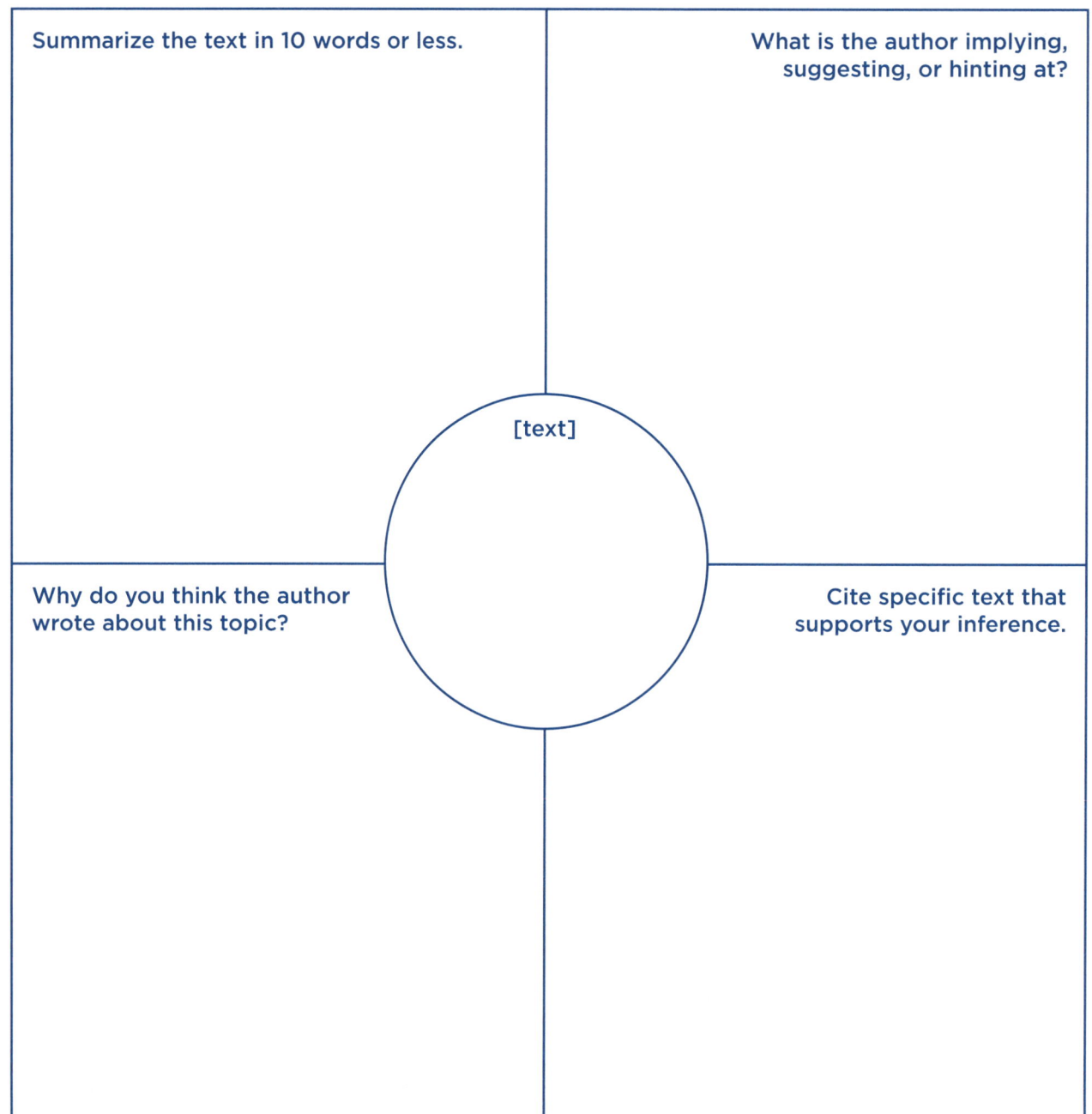

Positive, Negative, Interesting (PNI)

Topic:		
POSITIVE	**NEGATIVE**	**INTERESTING**

From *Advancing Differentiation: Thinking and Learning for the 21st Century* by Richard M. Cash, Ed.D., copyright © 2017. This page may be reproduced for use within an individual school or district. For all other uses, contact Free Spirit Publishing Inc. at www.freespirit.com/permissions.

Consider All the Issues (CAI)

ISSUE	PLUS	MINUS	INTERESTING

Priority Ladder

Issue:

MOST IMPORTANT
LEAST IMPORTANT

Synthesis 3 + 1

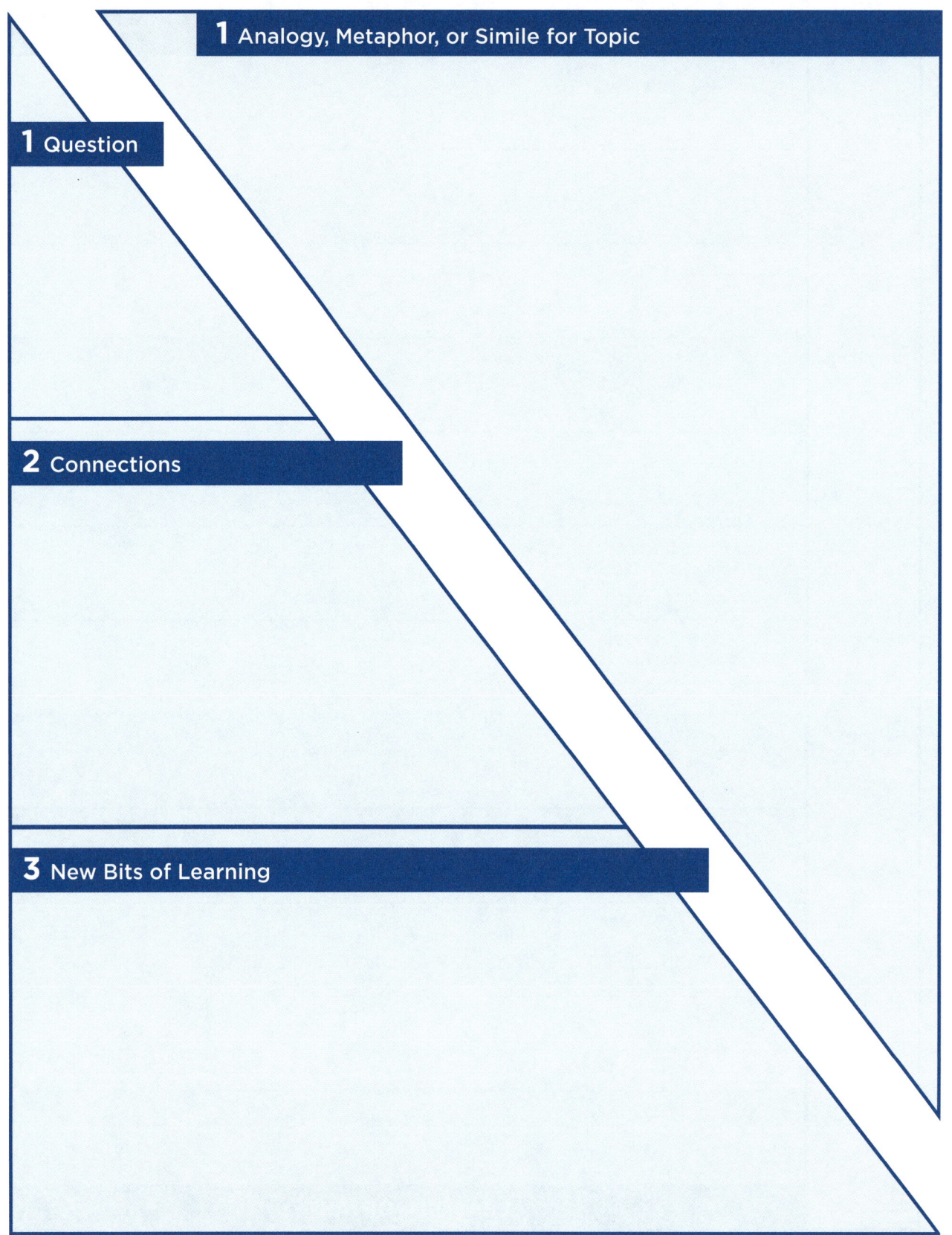

Structured Thinking Organizer (STO)

Directions:

1. On the left side of the triangle, write an analogy for the information presented. Then, explain why you chose this analogy.
2. On the right side of the triangle, write an analogy to define the *opposite* of the information presented. Explain why you chose this analogy.
3. Inside the triangle, draw a picture to represent the information presented. (The picture should *not* be an exact replica of the information.)
4. At the end of the unit of study, answer the five follow-up questions beneath the triangle.

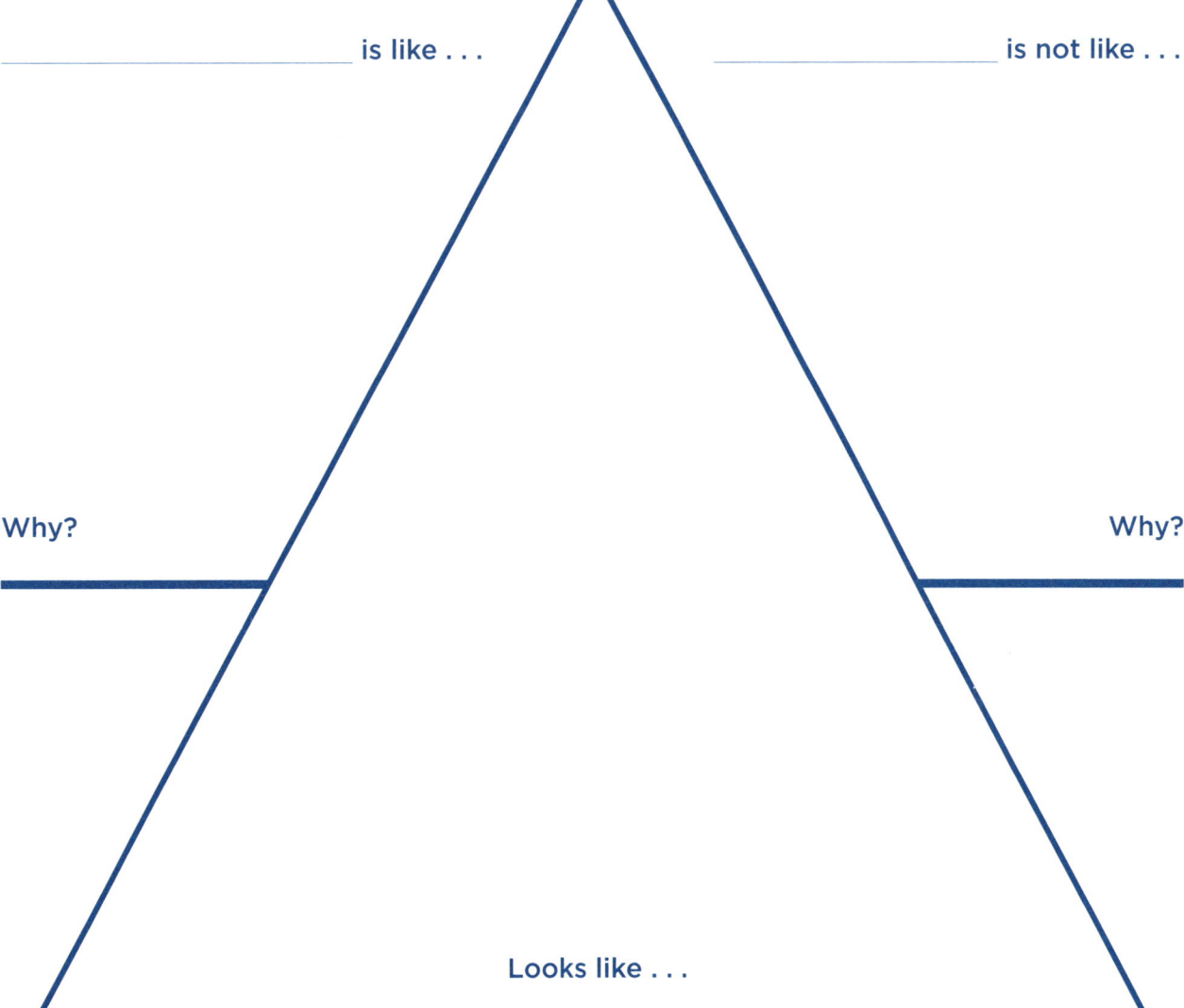

_____ is like . . .

_____ is not like . . .

Why?

Why?

Looks like . . .

Follow-Up Questions

1. What did you already know about this topic?
2. How can you connect this topic to your everyday life?
3. How would you explain this topic to another person?
4. What patterns do you see?
5. What new ideas did you come up with?

From *Advancing Differentiation: Thinking and Learning for the 21st Century* by Richard M. Cash, Ed.D., copyright © 2017. This page may be reproduced for use within an individual school or district. For all other uses, contact Free Spirit Publishing Inc. at www.freespirit.com/permissions.

Chapter 10

Creative Thinking: Stepping Outside the Box

> We are all creative, but by the time we are three or four years old, someone has knocked the creativity out of us. Some people shut up the kids who start to tell stories. Kids dance in their cribs, but someone will insist they sit still. By the time the creative people are 10 or 12, they want to be like everyone else.
>
> —Maya Angelou, author

Recent studies suggest that levels of creativity have declined in the United States.[1] The reasons for this decline may be related to schools being overwhelmed by the mandating of standards and assessments, making it difficult for teachers to efficiently infuse creativity into curriculum and instruction. Additionally, some feel that the skills of creativity are limited to art and music classes, which are being eliminated in many schools due to hard financial times.

Creativity, the act of producing something original and useful, is an essential skill for the twenty-first century and considered to be the number-one competency for leadership. Europe and Asia have placed substantial emphasis on idea generation and creative thinking in order to position themselves as world leaders economically, politically, and culturally. As we consider our students' futures, it is critical that we view creativity not only as a vital learning tool, but also as a crucial component in national confidence and success.

Brilliant researchers have authored many books on creativity—where it comes from and how to develop it. There are also substantial resources available to teachers that directly teach the art of creativity. My intent in this book is to offer a general overview of the idea of creativity; characteristics of creative individuals; general strategies of creativity; and how creativity can be infused within your daily routine, lessons, and curriculum. Creativity is natural to every person, but for many, this natural inclination toward creativity gets suppressed throughout their years in school. When we ask students for that one right answer, or we test them on reaching the correct solution, we may be inadvertently stifling the creative process. I am not suggesting that finding the right answer is not important, but rather that our heavy reliance on close-ended solutions is not reflective of thinking for the twenty-first century.

Students have access to all kinds of information instantaneously. Finding a solution to a problem can be as simple and quick as a click of a button. Creativity and creative thinking compel us to take time, think things through, wait until we have considered all the different options, stand back to see our ideas from a distance, and, finally, ponder "what next?" From the invention of the light bulb to space travel, creativity is what has enabled our society to advance and succeed. Demanding that our students master creative thinking will ensure our continued success.

---

1. Bronson, P., and A. Merryman. "The Creativity Crisis." *Newsweek* (July 10, 2010). Cited research by Dr. Kyung Hee Kim at the College of William and Mary.

What Is Creative Thinking?

Creativity is an essential ingredient that makes entrepreneurs, mathematicians, business leaders, artists, musicians, teachers, doctors, lawyers, and everyday people successful. Being able to think creatively is what distinguishes those who can do the job from those who can do the job better. But what exactly *is* creativity? We may "know it when we see it," but how do we help students master it if we can't specifically define it? This chapter provides some descriptions of creativity and strategies for how to engage students in being more creative and thinking more creatively.

Creative Thinking Is Making Something New or Improved

In general, creativity is the mental process used to imagine or invent through combining, changing, or reshaping existing ideas. In the simplest term: it is *the ability to make something new*. Creative individuals see multiple ways to solve problems. They are limber thinkers who are able to produce innovative products, ideas, and solutions. Creativity is also a process of refining and improving ideas and solutions. Creative ideas and products usually do not happen in a flash. The most creative innovations are the result of hard work, patience, persistence, and perseverance.

Creative Thinking Is the Other Side of Critical Thinking

Creative thinking can also be thought of as the flip side to critical reasoning. Whereas the main goal of critical reasoning is to come to one conclusion, the goal of creative thinking is to explore many ideas, generate several possibilities, and look for many "right" answers. Both types of thinking are vital to a successful life and are required for solving problems. Providing students the opportunity to hone the skills of creative thinking will help them develop tools to deal with new problems and situations. These tools will allow them to find answers that are not in books or at websites, create ideas that have not been considered, and apply new information in constructive ways.

Creative Thinking Is Inclusive and Aware

The act of creative thinking requires us to look, ask, and seek new ideas and answers. It inspires us to open our eyes to the world around us and see it with wonder. Creative thinkers have an awareness of things others miss. Creativity also requires the use of all our senses to accept many kinds of stimuli. Most importantly, creativity does not happen in a vacuum; it requires the multiple voices and views of others. Sir Kenneth Robinson, a leading authority on creativity, states that most original thinking comes through collaboration and being stimulated by other people's ideas.[2] Collaboration, diversity, the exchange of ideas, and building on others' achievements is at the heart of the creative process.

Creative Thinking Is Both Convergent and Divergent

In Chapter 7, two types of thinking were discussed: convergent thinking and divergent thinking. In summary, convergent thinking is the thinking that brings together information from various sources so that a solution can be found. Decisions are based on the facts coming toward an answer (see Figure 7.2). Whereas divergent thinking is intuitive, open-minded, and generative of many solutions (see Figure 7.1). Creativity is not always about coming up with the wackiest or most far-fetched ideas, nor is it aimless thinking. For an idea to work, it has to be doable, reasonable, and provide an outcome that is reliable. Therefore, to be an effective creative thinker, both convergent and divergent thinking are required. Divergent thinking opens up the possibilities and convergent thinking ensures the solution or idea is workable.

Characteristics of Creative Individuals

Dr. Robert Sternberg promotes the idea of making creativity a habit, something that all students should be expected to do. He states, "The main things that promote the habit are (a) opportunities to engage in it, (b) encouragement when people avail themselves of these opportunities, and (c) rewards when people

---

2. Azzam, A. M. "Why Creativity Now? A Conversation with Sir Ken Robinson." *Teaching for the 21st Century,* 67 (1) (September 2009): 22–26.

respond to such encouragement and think and behave creatively."[3] Following are the general characteristics of creative individuals as well as ideas for developing these characteristics in your students.

Creative Individuals Are Motivated

Students who are internally motivated are driven to seek out problems and find interesting solutions to those problems. Creative thinkers are motivated to know how things work, why things don't work, and how to make things work better. Creativity takes that drive to solve problems in a new way. Chapter 4 explains motivation in more detail.

Creative Individuals Have a Solid Knowledge Base

To be effective at creativity, a student must have a solid understanding of the content area. One cannot solve problems or make things better without a wide range of knowledge, both within the content area and across other content areas. This interconnectivity of knowledge allows the individual to create variations or combinations of ideas. For instance, having a solid knowledge base is especially important for creativity in mathematics. Mathematicians think flexibly and are able to efficiently problem solve because of their insights into and understanding of the workings of mathematics, not just due to their computational skills. (See specific tips for encouraging creativity—especially in math—on page 195.)

Creative Individuals Enjoy Challenges

Being creative is not necessarily an easy act. Creativity usually requires a lot of trial and error. If students do not have the inclination toward challenge, or have not faced intellectual challenges throughout their learning, creativity may be difficult. This is why some gifted or advanced learners are unwilling to be creative. They lack the resourcefulness of being able to cope with challenge and not succeeding instantly. Creative individuals must be willing to take on the challenge of finding new solutions and question their own beliefs, ideas, and assumptions. They also must be aware that they may not reach a conclusion quickly or come up with the right solution initially.

Creative Individuals Show Patience, Persistence, and Perseverance (P^3)

Our world today is one of instant gratification. We don't have to wait long before we find an answer (Google.com, Ask.com), eat a meal (fast food, microwave dinners), hear from a friend (social media, text messages, cell phones), or watch our favorite show whenever we want (DVRs, on-demand, streaming). Today's students have generally become less patient and often lack persistence and the ability to persevere at a task that doesn't have a quick and easy solution.

Creativity is hard work and requires the P^3 behaviors of patience, persistence, and perseverance (see page 106). While there are no quick and easy answers, being able to stimulate creative thinking quickly is necessary. However, as previously stated, creative thinking requires a solid knowledge base—this takes time and patience to build. Creative thinkers also must enjoy the challenge of creating—this takes determination. And they must not settle for the single "right" answer—this takes perseverance and stick-to-it-ness.

Strategies to Develop Creative Thinking

Building creativity in the classroom takes many forms. From brainstorming ideas for a writing assignment, to predicting an outcome of a science experiment, to doing an independent study, students are using creative thinking skills and talents every day in the classroom. In many cases, students don't even know they are being creative. By raising the students' awareness of creativity, you can help them understand the power of creative thought. To raise your students' creative consciousness, you need to infuse specific and directed creative thinking activities and exercises into your daily lessons. Introduce the activities as "creativity building" activities. Students need to be consciously aware of these activities and know there is an expectation of open-mindedness, novelty, and unconventional thought.

---

3. Sternberg, R. J. "Creativity Is a Habit." *Education Week* (February 22, 2006): 47–64.

One approach to developing creative thinking is through the four best-known creative thinking strategies: *fluency*, *flexibility*, *originality*, and *elaboration* (FFOE). These strategies may be used individually or in combination. The following activities and ideas can be used as "sponge" activities (to be used when you have a few minutes left and you want students to soak up all the learning they can), warmups to thinking, or as "brain breaks" (see Chapter 4, page 84). Engaging students in these strategies, both imbedded within the curriculum and as independent activities, can develop their habits of creative thinking and provide incentive for them to use creative thinking more often.

Encourage Fluency

Fluency is the action of coming up with as many ideas as possible. Encouraging fluency can help students overcome their anxiety of finding that "one right answer." Fluency activities can also be thought of as brainstorming. Brainstorming requires that in a group:

1. All members participate in some way, either through generating ideas or respectful listening.
2. All ideas are considered; there is no judgment (either positive or negative) and no put-downs.
3. All members work as quickly as possible; taking time to think through an idea may stifle creativity and encourage self-criticism.
4. All members listen to others' ideas and build on them.

Activities That Stimulate Fluency

- List as many [insert color] things as you can.
- List all the things you can think of that are [insert adjective].
- List all the things that come in pairs [or in threes, fours, etc].
- List as many compound words as you can.
- List as many three-syllable words as you can.
- List words that start with the letter [insert letter].
- List words that end with the letter [insert letter].
- List words with the [insert vowel or consonant] sound.
- List all the things that involve [insert concept; for example, truth, love, justice, independence].
- List things that are framed.
- List things that shine.
- List things that inspire.
- List things that open [or close].
- List activities for [insert season].
- List the possible uses for [insert object].
- List ways to represent [insert number or math concept].
- List the questions you would ask [insert person; for example, the president of the United States, Albert Einstein, Georgia O'Keefe].
- List all the things you might see at a [insert place].
- List things that can only be used once.
- List things that come in multiple colors.
- List items included on a road map.
- List things that are uneven.
- List ways our culture has been influenced by ideas or inventions from ancient civilizations.
- List items that use the metric system as a method of measurement.
- List ways to say hello in as many languages as you can.
- List all the ways to solve [insert problem].

Develop Flexibility

Flexibility is the ability to adapt to new situations and try various ways to approach and solve problems. It means not accepting the first and most obvious solution. It teaches students to look at problems and ideas from many different angles and perspectives. Questions that can stimulate flexibility are, "What other kinds of . . . ?" "What else does . . . ?" "What's another way to . . . ?

Activities and Questions That Stimulate Flexibility

- How many different ways can you categorize these items?
- Create a metaphor for . . .
- Use a metaphor/simile/analogy to describe . . .
- What items could be bought at a discount store that could be used to build a house?

- What items could be bought at a grocery store that could be used to stop a flood?
- What items could be bought at a hardware store that could be used to make a dress?
- What items might you find in a garage that could be used to tame a lion?
- How many different ways can you use a pencil?
- What's another way to solve this problem?
- What's another way to look at . . . ?
- What's another way to use . . . ?
- How else can you . . . ?
- Where else might you find . . . ?
- Show a different way to represent your answer.

Emphasize Originality

The concept of *lateral thinking*—the process of consciously changing your perspective in order to come up with an original idea—is another valuable strategy in creative thinking. Originality is the development of unique, unusual, and novel ideas. Novelty in thinking can be difficult for students because they may believe that "everything has already been thought of," or they may take the easy way out by using others' ideas. Being original or novel does not always mean coming up with something totally new. It can also mean taking an old idea or product and giving it a twist so that the outcome is distinctive.

Activities and Questions That Stimulate Originality

- From your list of items, which item did no one else think of?
- From your list of items, which item do you think is the most unique?
- Create a new use for a [insert object].
- Design a new use for [insert object].
- Share the most unusual occasion for writing a note or letter to someone.
- Create a new ending for [insert novel or film].
- Construct a workable plan for a new gardening tool.
- Design a device to clean a messy room.

Inspire Elaboration

Elaboration is the process of providing extensive and extended details. When students are pushed to "color in all the white spaces," they develop a more holistic sensibility for solution finding. Elaboration requires expanding, embellishing, extending, refining, and stretching ideas. Creativity demands this refinement and continual improvement. For any common product or utensil, manufacturers are constantly making improvements by building upon the collective creativity of the previous model. Take, for instance, a car—each year, the new model includes improvements over the previous year's model. Car companies make these improvements based on continual evaluation to make their cars faster, sleeker, more comfortable, more efficient, and more tuned to our needs. Creative thinkers never stop trying to make their ideas better.

Activities and Questions That Stimulate Elaboration

- Choose a word from your list and elaborate on it by creating a story, picture, poem, or song.
- How can you make a pencil more effective or interesting?
- Elaborate on this shape [show a circle, squiggle, line, square, or other shape].
- Write what happened before the story begins of the Three Little Pigs, *Romeo and Juliet*, or *Call of the Wild*.
- Elaborate on the sentence: "The dog barked in the night."
- How would you change the game of [insert game] so it could be played . . . ? (for example, How would you change the game of baseball so it could be played under water?)
- Write a technical manual to build the world's best peanut butter and jelly sandwich.
- Explain how you arrived at your answer to [insert problem].
- Using numbers only, give someone directions to a location.
- A thief has stolen the *Mona Lisa* painting from the Louvre Museum in Paris. She used three items to help her steal the painting [list three unrelated items such as an ice cube, piano, and crowbar]. How did she do it?

- Which month is the heaviest? Why?
- Which day is the sweetest/most sour? Why?
- What hour is the tallest/widest/narrowest? Why?

Creative Thinking Activities

In addition to the activities listed under each FFOE strategy (fluency, flexibility, originality, elaboration), the following activities also help develop creative thinking skills by stimulating multiple FFOE strategies at once.

Activity: SCAMPER with Sparking Words

▶ **Stimulates: flexibility, originality**
(*sparking words* = words to spark kids' thinking)

S = Substitute
What could you substitute on a . . . to make it better?
Instead of . . . I could use . . .
What if I change . . . ?

Sparking words: alternate, exchange, fill-in, rename, replace, reposition, change, stand in for, swap, switch, take the place of, proxy, use instead of

C = Combine
What would you combine with . . . to make it better?
If I put . . . with . . . it will create . . .

Sparking words: merge, blend, bring together, commingle, conjoin, unite, join, coalesce, mix, associate, package

A = Adapt
What could you adapt on a . . . to make it better?
How can you adapt the idea of . . . ?
If I change . . . it will . . .

Sparking words: change, alter, adjust, vary, amend, bend, fit, adapt, conform, copy, emulate, incorporate, transform

M = Modify (maximize/minimize)
How can I modify . . . to make it better?
Where might I put greater emphasis to make . . . better?
If I make . . . larger/smaller it will . . .

Sparking words: adapt, adjust, alter, change, grow, amend, vary, transform, mutate, curb, control, temper, modulate, make the most of, exploit, capitalize on, get the most out of, take advantage of, enlarge, increase, expand, amplify, make bigger, raise, lengthen, heighten, boost, augment, extend, reduce, diminish, lessen, curtail, decrease, play down, make light of, shorten, stretch out, overemphasize, overstress, underemphasize

P = Put to other use
How might I use . . . differently to make it better?
I can use . . . in this way:_____.
How might . . . use . . . ?

Sparking words: employ, utilize, exercise, apply, exploit, draw on, operate, work, handle, treat, manipulate, manage, spend, expend, exhaust, use up, consume, function, purpose

E = Eliminate
What can I eliminate from . . . to make it better?
What could I simplify to make . . . better/more efficient?
If I eliminate . . . it will . . .

Sparking words: get rid of, do away with, eradicate, abolish, remove, reduce, purge, exclude, excrete, expel, exterminate, jettison, kill, lessen, limit, liquidate, lower, moderate, minimize, modulate, pass over/on, reject, restrict, throw out, waste, wipe out/away

R = Revise (rearrange/reorder/reverse)
What can I revise to make . . . better?
If I revise . . . it can . . .

Sparking words: overturn, turn around, undo, annul, invalidate, repeal, quash, swap, transpose, switch, invert, change, opposite, contrary, converse, inverse, antithesis, other side, alter, modify, adjust, amend, correct, improve, rework, reorganize, reschedule, delay, reshuffle, regroup, restructure, sort out, alter, mix up, move around, mess up, upset, change around, withdraw, move backward/forward/around

Activity: Squiggle

▶ **Stimulates: fluency, flexibility, originality, elaboration**

(*Variation:* Dot—the same activity but using a single sticky dot.)

1. With a black felt pen or marker, draw a random "squiggle" on a piece of paper for each student. The squiggle can be identical for every student or completely different for each student.
2. Give the paper to the students and direct them to elaborate on their squiggle to create an original drawing.
3. Be sure to encourage your students to turn the paper around to get a different perspective of the squiggle until an idea is sparked in their head.
4. Direct students to fill in "all the white spaces" and be as elaborate as they can.
5. Students should spend at least five minutes elaborating on their drawing. For those students with the "I'm done" syndrome, say:
   ▸ Where might you add more colors or lines?
   ▸ What objects could you add that might be around your object?
   ▸ What objects could you add that might not typically be around your object?
   ▸ How could you use SCAMPER to make your drawing more elaborate?
6. Have students share their drawings.
7. To extend the learning, ask:
   ▸ What was most difficult about this activity?
   ▸ What would make this task easier?
   ▸ Why did you do what you did?
   ▸ How could you use this technique in other classes?

Activity: Think Fast!

▶ **Stimulates: fluency, flexibility**

1. Collect an assortment of odd objects (such as: empty tin can, one foot of plastic tubing, spoon, slinky, drumstick, hair brush, paper towel tube, tennis ball), and place them into a large bag.
2. Arrange students in small groups of no more than 10.
3. To warm up, give each group one of the objects.
4. Have them pass the object around the group once without saying anything. They are to appraise the object using all of their senses (for example, What does/might it smell/taste/sound/look/feel like?) and then come up with at least one idea of what the object *could* be (not what it really is). For instance, the group with the drumstick may think of ideas such as a microphone, baton, or stirring rod.
5. On the second pass around, the students share with each other their idea. No one can repeat what someone else has said. If their idea was used, they will need to come up with another idea.
6. After students are warmed up, change the objects in the group and begin again.
7. This time have the students pass the object around the group instantly sharing their idea of what the object could be.
8. Again, change the object in each group and this time students must pass the object around stating what it could be, but doing it as quickly as possible. I use: "Ready, set, think fast!" to begin this round of the game.
9. The group that passes the object around fastest and comes up with all different ideas is considered the "winner."

Variations on this activity

- Instead of only passing the object around once, have the students try to pass it around the circle as many times as they can without repeating an idea. (flexibility, elaboration)
- After each round have the students decide which of the ideas was the most original. (originality)
- Have one student suggest what the object could be, and then the others elaborate on that idea (for example, drumstick = a baton . . . used by a world famous conductor . . . who was captured by evil spies . . . and taken to an underground hideaway . . . where he was found and rescued because his baton had magic powers that could lull his captors to sleep . . . and so on. (elaboration)
- Each group member gets a different object and must create a new idea for his or her object. The students then collaborate with each other

to use the objects in a play-acted scene. (fluency, flexibility, originality, elaboration)
- Each group member gets a different object and the group works together to come up with one combined object or new idea. (fluency, flexibility, originality, elaboration)
- Each group member must pantomime (using no words or sounds) their idea for an object to get others to guess what the student has created. (fluency, flexibility, elaboration)

Activity: ROLE Cards

▶ **Encourages: fluency, flexibility, originality, elaboration**

1. Using four different color index cards, create four categories:

ROLE	OCCASION	LOCATION	EMOTION
Farmer	Birthday	At a lake	Happy
Banker	Wedding	In a castle	Sad
Server	Funeral	In a car	Tired
Dog catcher	Party	In a cave	Angry
Writer	Religious event	In a haunted house	Bored
Artist	Dinner	In a restaurant	Disgusted
Scientist	Breakfast	On a bus	Calm
Mathematician	Senate hearing	In the woods	Crabby
Inventor	Business meeting	In a grocery store	Smug
Juror	Trial	In a school	Snide
Judge	Fundraiser	In a hospital	Excited
Historian	Prom	On a street	Frightened
Reporter	Halloween	In the zoo	Kind
Soldier	Kentucky derby	In a barn	Jealous
Therapist	Book signing	In an office	Worried
Journalist	Graduation	At the beach	Upset
Character from a novel	Event in a novel	Location in a novel	Emotion in a novel

2. Divide the students into groups of four or small teams.
3. Have the groups pull one card randomly from each of the four ROLE categories.
4. Each group develops a scene based on the ROLE cards they have drawn.
5. Allow the groups 5 to 10 minutes to collaborate on their scene. Tell the groups they are not to use the words written on the ROLE cards.
6. Have students present their scene to the other groups.
7. The other groups try to guess what ROLE cards the group chose.

Variations on this activity
- Each student draws one card from each category and writes his or her own story using the ROLE cards as guides. (elaboration, originality)
- In teams, students create their own ROLE cards and swap with another team. (flexibility, originality, elaboration)
- Using a work of literature, students create ROLE cards to rewrite the ending (elaboration) or create the prequel (elaboration, originality).
- After all groups have performed, the class votes on which scene was the most original. (originality)
- The class receives the same randomly drawn ROLE cards and each student must create a story or scene based on the four cards. (elaboration, originality)
- Each student in a small group draws one ROLE card from each category and must create one scene using all the descriptors. (elaboration, originality)

Activity: What's the Question?

▶ **Stimulates: fluency, flexibility, originality, elaboration**

This game, like the game Jeopardy, begins with the answer and requires the students to provide the question. The intent of this game is to help students understand and appreciate that there may be more than one right answer to any question. Using the ROLE cards, give the "answer" to the students. Individually, in pairs, in small groups, or as a whole class, students come up with the most original, unique, or novel "question" to match the answer.

Example:
You: "Farmer."
Students: "Who is outstanding in their field?"

Variations on this activity

- Instead of using the ROLE cards, have students create their own "answers" using the most obscure information they can find. For example, Answer: "Westmoreland." Question: "Ralph deNeville was the First Earl of what?" (*Note:* This variation requires substantial research. Therefore, students will need ample time to find the questions—up to one week.)
- For younger students, use content information as a form of review. For example, Answer: "Winter." Question: "In what season is the sun closest to the Earth?"
- For a math variation: use equations. For example, Answer: "9." Question: "What is (3 x 12) – (3 x 9)?"

Activity: Everyday Art View

▶ **Stimulates: fluency, flexibility, originality, elaboration**

1. Post a reprint of a famous work of art.
2. Next to the work of art, post a list of questions that are used as either "sponge" activities, writing prompts, or discussion builders/guides.

Sample fluency activities

- List all the things you identify in this painting.
- List all the feelings you have when you view this painting.
- List all the colors you see in this painting.
- List questions for the artist about this painting.
- List all the things you think about when you view this painting.

Sample flexibility activities and questions

- Put the items you have identified from this painting into categories.
- Create a metaphor, simile, or analogy to describe this painting.
- The artist titled this painting _____. What other title might you give the painting, and why?
- If we turn the painting on its side, what might you see?
- Besides a museum, where might you find a painting like this?

Sample originality questions

- What is the most unique component of this work of art?
- Where is the most unusual place you might find a work of art such as this?
- What would be the most original way to view this work of art?
- Why is this work of art original?
- How does this work of art stimulate your imagination?

Sample elaboration activities and questions

- Write a poem, story, song, or sentence about this painting.
- What happened right before/after the scene represented in this painting?
- On a blank piece of paper, use two of the colors from this painting to create an extension of the painting.
- Why do you think the artist used the colors or ideas he or she did?
- Design a frame that would highlight the most important aspects of this painting, and explain your design.

Activity: Name 5

▶ **Stimulates: flexibility, fluency, elaboration**

1. Have students sit in a circle with one student sitting in the center.
2. Give a tennis ball or other small, soft object to a random student in the circle.
3. The student in center of the circle closes his or her eyes and says, "begin."
4. The object is quickly passed around the circle counter-clockwise, while everyone is perfectly silent.
5. At any point the student in the center says, "stop," and keeping his or her eyes closed, says to the person holding the object, "Name five _____ ."
   Sample Name 5 items:
   ▸ animals in the zoo
   ▸ facts that are devisable by 5
   ▸ terms from the unit of study
   ▸ compositions by Tchaikovsky
   ▸ students in the classroom (a great way to get students to know each other's names)
   ▸ important dates during the Civil War
6. The object is passed again while the person tries to complete the list of five before the object returns to him or her.
7. If the student is unable to complete the list of five before receiving the object again, he or she goes into the center of the circle.

Variations on this activity
Reverse the activity by having the student holding the object say "Name 5 . . . " to the student in the center of the circle.

Creative "Sponge" Activities

The following activities can be done when small bits of time remain, such as when students are waiting in the lunch line, waiting for the bell to ring, or waiting for you to collect lunch money or take attendance.

Activity: What If . . . ?

▶ **Stimulates: fluency, flexibility, originality, elaboration**

Use hypothetical thinking to warm up students' creativity. (See Chapter 9 for more on hypothetical thinking.)

- What if there were no rain this summer?
- What if there were no music?
- What if school lasted until 6 p.m. every day?
- What if we didn't use numbers?
- What if everyone spoke the same language?
- What if cars could fly?
- What if there were no gravity?
- What if houses were built entirely from inflexible materials?
- What if there were no Internet?
- What if time stood still?
- What if no one went to school?

Activity: Then What Happened?

▶ **Stimulates: elaboration, originality**

1. Write a beginning sentence on the board, such as: *We all boarded the bus for the field trip.*
2. Ask students, "Then what happened?"
3. Students take turns calling out the next sentence. To each one you respond, "Then what happened?"
4. This continues until all students have made a sentence contribution.

Variation on this activity
Students can either write their next sentence on the board, in their journal, or on a sheet of paper that is passed around the room.

Additional Creative Activity Ideas

Activity: Living Timeline

▶ **Stimulates: elaboration**
Students choose a point along a timeline and then act out or narrate it.

Activity: Role Play, Skits, or Plays

▶ **Stimulates: fluency, flexibility, elaboration**
To highlight their understanding of a character in a novel or in history, students take on the character's role and create a two- to five-minute presentation of a moment in the character's life.

Activity: Readers Theater

▶ **Stimulates: elaboration**
Students read from a script to dramatize a piece of literature. No memorization, costumes, sets, or acting skills are required. Students use their voices to elaborate on the words.

Activity: Research on a Creative Individual

▶ **Stimulates: elaboration**
Researching a creative individual in history or the present day can help students understand the complex nature of creativity and the successes and struggles creative people face.

In the differentiated classroom, creativity is an integrated tool necessary for success in the twenty-first century. When you enrich the learning environment with varied creative activities, students grow "smarter" because they naturally become more engaged in the learning process. Creativity requires the use of both content knowledge (facts and skills) and conceptual connections (linking ideas across the disciplines). Nurturing your students' creative potential does not stand in opposition to teaching in support of standards and assessments. It can be a complementary tool that highlights effective thinking and encourages achievement.

Building a Creative Classroom

Every classroom should be a creative classroom. Students learn best by playing with ideas. To engage students in a creative classroom, we need to actively encourage students to question, make connections, and visualize what might be. We must value, promote, and reward imagination and originality. This engagement comes through authentic experiences with problems that have multiple ambiguous solutions. Ambiguity is a fact of life and students must develop cognitive tools for dealing with it rather than avoiding it. Students can become accustomed to and work through ambiguity by being immersed in authentic activities—real-world examples and experiences. A creative classroom also encourages a willingness to be in the moment. So when real-world experiences happen, they are transformed into "teachable moments."

A classroom that nurtures creativity is one where there is never only one right answer. There is openness to finding new problems; new solutions and varied perspectives are expected. Students find it fun and adventurous to explore ideas and get involved in discussing problems. They are encouraged to share ideas with others and to talk about their progress. They learn to appreciate the different qualities in others' work and to value ways of working that are different from their own.

Students feel relaxed, supported, and "at home" in a creative classroom. Their thinking is valued and honored. They take intellectual risks and respond creatively to new situations. Teachers also know when to stand back and let students take the lead. However, the teacher is always there to make sure students are prompted and supported when needed. Students are guided through the process with the assistance of formative feedback provided by the teacher and other students.

Phrases That Encourage Creativity

Interesting.
I'm enjoying all your answers.
Keep going.
Keep thinking.
Dig deeper.
Tell me more.
Hmmmmmmm.
Carry on.
Exciting!
Fascinating!
Noted.
Elaborate on that idea.
Rich!
Expand on that.
Go on.
Continue.

Teachers in a creative classroom must model creative thinking, behaviors, and attitudes. Show students that you are a learner as well. Don't fear being creative with and for your students. This will create an open, constructive learning environment. On page 194 is a list of norms to strive for in a creative classroom. You might find a place to display this list in your classroom.

Creativity has never been more important than it is today. Students will face challenges and issues never before considered, and they will need to critically analyze the issues and come up with creative solutions to complex problems. Oftentimes, students don't consider math to be a subject where they can be creative. However, teachers can promote creativity in the ways students approach math problems, think about how to solve those problem, and craft plausible solutions. Refer to the form on page 195 to guide you in encouraging creativity in all of your classrooms, especially in your math classroom.

Norms of the Creative Classroom

1. Curiosity and questions are encouraged.

2. Problems can be solved in many ways.

3. Necessity is the mother of invention.

4. Judgment and criticism are suspended.

5. Patience, perseverance, and persistence are mandatory.

Encouraging Creativity

- Actively encourage students to question, make connections, visualize possible outcomes, and explore ideas.

- Promote and reward imagination, originality, curiosity, and questions.

- Ask open-ended questions such as, "What if . . .?" and "How might you . . . ?" to help students view topics from different perspectives.

- Value and praise what students do and say. Establish an atmosphere in which they feel safe to speak, take risks, and respond creatively.

- Create a fun, relaxed working environment to encourage students to be adventurous and explore ideas freely.

- Create conditions for quiet reflection and concentration to encourage students to work imaginatively.

- Make the most of unexpected events. When appropriate, put aside your lesson plan and "go with the moment," but never lose sight of your overall learning objectives.

- Be willing to stand back and let students take the lead. However, make sure that you are always on hand to provide prompts and support as needed.

- Join in activities and model creative thinking and behavior. Showing students that you too are a learner can help create an open, constructive learning environment.

- Help students develop criteria they can use to judge their own work, particularly its originality and value (this can be as simple as asking, "What makes a good . . . ?").

- Hold regular open discussions of the problems students are facing and how they can solve them. Encourage students to share ideas with others and to talk about their progress.

- Help students appreciate the different qualities in others' work and to value ways of working that are different from their own.

- Help students give and receive constructive feedback.

- Use authentic (real-life) problems and challenges with multiple possible solutions.

- Provide opportunities that create constructive discontent. Constructive discontent occurs when available tools may not be sufficient to solve a problem. It also describes the act of looking at products or services and inventing ways to make them better or more efficient to meet needs. In other words, "Necessity is the mother of invention."

- Maintain the belief that most problems can be solved.

- Help students suspend judgment/criticism.

- Develop perseverance, flexibility, risk taking, problem finding, and mistake making in yourself and your students.

Chapter 11

Problem Finding, Problem Solving, and Decision Making

Education is the most powerful weapon that you can use to change the world.

—*Nelson Mandela, civil rights leader*

Effective thinking and learning skills ultimately lead to making sound decisions. Good decisions are necessary for a productive and successful life. Making decisions often involves rooting out problems and devising solutions. People who have the ability to identify potential problems before they arise are better equipped to proactively approach a solution. Unfortunately, many people do not foresee problems, and when problems arise, they approach them in a reactionary, stressful way, relying on past practice and automatic "knee-jerk" responses to deal with them. Effective problem finders, problem solvers, and decision makers anticipate problems, strategize their decisions, and take action toward the best solution.

Simply teaching students how to find answers to problems is no longer enough in today's complex world. Only teaching problem solving suggests to our students that "if it isn't broken, don't fix it." This line of thinking is analogous to putting out fires rather than preventing them. Problem finding, however, helps students better define problems, think more proactively, and achieve higher quality solutions. Once a problem has been found, the act of decision making begins. Decision making should not be thought of as a linear process. When identifying and choosing alternatives, we all base our decisions on the values and preferences that fit best with our desires, goals, needs, or wants. Decision making can be defined as *the act of reducing uncertainty or doubt to produce the most reasonable choice.*[1]

This chapter provides you with a list of characteristics of effective problem finders, problem solvers, and decision makers; offers various steps to achieving quality outcomes; and includes graphic organizers that can assist students in the process. At the end is a list of barriers students face in making good decisions and strategies to help them overcome these barriers.

Characteristics of Effective Problem Finders, Problem Solvers, and Decision Makers

Successful problem finders, problem solvers, and decision makers view problems through many lenses. They look at issues from multiple perspectives, seek out information from various sources, and foresee roadblocks that may arise. Their traits include the following.

They Are Curious

Curiosity, rather than kill the cat, can often save it. Curious people are open to all evidence and activity surrounding them; they do not quickly ignore or discount new information.

---

1. Harris, R. "Introduction to Decision Making, Part 1." (virtualsalt.com/crebook5.htm).

They Are Flexible

They take "old" problems and look at them with "new" eyes. This outside-the-box thinking can create outside-the-box solutions that are more effective and efficient.

They Listen to What's *Not* Being Said and See What's *Not* Being Shown

A common error people make in solving problems is not paying attention to the unspoken, or negative space. Anticipating problems before they arise, discovering unique possibilities, and identifying what has been previously overlooked can lead to better solutions.

They Are Persistent and Patient

As is often repeated, there are no easy answers. The most difficult problems are also often the most challenging to find and solve. Therefore, students must put forth effort, persist, and be patient until a good solution can be found.

They Defer Judgment

It may take students a long time to think through ideas, issues, or information. Successfully solving problems and coming to good decisions often requires us to "sleep on it." Our brains need time to process, consider possible outcomes, and choose alternatives. Reaching a sound decision might mean delaying closure and taking the time to fully think things through.

They Are Reflective

Once a conclusion has been reached, good problem solvers review what they did, how they did it, and in what ways the outcome could have been different.

Finding Problems

The first step to arriving at good solutions and decisions is finding potential problems. Finding problems should not be seen as looking for trouble, but instead looking for ways to improve a situation, anticipate potential failures, or intercept an issue before it becomes negative. Following are examples of questions and activities that help build students' skills in problem finding.

- Come up with a list of improvements for how this classroom and school operates.
- What are some issues we can address in our classroom now in order to prevent them from becoming bigger problems in the future?
- Seek out potential problems the characters may face in this story.
- If we implement an all-electronic financial system in our government, what problems might we anticipate?
- Suppose we limit each person on Earth to one gallon of water per day. What problems can we expect?
- What problems could occur if school were held four days a week rather than five?
- What issues could arise if we were required to post all public signs in two languages?
- Scientists are considering creating a pill that can increase intelligence. What issues might we anticipate?

Activity suggestion: Take a current issue in your school or community, and frame the issue in a similar manner to these questions and activities.

Solving Problems

A common problem-solving process, known as the "I-FORD," guides students through five steps to identify a problem, gather facts, list and rank options, and make a decision.

Steps to Problem Solving: I-FORD

Identify: Define or shape the problem. What is the goal you want to achieve?

Facts: Gather the facts and data you need to make the best decision.

Options: List possible solutions or strategies to solve the problem.

Rank your options: Rate, rank, and test your options and strategies.

Decide: Make your decision, and implement and evaluate your solution.

The most effective problem solvers often follow these steps in both a linear and cyclical process (see **Figure 11.1**). In this process, the solver can always back up to the previous step and should continually evaluate each step along the way to see if he or she is coming close to a solution.

Within each of the five I-FORD steps, detailed in the next section, the 12 specific problem-solving strategies listed in the chart below Figure 11.1 are embedded and described, along with several graphic organizers.

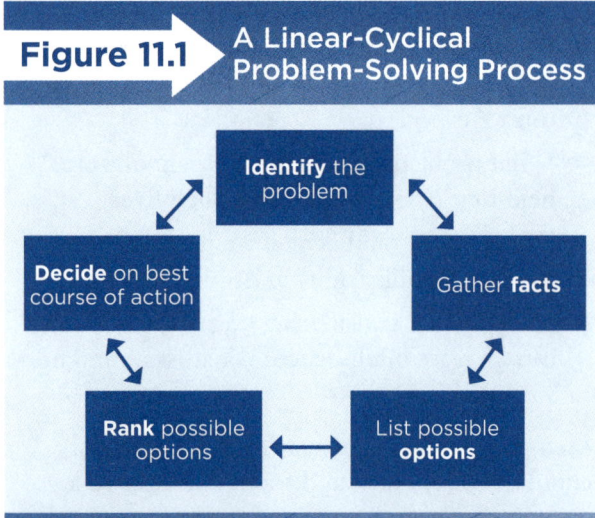

Figure 11.1 A Linear-Cyclical Problem-Solving Process

Strategies for Problem Solving

1. **Frame** the problem at its core in simple, descriptive language.
2. **Use graphics** (pictures, tables, diagrams) to dig deeper into the issues.
3. **Work backward** from possible outcomes.
4. **Use a different symbol system** to represent the problem in a new way.
5. **Share** your defined/refined problem with another person.
6. **Gather data** that may be helpful in solving the problem.
7. **Rephrase and confirm** the problem.
8. **Brainstorm** possible solutions or strategies.
9. **Test** possible solutions.
10. **Select** the best course of action.
11. **Implement** the action.
12. **Evaluate** your success.

The I-FORD Process Described

Step 1: Identify the Problem

Along with problem finding comes the art of shaping or defining the problem so that a quality solution can be found. In the problem-defining stage, students apply the strategy of *framing the problem at its core*. A technique to get to the core of a problem is the Five Whys to Therefore chart on page 206. See **Figure 11.2** for an example. After completing the example chart, I realized that my original problem, "I want a new car," had another problem embedded within it: "I need a new job." Simply stating that I needed a new car did not get to the real core of my problem. Once students reach their core problem, make sure they state it in simple descriptive language. Using overly elaborate or sophisticated language can muddy what needs to be accomplished and potentially aim the solution at the wrong issue.

Figure 11.2 Five Whys to Therefore: Example

Statement:
I want a new car.

Why:
Because I don't like paying for repairs.

Why:
Because it is costing me too much.

Why:
Because I don't have the extra cash.

Why:
Because I am not making enough money.

Why:
Because my current position doesn't pay what it should.

Therefore:
I need to find a job that pays better.

Another strategy for shaping or defining the problem is to *use graphics*, such as pictures, diagrams, or tables. Examples include the If-Then Mind Map for Decision Making (see **Figure 11.3**), the What Would Happen If . . . ? diagram (see **Figure 11.4**), and the What? So What? Now What? chart (see **Figure 11.5** on page 200). All

Chapter 11: Problem Finding, Problem Solving, and Decision Making **199**

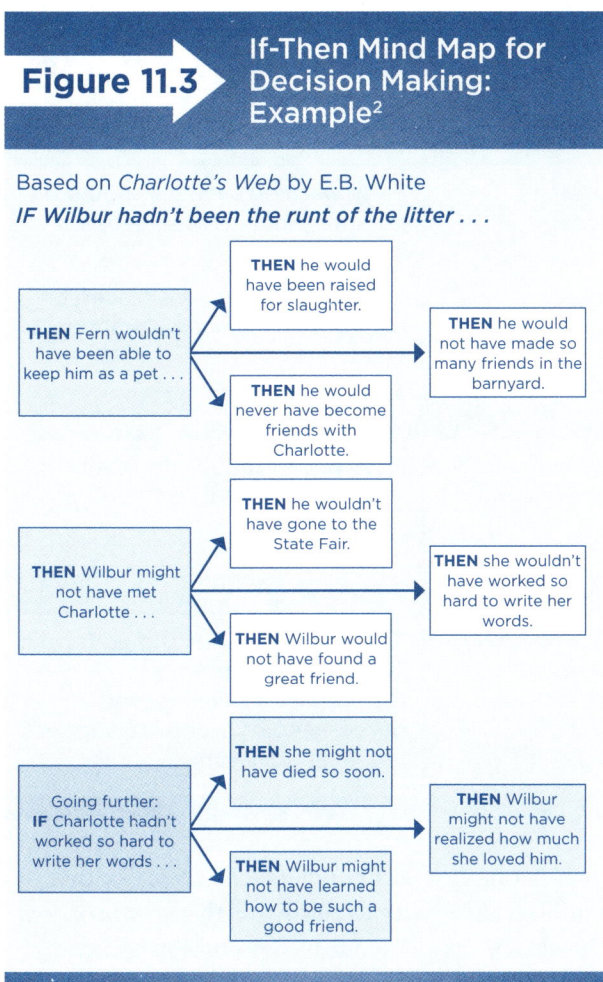

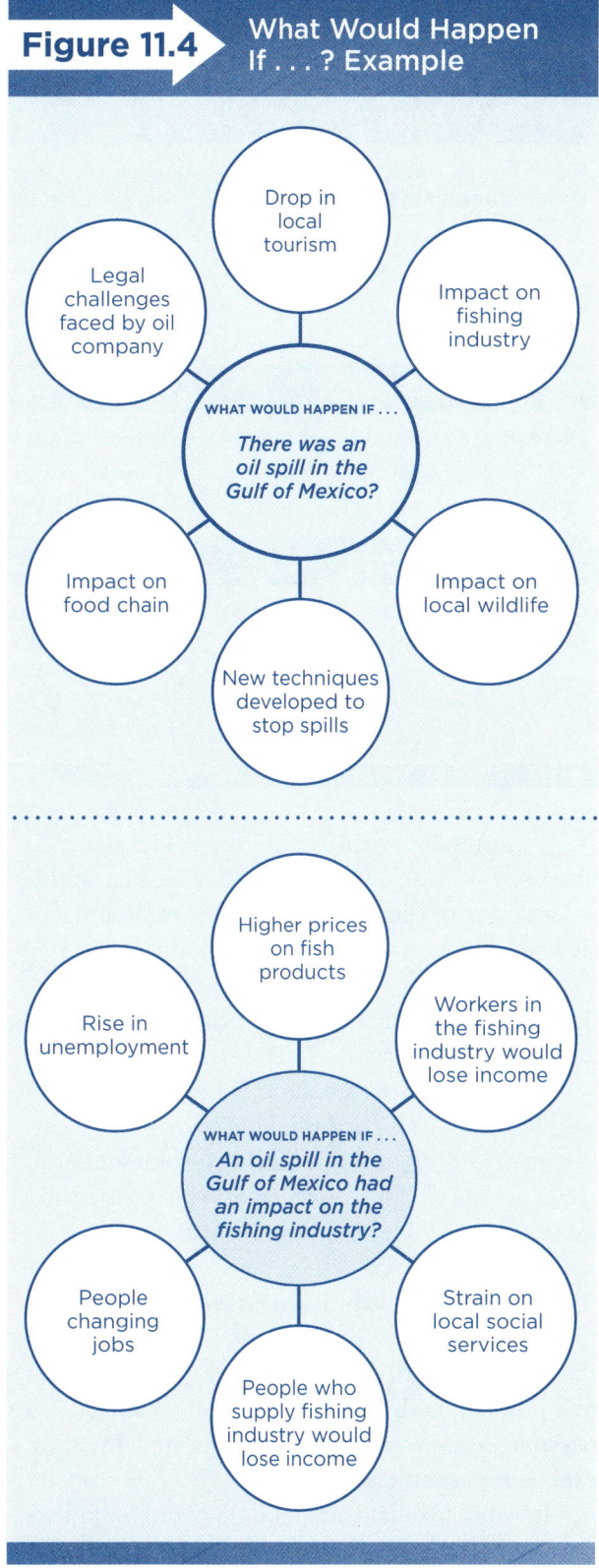

of these graphic organizers help the learner dig deeper into the issues, predict possible outcomes, or define possible obstacles. These graphics can also help identify potential causes for the problem.

Figure 11.3 can be used when multiple situations or issues could arise or need to be resolved. Remember, when having students do any sort of mind mapping, instruct them to keep their notations simple, clear, and concise. Mind maps are note-taking devices that provide an overview of a situation, offer keywords in solution finding, and help keep ideas organized. See a blank template on page 207.

Figure 11.4 is useful in hypothetical thinking situations or in predicting outcomes from actions. It offers the thinker a way to see how one situation can have an effect on or cause other interrelated situations or issues. From the example, you will see how one event leads to multiple secondary issues or situations. Have students select one of the secondary issues and do an additional mind map to find tertiary issues or situations that can or may arise. A blank template is provided on page 208.

2. Courtesy of Barbara Dullaghan, Bloomington Public Schools, Bloomington, MN.

Figure 11.5 — What? So What? Now What? Examples

WHAT?	SO WHAT?	NOW WHAT?
Flash floods destroy camping ground and kill 13 people.	Lives were lost due to the recreational use of local watersheds.	Early warning systems should be put into place to save people's lives. Limitations should be placed on recreational use of watershed areas.
Heart disease is the number one killer of women in the United States.	Heart disease in women may increase without more prevention and research.	More preventative information should be given to women.
Ethnic clashes in eastern Europe result in civil war.	Civil war in eastern Europe may lead to a major economic crisis that could impact the entire world.	The United Nations should form a negotiating team to help resolve the conflict as well as send in peace-keeping troops to support the local government.

The graphic organizer in Figure 11.5 was discussed previously in Chapter 8 as depicting the three stages of the Understand level of Bloom's Revised Taxonomy (see Figure 8.7 on page 154). A What? So What? Now What? chart helps students frame an issue, define ways the issue is important, and then describe actions that should be taken to solve or mitigate the situation. This model is an excellent tool to use for thinking through current events or coming up with local issues students could act upon. The model gives students a format for creating doable solutions. A blank template is provided on page 209.

Students can also use the previous graphics in the strategy of *working backward*. With this strategy, they would identify possible solutions or outcomes to a problem and, using the graphic organizers, cite possible domino or ripple effects of implementing each alternate solution.

In some problem situations, a stumbling block may lie in the way we are looking at the particular information or data. In this case, students can employ the strategy of *using a different symbol system* to clarify the issue. Sometimes the way the problem is represented (verbally, for instance) can distract or confuse its solver. When problems are framed in only one system or code (such as words), this can limit the ability to think creatively or broadly. Words convey many meanings and can confuse their receiver. For instance, take this problem:

Mary is six times the age of Sam. Sam is three times the age of Tina. Tina just celebrated her fourth birthday. How old are Mary and Sam?

Using a different symbol system (numbers versus words) can make the solution appear much simpler:

Tina (T) = 4

Sam (S) = 3T = 3 x 4 = 12

Mary (M) = 6S = 6 x 12 = 72

The following questions can be used to define a problem.

Questions Students Ask
- What is the problem?
- How can I describe it in my own words?
- What specific elements are involved?
- What am I being asked to do?
- What am I asked to show?
- Can I draw a picture or make a table, graph, or chart to better understand the problem?

- Can I show the problem using another symbol system (such as numbers versus words)?

Questions Teachers Ask
- Can you tell me, in your own words, what the problem is?
- What are your missing pieces of information?
- What information can you safely ignore?
- What assumptions are you making about this problem?
- What are you not defining about the problem that you should be?

Finally, another great idea for defining the problem is to *share the defined problem with another person*. Students must ensure they've captured the true essence of the issue. Enlisting another set of eyes or ears is very helpful in the problem-defining process.

Step 2: Find the Facts

Once the problem has been defined, students begin to *gather data* that may be helpful in the process of solving the problem. This may be as simple as listing information or creating graphic representations of what is known and unknown. In the Mary-Sam-Tina problem just described, we simply listed each of the individual's ages as stated in the problem. Here, students should also check to see if they have enough information to solve the problem. The solver must analyze the problem to check for information that is not stated or that may be taken for granted and also check that all information is in the same form or unit type. At this point, it is a good idea for solvers to step back from the problem and rephrase it to confirm what actually needs to be changed or corrected. (Use the Five Whys to Therefore chart on page 206.) The following questions can be used to find the facts of a problem.

Questions Students Ask
- What can be causing the problem?
- Where is it happening?
- When is it happening?
- How is it happening?
- With whom is it happening?
- Why is it happening?
- What are the (smaller) parts of this problem?
- What are the unknowns?

- What information can I gather from the problem?
- What information is missing or unnecessary?
- Is there a pattern in the information?
- Are there other problems like this that I can use as a model?
- Can I make a graph, chart, table, diagram, or equation with the information I have?

Questions Teachers Ask
- Define the possible causes of this problem.
- What are the smaller problems embedded within this problem?
- Define patterns that you see in this problem.
- Show me a graph, chart, table, diagram, or equation that you have created to help you define the problem.

Step 3: List Your Options

Next comes the strategy of *listing possible solutions or strategies to solve the problem*. Here is where students' brainstorming skills come in handy. Brainstorming involves the following process:

1. Generate as many ideas as possible.
2. Eliminate evaluation of ideas until all ideas have been shared.
3. Work quickly so as not to allow time for judgment.
4. Piggyback on others' ideas.

It is also helpful at this point for students to involve others in listing possible solutions. Other people may see the problem from a different point of view and may have a solution not already considered.

Step 4: Rank Your Options

After several ideas have been generated, students begin to analyze or *test possible solutions*. A list of the pros, cons, and additional questions that arise from each possible solution is created. A helpful tool at this point is to use either the PNI or CAI (see pages 177 and 178). Students should be careful not to evaluate any of the solutions at this point so they can keep an open mind about solutions that may have been previously unconsidered. After reviewing the various solutions, students are ready to *select the best course of action or strategy to solve the problem*.

Here is a list of possible problem-solving strategies students might test and rank:

- guess and check
- make a list
- draw a picture, diagram, table, or chart
- look for patterns
- solve a similar/simpler problem
- use a different symbol system
- act out the problem
- create a simulation
- work backward
- look at the problem from a different perspective

The following questions can be used to rank the strategies.

Questions Students Ask

- What should happen first, second, third, fourth, and so on, in this process?
- What resources will I need?
- How much time will the action take?
- Who is responsible for which steps?
- Which approaches are timely, appropriate, reasonable, realistic, cost-effective, efficient, and doable?
- What will the situation look like when the problem has been solved?
- How will I know when I've reached a solution?
- How do I check to see that each step has been followed?
- What might happen if I implement this solution? (Use the If-Then Mind Map for Decision Making or the What Would Happen If . . . ? templates on pages 207 and 208.)

Questions Teachers Ask

- Can you explain your plan to me?
- What have you tried so far?
- In what ways did you organize your information?
- What problems have you encountered before that resemble this problem?
- Why do you think your plan will work?
- How have you made sure that you have all the information you need?
- How will you know that you have reached a solution?
- In what ways have you checked your progress each step along the way?

Step 5: Decide on a Solution

Once the best course of action has been selected, problem solvers are now ready to *implement the action*. As they are implementing the action, have students check each step for accuracy along the way. After the action has been implemented, students must *evaluate* what changed, how it changed, and to what degree they will need to make adjustments to their actions. Also, they must determine if the solution makes sense in relation to the original problem. Critical at this stage are the P^3 behaviors: persistence, patience, and perseverance (see page 106).

The following questions can be used when deciding on a solution.

Questions Students Ask

- Did I solve the problem? If not, what do I need to do differently?
- Was the action I took effective and efficient?
- What did I learn from this problem-solving activity?
- Does my answer make sense?
- Could I have solved this problem another way?

Questions Teachers Ask

- How have you solved the problem?
- If you haven't solved the problem, what new direction will you take?
- How effective and efficient was your plan and solution?
- What have you learned from this experience?
- In what ways does your answer make sense?
- Could you have solved the problem in a different way?

If the problem has not been solved satisfactorily, students must begin the process again, making sure they have defined the problem well, gathered the appropriate data, listed all possible solutions, selected and implemented the right plan of action, and evaluated their success. Encourage students to look forward to a new decision, not to look back in regret. Remind them: If at first you don't succeed, try, try again!

Decision Making

Skills in decision making are required throughout the problem finding and solving process. Every step along the way requires students to produce reasonable choices based on the information available. However, making decisions is a complex process and is often one in which students have difficulty. They may be apprehensive about being creative or decisive because of stumbling blocks that get in the way of their thinking. In some cases, this is because students haven't been taught strategies to overcome these difficulties, or they have not met prior challenges that required them to work hard at solving a problem. Many very bright students struggle with decision making because of the lack of rigor or challenge in their early years of schooling.

Decision-making stumbling blocks include the following: (*Note:* You'll notice this list is similar to the list of reasons students underachieve on pages 66–67, because in many cases underachieving students have limited practice in the art of thinking.)

- fear of failure ("If I fail people will know I'm not that smart.")
- fear of success ("If I succeed people will expect me to succeed all the time.")
- lack of problem-solving skills
- lack of understanding the problem
- lack of challenge
- lack of interest
- lack of motivation
- lack of self-efficacy
- lack of perseverance
- too much or too little self-confidence
- spreading oneself too thin (taking on too many things)
- using the wrong abilities
- inability to translate thought into action
- lack of follow-through for getting the job done
- inability to complete tasks
- failure to initiate
- procrastination
- blaming others
- excessive self-pity
- excessive dependency
- focusing on personal difficulties
- being highly distractible or lacking in concentration

Overcoming Barriers to Decision Making

One major reason why students are reluctant to make decisions and risk failure is due to what cognitive psychologist Dr. Carol Dweck calls the *fixed mindset* (discussed previously in Chapter 5). Students with a fixed mindset believe their intelligence and abilities are fixed traits they are born with and cannot develop further. These students believe all the tests and documentations (grades, trophies, and certificates) are what define their success. Dweck states, "When people believe in fixed traits, they are always in danger of being measured by a failure."[3] Conversely, students with a *growth mindset* believe that all skills and abilities can be developed through dedication and hard work. A person with a growth mindset knows that what they are born with can be cultivated and built upon. "When people believe their basic qualities can be developed, failures may still hurt, but failures don't define them," writes Dweck.[4] When we teach students that they can improve their performance through a growth mindset, they are better able to overcome negative labels, bullying, difficult situations, stereotyping, and other perceived or real barriers. This may be especially valuable for students from culturally, linguistically, socially, or economically diverse backgrounds.

Develop Growth Mindset Conventions

A strategy to help students overcome difficult decision-making situations is to develop classroom conventions that address a growth mindset. Classroom conventions are different from rules; conventions are a way of doing business or acting within a given setting. Classroom conventions to encourage a growth mindset include the following:

Growth Mindset Conventions for the Teacher
As the teacher, I will . . .

- Present all skills and processes as learnable
- Model patience, persistence, and perseverance (P^3)

---

3. Dweck, C. S. *Mindset: The New Psychology of Success*. New York: Ballantine Books, 2006: 29.
4. Ibid, p. 39.

- Present all feedback as constructive toward future success

Growth Mindset Conventions for the Student
As the student, I will . . .
- Tackle all skills and processes as learnable
- Employ patience, persistence, and perseverance (P^3)
- Welcome all feedback as constructive toward my future success

Display these conventions in your classroom and have students (and yourself) recite them daily.

Support Students' Self-Confidence

Building students' confidence in themselves as learners and thinkers is another crucial strategy in helping them make sound decisions. As a teacher you can help build their confidence in the classroom, and you can also encourage parents to participate in confidence building.

Suggestions for parents to build their child's confidence:
- Show your child that you love challenges.
- Use your own mistakes as a learning tool.
- Discuss the effort you put forth each day.
- Display your continued learning.
- Provide constructive criticism to your child.
- When your child comes home from school, ask questions like:
  - What is one specific thing that you learned today?
  - What mistake did you make today that taught you something about yourself?
  - What did you try hard at today?
  - What is one thing that you were proud of in your learning today?
  - What is one thing that you would change about your learning today?
  - What specific goal will you set for yourself tomorrow?
- Give your child compliments that can build confidence, such as:
  - I'm proud of how much effort you put forth to achieve what you did.
  - Wow, you worked hard and that hard work paid off!
  - Your perseverance shows in your work.
  - I'm impressed at how patient you are when you face a challenge.
  - Even though you may not have achieved your goal, I can tell you tried your hardest.

Notice that all of the above statements focus not on ability but on *hard work* and *effort*.

Teach Students to Mobilize Their Resources

Another idea for helping students overcome decision-making barriers is to teach them how to mobilize their resources. When students know what they have and/or where to find what they need, they are better able to be creative and solve problems.

Steps to Mobilize Your Resources
1. Believe in yourself as the most valuable resource.
2. Utilize those around you (teachers, classmates, parents, or other adults).
3. Utilize the materials available.
4. Ask questions or ask for help.
5. Request, require, and/or advocate for more support, information, or resources.

Encourage Students to Take Risks

Finally, students need to know that making good decisions involves risk taking. Taking risks and making mistakes are actually valuable skills to be learned. Without risk and failure there is no growth; any success without risk or failure is pure luck. In fact, everything in life requires some level of risk and there will be some chances for failure. For example: Because I fear flying, I will decide to drive to my vacation destination. By avoiding my fear of flying, I've now increased my risk of being involved in a car crash. In another case, to avoid all risk, I will sit on the couch and watch TV. This choice will increase my risk for obesity, heart attack, or even an airplane crashing through my roof onto my sofa. Risk is a natural part of life and involves some levels of fear. This is a good thing, because it shows that we are human.

Practice decision making as a class by using the 12 Steps to Group Decision Making (see page 210).

A quality curriculum encourages students to develop and use problem finding and solving and stimulates good decision making. Effective instruction models and promotes successful problem finding and solving and supports students in making sound decisions. As stated at the beginning of Chapter 3, only quality curriculum and effective instructional practices can be differentiated. All students can problem find and solve; the distinction in a differentiated classroom is that varying levels of curricular activities are used to scaffold students so they are confident problem finders and to provide support structures for all students so they are willing to take risks to solve complex problems. Using the strategies and ideas listed in this chapter will help you find those "just right" activities to build students' abilities to problem find and solve so they are better equipped to make good decisions.

Five Whys to Therefore

Statement:

Why:

Why:

Why:

Why:

Why:

Therefore:

From *Advancing Differentiation: Thinking and Learning for the 21st Century* by Richard M. Cash, Ed.D., copyright © 2017. This page may be reproduced for use within an individual school or district. For all other uses, contact Free Spirit Publishing Inc. at www.freespirit.com/permissions.

If-Then Mind Map for Decision Making

TOPIC:

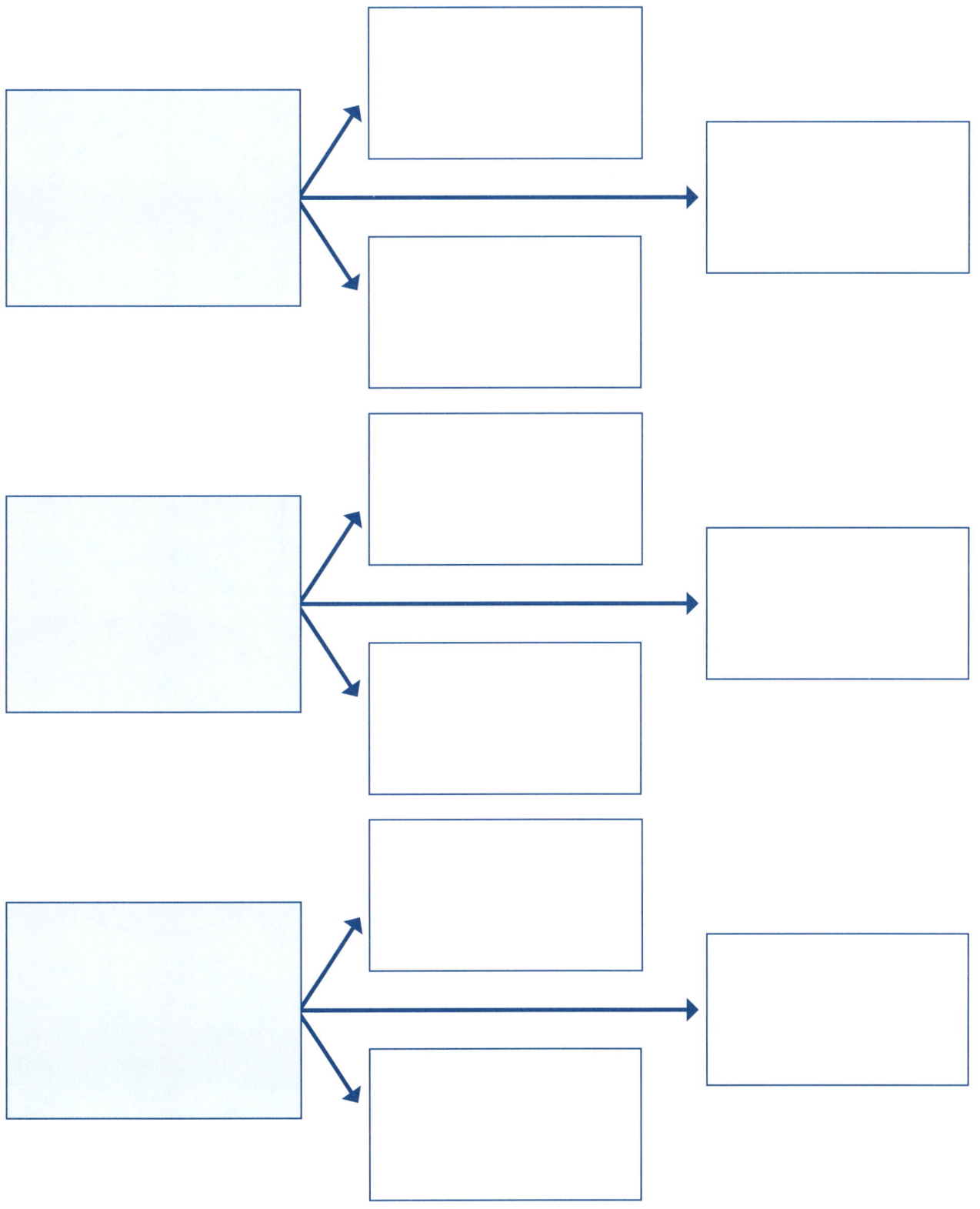

What Would Happen If . . . ?

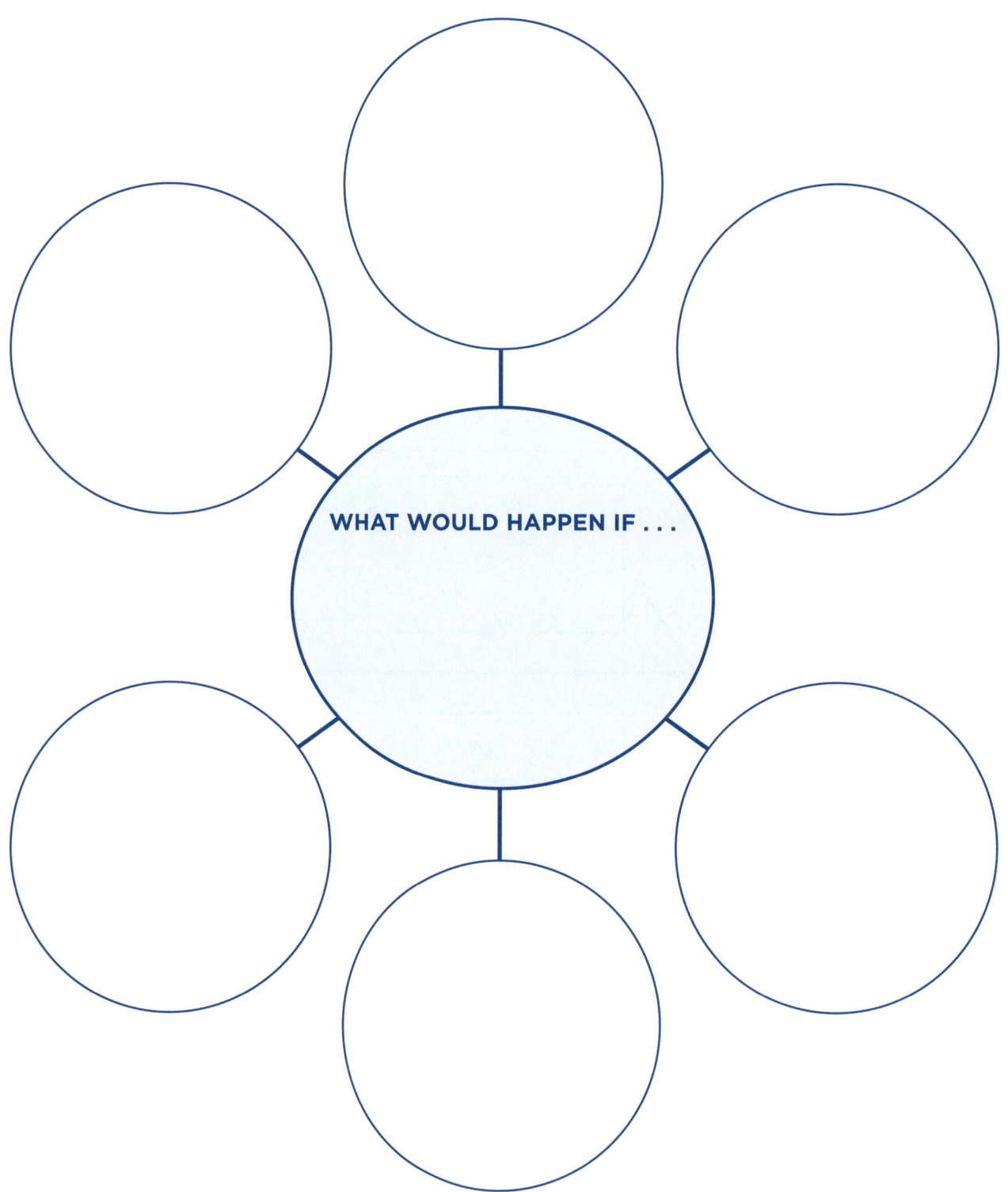

What? So What? Now What?

WHAT?	SO WHAT?	NOW WHAT?

WHAT?	SO WHAT?	NOW WHAT?

WHAT?	SO WHAT?	NOW WHAT?

12 Steps to Group Decision Making

Materials
Large chart paper

Colored adhesive dots (red, yellow, green)

Roles
Leader (keeps group on task)

Recorder (writes and records)

Timer (manages the time for each step)

1. Divide class into small groups of 5–8 students and designate 1 leader, 1 recorder, and 1 timer in each group.

2. Group leader defines the problem. *(1 minute)*

3. Each group member silently generates solutions. *(2 minutes)*

4. Using a round-robin format, group members share one idea. Recorder writes on a large sheet of paper exactly what was shared. Do not restate the individual's idea. No discussion other than clarifying questions is permitted at this point. The round-robin continues until all ideas have been shared. *(Maximum 10 minutes)*

5. Discussion and clarification. At this point individuals may ask clarification questions, discuss the particular implications of each idea, defend their ideas, compare ideas, or persuade others to favor their idea. *(5 minutes)*

6. Group members then rank the various ideas by assigning each idea one of the colored dots. *(1 minute)*

    Red: Most likely will NOT work

    Yellow: May be a possible solution

    Green: Most likely WILL work

7. Group leader then selects the ideas that generated the most green dots, or the ideas that generated the greatest likelihood of success.

8. Small groups come together and each group leader reports on the group's green dot decisions to the class. *(Maximum 5 minutes)*

9. The class votes on the various small-group decisions, ranking them the same way as in Step 6. *(1 minute)*

10. In case of a tie, groups may encourage others to vote for their solutions in a debate-style round-robin. *(1 minute)*

11. Repeat the class vote, this time using one red and one green dot. *(1 minute)*

12. Report the final decision to the class.

A Final Note

Pulling It All Together

Differentiation involves providing students with a variety of avenues through the content, enabling them to make sense and take ownership of the information through the process, guiding them to create products that represent their knowledge, and offering a nurturing environment that builds learner autonomy. **Figure 12.1** on page 212 connects these four aspects of differentiation with the essential twenty-first century thinking and learning tools presented in this book.

A quality curriculum is defined by content that clearly identifies major concepts that connect within and across disciplines, so students are better able to grasp conceptual meanings and form deep understandings. Additionally, as a teacher, you must be fully aware of the factual and procedural foundations embedded within the discipline and units of study. With this knowledge, you can effectively assess your students' knowledge base in facts, procedures, and concepts, and deliver content that encourages greater levels of problem finding and solving.

The processes of effective instruction are designed to build on students' prior knowledge and innate creativity to stimulate skill development for application within the discipline and in complex ways. Teachers know where students are in their ability to use critical, creative, and higher level thinking tools. If students need more scaffolding or more complexity when using these tools, teachers have multiple resources and strategies to support these needs. Students are then encouraged to develop products that represent their learning through unique and original performances. These performances can look very different from student to student, depending on his or her learning preference or necessity of expression.

The hallmark of success in the twenty-first century is the ability to generate unique and original ideas or products and be able to put them to use in practical ways. We must develop these abilities in our students by promoting various ways for students to express their thinking and learning. In the classrooms of the future, learning will take place in many different types of settings and venues. Students will be learning beyond the classroom walls. They will be communicating and collaborating with others around the world with the click of a button. Educators must be able to differentiate the learning environment so it is structured in ways that respect the learners' differing brain requirements, and it nurtures and supports the natural curiosity and creativity of our students.

Figure 12.1 Connecting Differentiation and 21st Century Thinking and Learning

Content
The curriculum is rich in deep concepts and ideas that encourage students to investigate beyond the facts. Some students expand on fundamental ideas, while others develop new ideas in the discipline. Students are encouraged to solve real-world problems using learned knowledge.

Process
Engaging instructional practices teach students the essential skills of the twenty-first century, such as critical and creative thinking. Some students require more direct instruction on these skills, while others develop risk-taking skills to expand on the usage of these tools.

DIFFERENTIATION

Product
Students construct meaningful products that represent their learning of new ideas, skills, and processes. Outcomes are designed to encourage students to problem solve through critical thinking and also to construct useful products. Some students are able to represent their ideas through music, drama, prose, or graphic representation, while others choose to represent their learning through speech, artistic design, multimedia, or other avenues.

Environment
The learning setting is designed to acknowledge brain compatibility and the need for enrichment and stimulation. Learning happens for some students inside of the classroom, while for others it may happen via the Internet or in authentic nonclassroom locations. In the twenty-first century, learning is increasingly occurring beyond the classroom walls.

Conclusion

My parents went to school in the late 1930s and early 1940s. My mother graduated from high school with only the prospects of going to college to become a teacher or nurse. My mother's strength was in math, so she was encouraged to proceed to clerical school to become a secretary, which she did. My father left school after completing eighth grade, because school held very little interest to him. In my father's day, a high school degree was not a necessity for getting a job. His only real prospect was to enter the military where he could earn his GED. My parents successfully raised five children without either of them attending a post-secondary institution.

My siblings and I graduated from high school in the mid-1970s. We all went on to college with career prospects far different from those afforded to our parents. Avenues were opening up in the computer sciences—the first computer I saw took up an entire classroom and required its own air conditioner—and healthcare. In addition, the options we had available to us post-college were greater and far more diverse than those available to our parents 30 years earlier. All of us ended up in the field of education, which is surprising given the fact neither of our parents attended college, and one did not even complete high school.

Students who will be graduating from high school in the coming decades of the twenty-first century will have many more options available to them than existed 30 years ago for my siblings and me, and exponentially more options than my parents had in the mid-twentieth century. The level of workforce needs has changed—and will continue to change—from skill application to knowledge development. Knowledge workers of the twenty-first century will be required to be FIT: **F**lexible, **I**nnovative thinkers, and **T**ech-savvy to increasingly greater degrees.

As discussed in Chapter 1, the use and application of technology in the classroom is essential for our students to be prepared for their futures. Our role with students is to guide them by employing technology in a thoughtful manner to enhance and enrich all of our lives. If used in this way, computers, smartphones, tablets, applications, video games, software programs, projectors, clickers, and other devices provide unparalleled learning tools that increase students' resourcefulness, productivity, and creativity. They also appeal to the visual, interactive learning preferences of many of today's students. However, while technology can benefit, improve, and enhance our lives and the lives of our students, it cannot do our thinking for us.

All students can learn and think at advanced levels, and they will need practice and coaching to get there. To assist them in our full capacity as teachers, we must remember these key points:

- We must model our own thinking and learning processes for our students.
- We must infuse thinking and learning processes into the classroom and curriculum on a daily basis.
- We must expect students to use and discuss their thinking.
- We must honor, value, and celebrate all kinds of student thinking, even if we don't agree with it.
- We must support students in their ability to connect what is learned in the classroom to what goes on outside the classroom walls.

By embracing this book's ideas for infusing effective twenty-first century thinking and learning skills into your classroom and curriculum, and implementing its strategies, templates, and models, you can be assured that your students will be more actively engaged in learning and will advance their thinking processes to increase their chances of success in this rapidly advancing society.

References and Resources

Afflerbach, P., P. Pearson, and S. G. Paris. "Clarifying Differences Between Reading Skills and Reading Strategies." *The Reading Teacher, 61 (5)* (2008): 364–373.

Anderson, L. W., and D. R. Krathwohl (Eds.). *A Taxonomy for Learning, Teaching, and Assessing: A Revision of Bloom's Taxonomy of Educational Objectives*. New York: Longman, 2001.

Azzam, A. M. "Why Creativity Now? A Conversation with Sir Ken Robinson." *Teaching for the 21st Century, 67 (1)* (September 2009): 22–26.

Beecher, M. *Developing the Gifts and Talents of All Students in the Regular Classroom*. Austin, TX: Prufrock, 1995.

Bellanca, J., and R. Fogarty. *Catch Them Thinking*. Arlington Heights, IL: IRI/Skylight, 1986.

Ben-Hur, M. *Concept-Rich Math Instruction: Building a Strong Foundation for Reasoning and Problem Solving*. Alexandria, VA: ASCD, 2006.

Bloom, B. S. *Taxonomy of Educational Objectives, The Classification of Educational Goals, Handbook I: Cognitive Domain*. White Plains, NY: Longman, 1956.

Bronson, P., and A. Merryman. "The Creativity Crisis." *Newsweek* (July 10, 2010). Cited research by Dr. Kyung Hee Kim at the College of William and Mary.

Cash, R. M. *Self-Regulation in the Classroom: Helping Students Learn How to Learn*. Minneapolis: Free Spirit Publishing, 2016.

Casserly, M. "10 Jobs That Didn't Exist 10 Years Ago." *Forbes.com* (May 11, 2012) (forbes.com/sites/meghancasserly/2012/05/11/10-jobs-that-didnt-exist-10-years-ago).

Chappuis, J., et al.. *Classroom Assessment for Student Learning*. Upper Saddle River, NJ: Pearson, 2014.

Cole, R. W., ed. *Educating Everybody's Children: Diverse Teaching Strategies for Diverse Learners*. Alexandria, VA: ASCD, 2008.

———. *More Strategies for Educating Everybody's Children*. Alexandria, VA: ASCD, 2001.

Collaborative for Academic, Social, and Emotional Learning (CASEL). "What Is Social and Emotional Learning?" (casel.org/social-and-emotional-learning)

Colvin, G. *Talent Is Overrated: What Really Separates World-Class Performers from Everybody Else*. New York: Portfolio Publishing, 2008.

Cotton, K. "Close-Up #11: Teaching Thinking Skills." *School Improvement Research Series Report*. Northwest Regional Educational Laboratory (NWREL), 1991.

Cox, A. J. *No Mind Left Behind: Understanding and Fostering Executive Control—The Eight Essential Brain Skills Every Child Needs to Thrive*. New York: Perigee Books, 2007.

Csikszentmihalyi, M. *Finding Flow: The Psychology of Engagement with Everyday Life*. New York: Basic Books, 1997.

Danielson, C. *Enhancing Professional Practice: A Framework for Teaching*. Alexandria, VA: ASCD, 2007.

———. *The Framework for Teaching Evaluation Instrument, 2013 Edition*. Princeton, NJ: The Danielson Group, 2014.

Dean, B. "Wisdom" (www.authentichappiness.sas.upenn.edu/newsletters/authentichappinesscoaching/wisdom).

Dosomething.org. "11 Facts About Education and Poverty in America" (dosomething.org/us/facts/11-facts-about-education-and-poverty-america).

Drucker, P. F. "The Next Workforce: Knowledge Workers Are the New Capitalists." *The Economist* (November 2001).

Dweck, C. S. *Mindset: The New Psychology of Success.* New York: Ballantine Books, 2006.

EDUCAUSE. "Things You Should Know About... Flipped Classrooms." (February 2012) (net.educause.edu/ir/library/pdf/ELI7081.pdf).

Elder, L., and R. Paul. *Guide to Critical Thinking.* Dillon Beach, CA: Foundation for Critical Thinking, 2009.

Eliot, L. "The Truth About Boys and Girls." *Scientific American Mind* (May/June 2010).

Elliot, A. J., and C. S. Dweck, eds. *Handbook of Competence and Motivation.* New York: Guilford Press, 2005.

Erickson, H. L. *Concept-Based Curriculum and Instruction: Teaching Beyond the Facts.* Thousand Oaks, CA: Corwin Press, 2002.

———. *Concept-Based Curriculum and Instruction for the Thinking Classroom.* Thousand Oaks, CA: Corwin Press, 2007.

Erlauer, L. *The Brain-Compatible Classroom: Using What We Know About Learning to Improve Teaching.* Alexandria, VA: ASCD, 2003.

Erwin, J. C. *The Classroom of Choice: Giving Students What They Need and Getting What You Want.* Alexandria, VA: ASCD, 2004.

Ettling, M. "Workforce 2020: How Ready Are You?" *Forbes.com* (Sept. 11, 2014) (forbes.com/sites/sap/2014/09/11/workforce-2020-how-ready-are-you).

Fisher, D., and N. Frey. *Checking for Understanding: Formative Assessment Techniques for Your Classroom.* Alexandria, VA: ASCD, 2014.

Fredricks, J. A., P. C. Blumenfeld, and A. H. Paris. "School Engagement: Potential of the Concept, State of the Evidence." *Review of Educational Research,* 74 (1) (Spring 2004): 59–109.

Gentry, M., and R. K. Gable. *My Class Activities: A Survey Instrument to Assess Students' Perceptions of Interest, Challenge, Choice, and Enjoyment in Their Classroom.* Mansfield Center, CT: Creative Learning Press, 2001.

Giroux, H. A. "Toward a Pedagogy of Critical Thinking." In *Re-Thinking Reason: New Perspectives on Critical Thinking.* K. S. Walters (Ed.). Albany, NY: State University of New York Press, 1994.

Girsch, M., and C. Girsch. *Fanning the Creative Spirit: Two Toy Inventors Simplify Creativity.* St. Paul, MN: Creativity Central, 2005.

Given, B. K. *Teaching to the Brain's Natural Learning Systems.* Alexandria, VA: ASCD, 2002.

Global Digital Citizen Foundation (globaldigitalcitizen.org).

Goodwin, B., and K. Miller. "Research Says / Evidence on Flipped Classrooms Is Still Coming In." *Educational Leadership,* 70 (6) (March 2013): 78–80.

Graham, S., and C. Hudley. "Race and Ethnicity in the Study of Motivation and Competence." In *Handbook of Competence and Motivation.* A. J. Elliot and C. S. Dweck (Eds.). New York: Guilford Press, 2005.

Gurian, M., and K. Stevens. *The Minds of Boys: Saving Our Sons from Falling Behind in School and Life.* San Francisco, CA: Jossey-Bass, 2005.

Guskey, T. R., ed. *The Teacher as Assessment Leader.* Bloomington, IN: Solution Tree Press, 2009.

Harris, R. "Introduction to Decision Making, Part 1." (virtualsalt.com/crebook5.htm).

Hattie, J. *Visible Learning.* New York: Routledge, 2009.

Heacox, D. *Differentiating Instruction in the Regular Classroom: How to Reach and Teach All Learners.* Minneapolis: Free Spirit Publishing, 2012.

———. *Making Differentiation a Habit: How to Ensure Success in Academically Diverse Classrooms.* Minneapolis: Free Spirit Publishing, 2009.

Heacox, D., and R. M. Cash. *Differentiation for Gifted Learners: Going Beyond the Basics*. Minneapolis: Free Spirit Publishing, 2014.

Institute for the Future. "Future Work Skills 2020." Palo Alto, CA: Institute for the Future for the University of Phoenix Research Institute, 2011. (iftf.org/uploads/media/SR-1382A_UPRI_future_work_skills_sm.pdf).

Jensen, E. *Arts with the Brain in Mind*. Alexandria, VA: ASCD, 2001.

———. *Brain-Based Learning*. Thousand Oaks, CA: Corwin Press, 2008.

———. *Teaching with Poverty in Mind: What Being Poor Does to Kids' Brains and What Schools Can Do About It*. Alexandria, VA: ASCD, 2009.

Johnson, E. B. *Contextual Teaching and Learning: What It Is and Why It's Here to Stay*. Thousand Oaks, CA: Corwin Press, 2002.

Joint Committee on National Health Education Standards. *National Health Education Standards: Achieving Excellence*. Atlanta: American Cancer Society, 2007.

Jukes, I., T. McCain, and L. Crockett. *Understanding the Digital Generation*. Thousand Oaks, CA: Corwin Press, 2010.

Koob, G. F., et al. "Stress, Performance, and Arousal: Focus on CRF." *National Institute on Drug Abuse Research Monograph*, 97 (1990): 163–176.

Leong, D. J., and E. Bodrova. "Developing Self-Regulation: The Vygotskian View." *Academic Exchange Quarterly* (Winter 2006).

Lombardi, M. M. "Authentic Learning for the 21st Century: An Overview." ELI Paper 1. Educause Learning Initiative (May 2007).

Marzano, R. J. "The Marzano Teacher Evaluation Model." Marzano Research Laboratory (August 2011).

———. *Transforming Classroom Grading*. Alexandria, VA: ASCD, 2000.

Marzano, R. J., and J. S. Kendall. *The New Taxonomy of Educational Objectives*. Thousand Oaks, CA: Corwin Press, 2007.

Marzano, R. J., D. J. Pickering, and J. E. Pollock. *Classroom Instruction that Works: Research-Based Strategies for Increasing Student Achievement*. Alexandria, VA: ASCD, 2001.

Mead, M. *Coming of Age in Samoa: A Psychological Study of Primitive Youth for Western Civilisation*. New York: William Morrow, 1928.

Murphy, P. K., and P. A. Alexander. *Understanding How Students Learn: A Guide for Instructional Leaders*. Thousand Oaks, CA: Corwin Press, 2006.

National Center for Education Statistics. "Family Characteristics of School-Age Children." *The Condition of Education 2016* (nces.ed.gov/programs/coe/pdf/coe_cce.pdf).

National Research Council. *How People Learn: Brain, Mind, Experience, and School (Expanded Edition)*. Washington, DC: National Academy Press, 2000.

Neu, T. W., and R. Weinfeld. *Helping Boys Succeed in School: A Practical Guide for Parents and Teachers*. Waco, TX: Prufrock Press, 2007.

Newmann, F. M., W. G. Secada, and G. G. Wehlage. *A Guide to Authentic Instruction and Assessment: Vision, Standards and Scoring*. Madison, WI: Wisconsin Center for Educational Research, 1995.

Nussbaum, P. D., and W. R. Daggett. *What Brain Research Teaches About Rigor, Relevance, and Relationships: And What It Teaches About Keeping Your Own Brain Healthy*. Rexford, NY: International Center for Leadership in Education, 2008.

O'Connor, K. *How to Grade for Learning: K–12*. Thousand Oaks, CA: Corwin Press, 2009.

Oxford Economics. "Workforce 2020: Building a Strategic Workforce for the Future." (2015) (oxfordeconomics.com/workforce2020).

Partnership for 21st Century Learning (p21.org/our-work/p21-framework).

Pearson, P. D., and M. C. Gallagher. "The Instruction of Reading Comprehension." *Contemporary Educational Psychology, 8* (1983): 317–345.

Piirto, J. *Understanding Creativity.* Scottsdale, AZ: Great Potential Press, 2004.

———. *Understanding Those Who Create.* Scottsdale, AZ: Great Potential Press, 1998.

PwC. "The Future of Work: Reshaping the Workplace." (2014) (pwc.com/gx/en/issues/talent/future-of-work.html).

Reeves, D. B. *Making Standards Work: How to Implement Standards-Based Assessments in the Classroom, School, and District.* Denver, CO: Advanced Learning Press, 2002.

Reeves, T. C., J. Herrington, and R. Oliver. "Authentic Activities and Online Learning." In *Research and Development in Higher Education: Quality Conversations Vol. 25.* T. Herrington (Ed.). Perth, Australia: Higher Education Research Development Society of Australasia, 2002.

Renzulli, J. S., M. Gentry, and S. M. Reis. *Enrichment Clusters: A Practical Plan for Real-World, Student-Driven Learning.* Waco, TX: Prufrock Press, 2014.

Right Question Institute (rightquestion.org).

Robinson, K. *The Element: How Finding Your Passion Changes Everything.* New York: Penguin Books, 2009.

———. *Out of Our Minds: Learning to Be Creative.* Oxford, United Kingdom: Capstone Publishing, 2011.

Ryan, R. M., and E. L. Deci. "Self-Determination Theory and the Facilitation of Intrinsic Motivation, Social Development, and Well-Being." *American Psychologist* (January 2000): 68–78.

Sams, A., and J. Bergmann. "Flip Your Students' Learning." *Educational Leadership, 70 (6)* (March 2013).

Savery, J. R., and T. M. Duffy. "Problem-Based Learning: An Instructional Model and Its Constructivist Framework." In *Constructivist Learning Environments: Case Studies in Instructional Design.* B. G. Wilson (Ed.). Englewood Cliffs, NJ: Educational Technology Publications, 1998: 135–148.

Schultz, W., P. Dayan, and P. R. Montague. "A Neural Substrate of Prediction and Reward." *Science, 275* (1997): 1593–1599.

Sheffield, L. J. *Extending the Challenge in Mathematics: Developing Mathematical Promise in K–8 Students.* Thousand Oaks, CA: Corwin Press, 2003.

Smilkstein, R. *We're Born to Learn: Using the Brain's Natural Learning Process to Create Today's Curriculum.* Thousand Oaks, CA: Corwin Press, 2011.

Sousa, D. A. *How the Brain Learns.* Thousand Oaks, CA: Corwin Press, 2011.

Sousa, D. A., and C. A. Tomlinson. *Differentiation and the Brain: How Neuroscience Supports the Learner-Friendly Classroom.* Bloomington, IN: Solution Tree Press, 2011.

Sternberg, R. J. "Creativity Is a Habit." *Education Week* (February 22, 2006): 47–64.

———. "Schools Should Nurture Wisdom." In *Teaching for Intelligence.* B. Z. Presseisen (Ed.). Arlington Heights, IL: Skylight Training and Publishing, 1999: 55–82.

———. *Successful Intelligence: How Practical and Creative Intelligence Determine Success in Life.* New York: Plume Books, 1996.

———. *Wisdom, Intelligence and Creativity Synthesized.* New York: Cambridge University Press, 2003.

Sternberg, R. J., and E. L. Grigorenko. *Teaching for Successful Intelligence: To Increase Student Learning and Achievement.* Thousand Oaks, CA: Corwin Press, 2007.

Sternberg, R. J., and R. Subotnik, eds. *Optimizing Student Success with the Other Three Rs: Reasoning, Resilience, and Responsibility.* Greenwich, CT: Information Age Publishing, 2006.

Strong, R. W., H. F. Silver, and M. J. Perini. *Teaching What Matters Most: Standards and Strategies for Raising Student Achievement.* Alexandria, VA: ASCD, 2001.

Sylwester, R. *How to Explain a Brain: An Educator's Handbook of Brain Terms and Cognitive Processes.* Thousand Oaks, CA: Corwin Press, 2005.

Taba, H. *Curriculum Development: Theory and Practice.* New York: Harcourt Brace and World, 1962.

Tomlinson, C. A. *The Differentiated Classroom: Responding to the Needs of All Learners.* Alexandria, VA: ASCD, 2014.

———. *Fulfilling the Promise of the Differentiated Classroom: Strategies and Tools for Responsive Teaching.* Alexandria, VA: ASCD, 2003.

———. *How to Differentiate Instruction in Mixed-Ability Classrooms.* Alexandria, VA: ASCD, 2001.

Tomlinson, C. A., and M. B. Imbeau. *Leading and Managing a Differentiated Classroom.* Alexandria, VA: ASCD, 2010.

Tomlinson, C. A., and J. McTighe. *Integrating Differentiated Instruction & Understanding by Design: Connecting Content and Kids.* Alexandria, VA: ASCD, 2006.

Tomlinson, C. A., and T. R. Moon. *Assessment and Student Success in a Differentiated Classroom.* Alexandria, VA: ASCD, 2013.

Treffinger, D. J., ed. *Creativity and Giftedness.* Thousand Oaks, CA: Corwin Press, 2004.

VanTassel-Baska, J., and C. A. Little. *Content-Based Curriculum for High-Ability Learners.* Waco, TX: Prufrock Press, 2011.

Vygotsky, L. S. *Mind in Society: The Development of Higher Psychological Processes.* Cambridge, MA: Harvard University Press, 1978.

Walters, K. S., ed. *Re-Thinking Reason: New Perspectives in Critical Thinking.* Albany, NY: State University of New York Press, 1994.

Ward, B. A. "Instructional Grouping in the Classroom." Washington, DC: Office of Educational Research and Improvement (OERI), U.S. Department of Education, November 1987.

Wiggins, G. and J. McTighe. *Understanding by Design.* Alexandria, VA: ASCD, 2005.

Wolfe, P. *Brain Matters: Translating Research into Classroom Practice.* Alexandria, VA: ASCD, 2010.

Wormeli, R. *Fair Isn't Always Equal: Assessing and Grading in the Differentiated Classroom.* Portland, ME: Stenhouse Publishers, 2006.

Zimmerman, B. J. "Becoming a Self-Regulated Learner: An Overview." *Theory into Practice, 41 (2)* (Spring 2002): 64–70.

———. "Investigating Self-Regulation and Motivation: Historical Background, Methodological Developments, and Future Prospects." *American Educational Research Journal, 45* (2000): 166–183.

Zimmerman, B. J., S. Bonner, and R. Kovach. *Developing Self-Regulated Learners: Beyond Achievement to Self-Efficacy.* Washington, DC: American Psychological Association, 1996.

Zimmerman, B. J., and A. Kitsantas. "Developmental Phases in Self-Regulation: Shifting from Process Goals to Outcome Goals." *Journal of Educational Psychology, 89 (1)* (1997): 29–36.

———. "The Hidden Dimension of Personal Competence: Self-Regulated Learning and Practice." In *Handbook of Competence and Motivation.* A. J. Elliot and C. S. Dweck (Eds.). New York: Guilford Press, 2005.

Index

Page numbers in *italics* refer to figures; those in **bold** refer to reproducible forms.

A

Abstract conceptual knowledge, 31, *32*
Achievement
   cycle of progression, *102*
   grouping based on, 13
   intrinsic motivation and, 67, *110*
   reasons for underachievement, 66–67
Advancement Via Individual Determination (AVID), 17
Affect, as dimension of self-regulation, *100*, 101
Ambiguity
   integrating into curricula, 57, 130, 192
   as learning tool, 57
   student appreciation of, 129
Amygdala, 69
Analytical learning dimension, 76–77
Analyze level, Bloom's revised taxonomy, *149*, 155
Anderson, Lorin, 147
Annotating, as reading strategy, 163
Answer-checking skills, 106
Apply level, Bloom's revised taxonomy, *149*, 154–155
Arguments, evaluating, 108, 165
Assessment
   as basis for guided thinking, 132
   at Bloom's taxonomic levels, 147–148, 153–157
   goals and uses of, 77, *78*
   grading practices, 17, 79, 80
   knowledge level assessment, 30, 45
   motivation strategies based on, **99**
   role in differentiation, 13, 16
   in Teaching and Learning Continuum model, 120, *121*
   types of, 17, 77–80
Authentic audiences, presentations to, 114
Authentic tasks and activities
   as characteristic of thinking curriculum, 130
   creativity and, 192
   designing, 57–59
   examples, 154–155
Automatic performance, 69, 147
Autonomy
   assessment and, 120, *121*
   in goal setting, 102
   importance of, 113, 114–115
   See also Teaching and Learning Continuum (TLC)

B

Barometer groups, 14
Behavior, as dimension of self-regulation, *100*, 101
Bill of rights, classroom, 104
Bloom, Benjamin, 30, 146

Bloom's Taxonomy
   assessment associated with, 147–148, 156–157
   examples, *150–153*
   overview, 30, 146, *147*
   revision, 147–148, *149*, 154–157
Boy-friendly classrooms, **81–82**
Brain breaks, **84**, 185
Brain-compatible learning environments
   need for, 68
   role of emotion and attention, 66
   strategies for creating, **83**, 103–104
Brain physiology, 68–71, 130
Brain stem, 68, *69*, 70, *70*
Brainstorming, 185, 201
Buddy systems, 14, 105

C

CAI. *See* Consider All the Issues (CAI) tool
Centers, learning, 107, 108–109
Cerebellum, 68–69, *69*, 70, *70*
Cerebral cortex, *70*, 70–71, *71*, *72*
Challenging activities, need for, 74
Check-ins, 134–135
Choices, need for, 73–74
CIM. *See* Cross-Impact Matrix (CIM) graphic organizers
Classroom practices
   for advancing learning, 60, **61**, 62
   autonomy, encouraging, 114–115
   bill of rights, 104
   boy-friendly classrooms, **81–82**
   brain breaks and sponge activities, **84**, 185, 191
   brain-compatible environments, strategies for, **83**, 103–104
   characteristics of thinking classrooms, 129, **138**
   communities of scholars, establishing, 103–104
   conventions, establishing, 104, 203–204
   creativity, building, 192–193, **194**, **195**
   elements and indicators of differentiated classrooms, 19, **21**, **24–27**
   learning centers and stations, 107–109
   motivating classroom, pathway to building, 73–74, *74*
   oversight councils, 104
   restorative justice, 104
   rigorous curriculum, developing, 55–59, 60
   routines, 106
   student-centered classrooms, 103–107, **111**, **112**
   students' needs, wants, and requirements, addressing, 73, *73*–74
   supportive environments, 105
   tiering assignments and activities, **64–65**
   12 Steps to Group Decision Making, **210**
   walkthroughs, 60, **63**
   See also Creativity/creative thinking; Critical thinking; Curricula; Teachers

Clock/map partners, 13–14
Coached instruction, 114, 117–119, *118*, *121*
Coaching, for teachers, 18–19
Cognition, as dimension of self-regulation, *100*, 101. *See also* Brain physiology
Collaboration of students
 authentic tasks, 57
 creativity and, 183
 grouping students, 12–14
 student interests, using, 75
 12 Steps to Group Decision Making, **210**
Communication
 need for competence in, 2, 29, 127
 technologic developments, 126
Communities of scholars, establishing, 103–104
Compare and contrast graphic organizers, 161, *162*, **174**
Competence/competencies
 cross-cultural, 127
 defined, 67
 self-regulation and, 100, 101
 student need for, 73
 in Teaching and Learning Continuum model, 113, 115
 thinking curriculum and, 130
 for twenty-first century workforce, 2, *28*, 28–29, 127
 See also Motivation
Complete an incomplete questioning strategy, 168
Complexity
 creating, 56
 Digging Deeper Matrix (DDM), *150–153*, 157
 student appreciation of, 129
 See also Rigorous curriculum
Comprehension level, Bloom's revised taxonomy, *149*, 153–154, *154*
Concept development
 effective curricula and, 56
 generalizations, 33, *36*
 importance of, 30
 interconnected concept model, *42*, 42–43
 mapping year-long concepts, 42, *43*, *44*, **51**
 principles and theories, 36
 relationships-rigor-relevance model, 33, *36*
 sample lesson plan, 33, *34–35*
 unit plans, 43–45, *46–48*
 worksheet, *36*, **49**
Conceptual knowledge
 defined, 29, 31
 objectives, developing, 37
 types of concepts, 31, *32*, 33
Concrete knowledge, 31
Confidence. *See* Self-confidence
Connectedness
 connected thinkers, 128
 curriculum map example, *44*
 need for, 73
Conscious performance, 147
Conscious thinking, 159. *See also* Critical thinking
Consider All the Issues (CAI) tool, 171, **178**, 201
Consultative instruction, 114, *119*, 119–120, *121*

Content
 content-based concepts, 31
 differentiation of, 12
Content-based essential questions (CEQ), 39–40, 43–45
Content standards
 Breaking Down the Essentials template, **50**
 language arts example, *41*
 mathematics examples, *38*, *40*
Contextualizing, as reading strategy, 165
Control, student need for, 73
Conventions
 classroom, 104
 mindset, 203–204
Convergent thinking, 128, *128*, 183
Conversations, substantive, 59
Cooperative groups, 14
Cortex, *70*, 70–71, *71*, 72
Create level, Bloom's revised taxonomy, *149*, 156
Creativity/creative thinking
 characteristics of creative individuals, 183–184
 classroom practices, 192–193, **194**, **195**
 compared to critical thinking, 159, 183
 creative learning dimension, 76
 decline in, 182
 definition and overview, 182–183
 importance of, 127, 182, 193
 learning preferences and, 76
 in mathematics, 184, 193
 strategies and activities for encouraging, 184–192, **195**
Critical thinking
 compared to creative thinking, 159, 183
 definition and overview, 159–160
 general strategies, 160–161, *161*, *162*, *163*, *164*
 mathematics strategies, 166
 questioning strategies, 167–169
 reading strategies, 161–163, 165
 science strategies, 166–167
 tools for, 169–172, *170*, *172*, **173–181**
 writing strategies, 165–166
Cross-cultural competencies, 127
Cross-Impact Matrix (CIM) graphic organizers, 161, *163*, **175**
Cross-lateral brain activities, **84**
Cultural diversity, 72
Curricula
 adapting and enhancing, importance of, 1–3
 characteristics of a thinking curriculum, 129–130, **139**
 conceptual knowledge, importance of teaching about, 30
 decision making, emphasis on, 205
 differentiation of, 12
 essential questions, creating, 38–40
 hierarchy of knowledge, 29–30, *30*
 interdisciplinary themes, 2, 29
 key components, 30–31, 33, 36–37
 mapping year-long concepts, 42, *43*, *44*
 objectives, developing, 37–38, *38*
 principles for advancing learning, 60, **61**

problem finding and solving, emphasis on, 205
quality, defining, 211
rigor, infusing, 56–60, 157
twenty-first century goals, 30
unit questions, developing, *40*, 40–42, *41*
Curriculum mapping
concept development, 42–43
examples, *43*, *44*
template, **51**
unit plans, developing, 43–45, *46–48*

D

Danielson, Charlotte, 18
DDM. *See* Digging Deeper Matrix (DDM)
Dean, Ben, 104
Deci, Edward, 114
Decision making
characteristics of effective decision makers, 196–197
definition, 196
If-Then Mind Map for Decision Making, 199, *199*, **207**
strategies for overcoming barriers, 203–205
12 Steps to Group Decision Making, **210**
Deductive reasoning, 160
Descartes, René, 132
Didactic instruction, 114, 116, *117*, *121*
Differentiated instruction
connecting to twenty-first century thinking and learning, 1–2, 211, *212*
content/curriculum, 12, 211, *212*
determining need for, 15
elements and indicators of differentiated classrooms, 19, **21, 24–27**
flipped classrooms, 11–12
group work, 12–14
learning environments, 10–12, *212*
myths about and characteristics of, 15–17
teacher coaching and evaluation, 18–19
teacher survey, **22–23**
time commitment for, 17
Digging Deeper Matrix (DDM)
examples, *150–153*
overview, 157
template, **158**
Disassociated terms, for Internet searches, 108
Discrimination, impact on learning, 72
Discussions
about student writing, 166
substantive conversations, 59
See also Questions/questioning
Divergent thinking, 128, *128*, 183
Diversity
creativity and, 183
impact on learning, 72
Downshifting, to reptilian brain, 70
Dweck, Carol, 67, 102, 116, 203

E

E³ (enrichment, extension, enhancement) learning activities, 107

E⁴ (effective, engaging, exciting, enriching) curricula, 56–59, 60
Editing, as writing strategy, 166
Elaborate rehearsal (ER), **94**
Elaboration
activities for stimulating, 186–187, 188–192
creativity and, 186
Elliott, Andrew, 67
Emotional relevance of activities, 56–57
Empathy, building, 104–105
Engagement of students, 56–57. *See also* Motivation
English language arts
content-based concepts, 31
content standard example, *41*
tiered activities, **64, 65**
Environment
brain-compatible environments, strategies for, **83**, 103–104
differentiation of, 10–12
See also Classroom practices
Erickson, H. Lynn, 42
Essential questions
creating, 38–40
examples, *40*, *41*, 42–43, *43*, *44*
template, **50**
Ethnic/racial diversity, 72
Evaluate level, Bloom's revised taxonomy, *149*, 155–156
Everyday Art View activity, 190
Exit slip/entrance ticket, **96**
Experts, students as, 75
Expert sources, consulting, 58
Extrinsic motivation, 67

F

Facebook, 126
Facilitated instruction, 114, 117, *117*, *121*
Factual knowledge
defined, 29, 30, *30*
objectives, developing, 37
Feedback
growth mindsets and, 116, 203
providing to students, 106, 117, 148
using assessment as, *78*
See also Assessment
Feldhusen, John, 10
Five Whys to Therefore chart, 198, *198*, **206**
Fixed mindsets, 102–103, 116, 203
Flexibility
activities for stimulating, 185–186, 187–192
creativity and, 185
need for, 127
Flexible grouping practices, 12–14, 16–17
Flipped classrooms, 11–12
Fluency
activities for stimulating, 185, 187–192
creativity and, 185
Formative assessments
as basis for guided thinking, 132
at Bloom's taxonomic levels, 147–148, *149*, 156–157

knowledge level assessment, 30, 45
1- to 3-minute coaching activity, *79*
overview, 17, 78–80
read-write-pair-share activity, *79*
roundtable review and reflection, **97–98**
in Teaching and Learning Continuum model, 120, *121*
think-pair-share activity, *79*
3-2-1 exit slip/entrance ticket, **96**
tiered review/practice activity, *80*
Four square concept maps, 78, **95**
Framework for Teaching Evaluation Instrument, 18
Free writing strategy, 166
Friendship-based grouping, 13
Frontal lobe, 70–71, *71*, 130
Fun, need for, 74

G

Gender differences
    boy-friendly classrooms, strategies for, **81–82**
    hippocampus, 69
    learning preferences, 69, 71–72
Generalizations
    sense-making approach, 33, *36*
    teaching about, 33, 44
    unit plan examples, 44–45
Gifted and talented students
    differentiation for as myth, 16
    historical perspective, 10
    lack of creativity, 184
    passion projects, 75
Global Digital Citizen Foundation, 2
Goals
    building self-regulation, 102, *110*
    curricular, 30
    SMART goals, *110*, 132, 134
    See also Objectives
Grading practices, 17, 79, 80
Gradual Release of Responsibility model of teaching, 115, *115*
Graphic organizers
    comparing and contrasting, 161, *162*, **174**
    Cross-Impact Matrix, 161, *163*, **175**
    If-Then Mind Map for Decision Making, 199, *199*, **207**
    Justify Your Thinking, **176**
    sequencing and prioritizing, 161, *164–165*
    spider diagram, *161*, **173**
    T-chart, 161, *162*
    Venn diagram, 161, *162*
    What? So What? Now What? chart, *154*, 200, *200*, **209**
    What Would Happen If . . . ? diagram, 199, *199*, **208**
Group work
    benefits of, 12
    group decision making, **210**
    group discussions, 166
    special interest groups (SIGs), **91**
    student interests, using, 13, 75
    tips for, 12
    types of groups, 13–14, 16–17
Growth mindsets, 103, 116, 203–204

GT acronym, 10
Guided thinking, 131–132, *133*, **142**

H

Hattie, John, 79
Heacox, Diane, xi, 113
Hierarchy of knowledge, 29–30, *30*
Higher order thinking skills (HOTS)
    Digging Deeper Matrix, *150–153*, 157, **158**
    for gifted and talented students, 10
    incorporating in instruction, 135
    students' right to, 146
    See also Rigorous curriculum
Highlighting, as reading strategy, 163, 165
Hindbrain, 68–69, *69*
Hippocampus, 69
History instruction
    Digging Deeper into Bloom's example, *151*
    guided thinking example, *133*
    See also Social studies instruction
Hypothetical thinking
    sample questions and activities, 168–169
    What Would Happen If . . . ? diagram, 199, *199*, **208**

I

I Chart, **85**
I-FORD problem solving process, 197–202, *198*, *199*, *200*
If-Then Mind Map for Decision Making, 199, *199*, **207**
Impulse control, developing, 106. *See also* Self-regulation
Independence. *See* Autonomy
Individualization, compared to differentiation, 15
Inductive reasoning, 160
Inferring, as reading strategy, 165, **176**
Information, validation of, 160–161
Institute for the Future, 28, 29, 126, 127
Intellectual laziness, 19, 126
Interactions, curriculum map example, *43*
Interdisciplinary themes, 2, 29
Interest-based instruction
    differentiating by interest, 14–15
    engaging students, 56–57
    grouping students, 13
    motivating students, 74–76, **91**
    passion projects, 75–76, **89–90**
    Rank Your Interests form, 75, *75*, **88**
    What Interests Me: Topic Preview, **86**
Internet searches
    disassociated terms, use of, 108
    intellectual laziness and, 19
Intrinsic motivation, 67, *68*, *110*, 115–116
Intuitive thinkers, 127
iPads, 126

J

Jensen, Eric, 73
Jigsaw group work, 13
Journaling, **94**, 106
Justify Your Thinking graphic organizer, **176**

K

Kaplan, Sandra, 10
Kindles, 126
KIQ charts, 74–75, **87**
Kitsantas, Anastasia, 101
Knowledge
    assessment of, 30, 45
    as basis for creativity, 184
    Bloom's revised taxonomy, 148, *149*
    conceptual, 29, 31, 33
    factual, 29, 30
    hierarchy of, 29–30, *30*
    procedural, 29, 30–31
    pyramid of, *37*
Knowledge workers, 28, 213
Krathwohl, David, 147

L

Language arts. *See* English language arts
Lateral thinking, 186
Learning
    ability dimensions, 76–77, **92–93**
    autonomy, importance of, 113, 114
    brain domains, 68–71
    dimensions of, 29–30, *30*
    gender differences, 69, 71–72
    Gradual Release of Responsibility model, 115, *115*
    jigsaw puzzle analogy, 33
    learning styles activity, **92–93**
    mindsets and, 102–103
    poverty and, 72–73
    race, ethnicity, and cultural considerations, 72–73
    readiness for, 29
    self-determination theory, 115–116
    self-regulation theory, 100–102, *101*, *102*
    10:2/20:2 rule, 106
    zone of proximal development (ZPD) theory, 56
    See also Knowledge
Learning centers and stations, 107–109
Learning preferences
    instruction based on, 13, 15
    motivation strategies based on, **94**
    Sternberg model of abilities, 76–77, **92–93**
Lifelong learners, 113
Limbic system, 69, *69*, 70, *70*
Linguistic diversity, 72
Literature circles, 13
Living Timeline activity, 191
Locus of control, *110*

M

Marzano, Robert, 18
Mathematics instruction
    content-based concepts, 31
    content-specific generalizations, 44
    creativity and, 184, 193, **195**
    critical thinking strategies, 166
    Digging Deeper into Bloom's example, *152–153*
    example objectives, *38*
    guided thinking example, *133*
    math standards examples, *38*, *40*
    tiered activities, **64, 65**
    universal concepts, 31, *32*
Metacognition
    Bloom's taxonomy and, 148
    definition and overview, 105, *110*, 132
    strategies for development of, 105–106
    student perception questionnaire, 132, **143**
    teaching about, 132
Midbrain, 69, *69*, 70, *70*
Mind maps, 199, *199*, **207**
Mindsets, 102–103, 116, 203–204
Minority students, 72
Motivation
    assessment as basis for, **99**
    creativity and, 184
    defined, 67
    intrinsic versus extrinsic, 67, *68*
    learning preferences and, 76–77, **92–93**
    pathway to building a motivating classroom, 73–74, *74*
    student interests, using, 74–76, *75*, **91**
    in Teaching and Learning Continuum model, 115–116
Multi-Tiered System of Supports (MTSS), 16, 17

N

Name 5 activity, 191
National Center for Education Statistics, poverty statistics, 72
Neocortex, 130
No Easy Answers tool, 172
Note taking, as reading strategy, 163

O

Objectives
    Bloom's taxonomy of, 30
    curricular, 37–38
    example math standard, *38*
    See also Goals
Occipital lobe, 71, *71*, 72
1- to 3-minute coaching activity, *79*
Open-ended questions, 38–39
Originality
    activities for stimulating, 186, 187–192
    creativity and, 186
Oversight councils, 104
Oxytocin, 72

P

P³ (persistence, patience, and perseverance)
    as basis for creativity, 184
    as classroom conventions, 104
    in problem solving, 197, 202
    strategies for developing, 106–107
Parents
    as homework coaches, **81**
    suggestions for supporting self-confidence, 204
Parietal lobe, 71, *71*
Partnership for 21st Century Learning, 28–29

Passion projects, 75–76, **89–90**
Peer review of writing, 166
PL. *See* Priority Ladder (PL) tool
PNI. *See* Positive, Negative, Interesting (PNI) tool
Point of view, analyzing, 167–168
Portable skills, 58
Positive, Negative, Interesting (PNI) tool, 169–170, *170*, **177**, 201
Positive Behavioral Interventions and Supports (PBIS), 17
Poverty, impact on learning, 72–73
Practical learning dimension, 77
Praise. *See* Feedback
Preassessments
    four square concept maps, *78*, **95**
    KIQ charts, 74–75, **87**
    overview, 17, 78
    in Teaching and Learning Continuum model, 120, *121*
Prefrontal cortex, 70–71, 130
Principles, in concept development, 36
Priority Ladder (PL) tool, 171, *172*, **179**
Problem finding
    characteristics of effective problem finders, 196–197
    example activities, 197
    importance of, 196
Problem solving
    characteristics of effective problem solvers, 196–197
    graphic organizers, *198*, 198–200, *199*, *200*
    I-FORD process, 197–202, *198*, *199*, *200*
    need for skills, 127, 196
    strategies, 107, 198
    student/teacher questions, 200–201, 202
Procedural knowledge
    cerebellum, role of, 68–69
    defined, 29, *30*, 30–31
    objectives, developing, 37
Process, differentiation of, 12–14
Product, differentiation of, 14
Proofreading skills, 106
Provocative topics, 57, 58
Publication of student writing, 166
Pyramid of knowledge, *37*

Q

Questions/questioning
    about problem solving, 200–201, 202
    adjusting questioning practices, **99**
    content-based essential questions (CEQ), 39, 43–45
    critical thinking strategies, 167–169
    essential questions, constructing, 38–40, *40*, *41*
    sequential questioning, 104
    steps to asking good questions, 135–136, *136*
    for students before turning in work, 106
    substantive conversations, 59
    unit questions, *40*, 40–42, *41*
    universal essential questions (UEQ), 39, 43–44

R

Racial identity, and learning, 72
Random instructional grouping, 14
Rank Your Interests form, 75, *75*, **88**
Readers Theater activity, 192
Readiness-based instruction, 13, 14
Reading instruction
    critical thinking strategies, 161–163, 165
    Cross-Impact Matrix example, *163*
    If-Then Mind Map example, 199, *199*, **207**
    PNI example, *170*
Read-write-pair-share activity, *79*
Recall level, Bloom's revised taxonomy, 148, *149*, 153
Reciprocal teaching, **99**
Reflection
    in cycle of progression of achievement, 101–102, *102*
    encouraging, 106
    as reading strategy, 165
    Student Reflection Log, 135, **145**
Relationships-rigor-relevance model, 33, *36*
Renzulli, Joseph, 10
Reptilian brain, 70, *70*
Research on a creative individual activity, 192
Research strategies for authentic learning, 57–58
Resiliency, need for, 127
Response to Intervention (RTI), 17
Response to Intervention (RTI) model, 16
Responsibility for learning, 73
Restorative justice, in classrooms, 104
Reversal of thinking strategy, 169
Right Question Institute, 135
Rigorous curriculum
    defined, 55
    Digging Deeper Matrix (DDM), *150–153*, 157
    E^4 curricula, 55–56
    strategies for, 60
    teachers' roles, 55–56
    tiering assignments and activities, **64–65**
Risk taking, in decision making, 204
Robinson, Kenneth, 183
ROLE cards activity, 189
Role play activity, 192
Roundtable review and reflection, **97–98**
Row/column grouping, 13
Ryan, Richard, 114

S

SCAMPER thinking technique, *131*, 187
Scanning, as reading strategy, 162
Scholars, communities of, 103–104
Science instruction
    content-based concepts, 31
    content-specific generalizations, 44
    critical thinking strategies, 166–167
    Digging Deeper into Bloom's example, *150*
    Rank Your Interests example, *75*
    spider diagram example, *161*
    tiered activities, **64, 65**
    unit plan example, *46–48*

Self-confidence
  autonomy and, 114
  in decision making, 204
  in Teaching and Learning Continuum model, 114, 115–116
Self-determination theory, 115–116
Self-direction. *See* Autonomy
Self-efficacy, 102, *110*
Self-esteem, 113, 132
Self-evaluations, 106
Self-regulation
  Bloom's taxonomy and, 148
  communities of scholars, establishing, 103–104
  development of, necessary understandings for, 109, *110*
  incorporating in unit plans, 45
  learning centers and stations, 107–109
  metacognitive skills, 105–106, *110*, 132, 148
  need for, 127
  P³ (persistence, patience, and perseverance), 104, 106–107
  phases of, 101–102, *102*
  related concepts, 31
  self-determination theory and, 115–116
  supportive environments for, 105
  theoretical background, 100–102, *101*, *102*
  wisdom and empathy, developing, 104–105
  See also Social and emotional learning (SEL)
Sense-making approach to instruction, 33, *36*
Sequence Chain tool, *164*
Sequencing and prioritizing graphic organizers, 161, *164–165*
Sequential questioning, 104
Sequential thinkers, 127
Series of Events tool, *165*
Serotonin, 72
Sheltered Instruction Observation Protocol (SIOP), 17
Short-term goals, setting, 102
Skimming, as reading strategy, 162
Skits and plays, 192
SMART goals, *110*, 132, 134
Social and emotional learning (SEL)
  gender differences and, 71–72
  in unit plans, 45
  See also Self-regulation
Social awareness, need for, 127
Social connections, grouping based on, 13–14
Social media, 126
Social studies instruction
  content-based concepts, 31
  content-specific generalizations, 44–45
  Cross-Impact Matrix example, *163*
  PNI example, *170*
  tiered activities, **64**, *65*
  What? So What? Now What? examples, *154*, *200*
  What Would Happen If . . . ? example, *199*
Special interest groups (SIGs), **91**
Spider diagram graphic organizers, *161*, **173**
"Sponge activities," 185, 191

Squiggle activity, 188
Standardized tests, 16, 80
Stations, learning, 107–109
Stereotyping, impact on learning, 72
Sternberg, Robert, 76, 104, 113, 183–184
Sternberg model of abilities, 76–77, **92–93**
STO. *See* Structured Thinking Organizer (STO)
Structured Thinking Organizer (STO), 172, **181**
Student-centered classrooms
  learning centers and stations, 107–109
  strategies for creating, 103–107
  student checklist, **111**
  teacher checklist, **112**
  teacher responsibilities, 103
Student Perception Questionnaire, 132, **143**
Student Reflection Log, 135, **145**
Study buddies, 14
Substantive conversations, 59
Successful intelligence, 76–77
Summative assessments
  knowledge level assessment, 45
  overview, 17, 80
  in Teaching and Learning Continuum model, 120, *121*
Supportive classrooms, developing, 105
Support of students, need for, 73
Surveys and inventories
  student interests, 74, *75*
  10 Elements of a Differentiated Classroom Survey, **22–23**
Symbol systems, 169, 200
Synthesis 3+1 tool, 172, **180**
Synthesis level, Bloom's revised taxonomy, *149*, 156

T

Taxonomy of educational objectives, 30
Taxonomy of Educational Objectives, The Classification of Educational Goals, Handbook I: Cognitive Domain (Bloom), 146
T-chart graphic organizers, 161, *162*
Teacher Evaluation Model, 18
Teachers
  autonomy development and, 114–115, 116–120, *121*, **122–123**
  changing roles of, 126–127
  coaching strategies and observations, 18–19
  creativity development and, 193, **195**
  evaluation of, 18, **22–23**, **24–27**
  growth mindset conventions for, 203–204
  indicators of differentiated instruction, **24–27**, 211
  key points for, 211, 213
  problem solving questions for, 201, *202*
  responsibilities in student-centered classrooms, 103, **112**
  time commitment for differentiation, 17
  tips for learning centers and stations, 108–109
Teaching and Learning Continuum (TLC)
  levels of, 114, 116–120, *117*, *118*, *119*
  overview, 113–114, **122–123**
  theoretical framework, *115*, 115–116

Technology
    adaptability, need for, 127
    developments in, 126, 213
    flipped classrooms, 11–12
    impact on thinking skills, 126, 213
    pros and cons, *20*
    role in differentiation, 10–11, 19
Temporal lobe, 71, *71*
10 Elements of a Differentiated Classroom, **21**
10 Elements of a Differentiated Classroom Survey, **22–23**
10:2/20:2 rule, 106
Textbooks
    previewing, 74
    role of, 59
Then What Happened? activity, 191
Theories, in concept development, 36
Think Fast! activity, 188–189
Thinking
    classroom characteristics, 129, **138**
    competencies and themes, 2
    convergent versus divergent thinking, 128, *128*, 183
    curriculum characteristics, 129–130, **139**
    definition, 127
    guided thinking, 131–132, *133*, **142**
    higher order skills, 10, 135, **146**
    hypothetical thinking, 168–169
    importance of, 2, 19
    inductive versus deductive reasoning, 160
    lateral thinking, 186
    lesson formats, *131*, **140–141**
    reflection logs, 135, **145**
    reversal of thinking strategy, 169
    steps to asking good questions, 135–136, *136*
    strategies for developing, 130–136, *131*, *133*
    student characteristics, 129, **137**
    types of thinkers and thinking, 127–128
    unconscious versus conscious thinking, 159
    See also Creativity/creative thinking; Critical thinking
Thinking journals, 106
Think-pair-share activity, *79*
3-2-1 exit slip/entrance ticket, **96**
Tiered activities, **64–65**, *80*
TLC. *See* Teaching and Learning Continuum (TLC)
Tomlinson, Carol Ann, 55, 107
Topic previews, *75*, **86**
Tracking, compared to differentiation, 16
Transparency-level skills, 2
Twitter, 126

U
Unconscious thinking, 159
Underachievement, reasons for, 66–67
Understand level, Bloom's revised taxonomy, *149*, 153–154, *154*
Unit plans
    developing, 43–45
    example, *46–48*
    template, **52–54**
Unit questions
    developing, 40–42
    examples, *40*, *41*
Universal concepts, 31, *32*, 33, 44
Universal essential questions (UEQ), 39, 43–44

V
Validating information, 160–161
VanTassel-Baska, Joyce, 10
Venn diagram graphic organizers, 161, *162*
Verbal repetition, 105
Visible Learning (Hattie), 79
Vygotsky, Lev, 56

W
Wait time, providing, 107, 135
Walkthroughs, 60, **63**
Ways of learning. *See* Learning preferences
Webbing strategy, 168
What If . . .? activity, 191
What Interests Me: Topic Preview, **86**
What? So What? Now What? chart, *154*, 200, *200*, *209*
What's the Question? activity, 190
What Would Happen If . . . ? diagram, 199, *199*, **208**
Wisdom, building, 104–105
Workforce skills
    changes in, 126, 213
    essential competencies and skills, 2, *28*, 28–29
    forces driving change, 29
    future skills, 127, 213
    need for knowledge workers, 28
Working backward problem solving strategy, 200
Work plans, creating, 132, 134–135, **144**
Writing
    critical thinking strategies, 165–166
    journaling, **94**, 106

Y
YouTube, 126

Z
Zimmerman, Barry, 101
Zone of proximal development (ZPD) theory, 56

About the Author

Dr. Richard M. Cash is an award-winning author and educator who has worked in the field of education for over 25 years. His range of experience includes teaching, curriculum coordination, and program administration. Currently, he is an internationally recognized education consultant, and his work has taken him throughout the United States, Canada, the Czech Republic, China, England, Indonesia, Saudi Arabia, Mexico, Poland, Qatar, Spain, South Korea, and Turkey.

Richard received his doctorate in educational leadership and a master's degree in curriculum and instruction from the University of St. Thomas in Minneapolis, Minnesota. He has a bachelor's degree in education from the University of Minnesota and a bachelor's degree in theater from the University of Wisconsin, Eau Claire. For over 10 years, he codirected a children's theater company in Minnesota and coauthored four award-winning children's plays. In 2011, Richard was the recipient of the National Association for Gifted Children's Early Leader Award, recognizing his leadership in programming for gifted children. In 2016, he was named a "Friend of the Gifted" by the Minnesota Educators of the Gifted and Talented.

Richard's areas of expertise are educational programming, rigorous and challenging curriculum design, differentiated instruction, 21st Century Skills, brain-compatible classrooms, gifted and talented education, and self-regulated learning. His book *Differentiation for Gifted Learners: Going Beyond the Basics* (coauthored with Diane Heacox) won the Legacy Book Award for Educators. His book *Self-Regulation in the Classroom: Helping Students Learn How to Learn* was published in 2016. Richard lives in Minneapolis, Minnesota. His website can be found at nrich.consulting.

Richard offers on-site professional development on differentiated instruction, thinking skills, brain-compatible learning, creativity, and gifted education, among other topics. He provides one-on-one consulting as well as group workshops. To learn more, visit **nrich.consulting** or email **speakers@freespirit.com**.

Other Great Resources from Free Spirit

Self-Regulation in the Classroom
Helping Students Learn How to Learn
by Richard M. Cash, Ed.D.

Teachers, administrators, counselors, grades K–12

184 pp.; paperback; 8½" x 11"; includes digital content

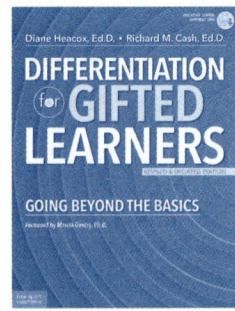

Differentiation for Gifted Learners
Going Beyond the Basics (Revised & Updated Edition)
by Diane Heacox, Ed.D. and Richard M. Cash, Ed.D.

K–8 teachers, gifted education teachers, program directors, administrators, instructional coaches, curriculum developers

264 pp.; paperback; 8½" x 11"; includes digital content

Making Curriculum Pop
Developing Literacies in All Content Areas
by Pam Goble, Ed.D., and Ryan R. Goble, M.A.

Teachers, administrators, curriculum directors, grades 6–12

224 pp.; paperback; 8½" x 11"; includes digital content

Teaching Gifted Children in Today's Preschool and Primary Classrooms
Identifying, Nurturing, and Challenging Children Ages 4–9
by Joan Franklin Smutny, M.A., Sally Yahnke Walker, Ph.D., and Ellen I. Honeck, Ph.D.

Teachers, grades preK–3

248 pp.; paperback; 8½" x 11"; includes digital content

Teaching Gifted Kids in Today's Classroom
Strategies and Techniques Every Teacher Can Use (Updated 4th Edition)
by Susan Winebrenner, M.S., with Dina Brulles, Ph.D.

Teachers and administrators, grades K–12

256 pp.; paperback; 8½" x 11"; includes digital content

Making Differentiation a Habit
How to Ensure Success in Academically Diverse Classrooms (Updated Edition)
by Diane Heacox, Ed.D.

Teachers and administrators, grades K–12

192 pp.; paperback; 8½" x 11"; includes digital content

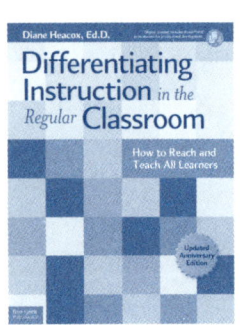

Differentiating Instruction in the Regular Classroom
How to Reach and Teach All Learners (Updated Anniversary Edition)
by Diane Heacox, Ed.D.

Teachers and administrators, grades K–12

176 pp.; paperback; 8½" x 11"; includes digital content

Many Free Spirit teacher resources include free, downloadable PLC/Book Study Guides. Find them at **freespirit.com/PLC**.

Interested in purchasing multiple quantities and receiving volume discounts?
Contact edsales@freespirit.com or call 1.800.735.7323 and ask for Education Sales.

Many Free Spirit authors are available for speaking engagements, workshops, and keynotes.
Contact speakers@freespirit.com or call 1.800.735.7323.

For pricing information, to place an order, or to request a free catalog, contact:

Free Spirit Publishing Inc. • 6325 Sandburg Road, Suite 100 • Minneapolis, MN 55427-3674
toll-free 800.735.7323 • local 612.338.2068 • fax 612.337.5050
help4kids@freespirit.com • freespirit.com